ZERO AT THE BONE

Bryce Marshall and Paul Williams

POCKET STAR BOOKS

New York   London   Toronto   Sydney   Tokyo   Singapore

For Jimmie, who gave us the key,
and for Diane, whose patience and support,
miraculously, never wavered

An *Original* Publication of POCKET BOOKS

 A Pocket Star Book published by
POCKET BOOKS, a division of Simon & Schuster
1230 Avenue of the Americas, New York, NY 10020

Acknowledgments

The authors would like to thank Mary Chessum, Peter Griffen, Debbie Hoyt, Margorie McNulty, Patrick McNulty, Patrick McNulty Jr., Roger O'Shields, Viola O'Shields, Steven Sanders, Manuel Ulibarri, and others who wish to remain anonymous, for their time, their candor, and their insight; *The Looking Glass* newspaper of Waldron, Arkansas, and Dave Sheppard of the *El Paso Times*'s Alamogordo bureau for sharing their files with us; the staff of the New Mexico Social Services office in Alamogordo; the United States Air Force recruiting office in Little Rock; John Irwin, for keeping us posted; Tom Honeycutt, George Waldron, and David Kern of *Arkansas Business* magazine, whose gift of time saved us many tedious hours; Lequetta Singleton and others at the Russellville Police Department, as well as Sandra Butler at the Pope County Sheriff's Office, whose courtesy and efficiency were a delight; James Ward for his criticism, creativity, and constant support; Martin's Computer Repair of Little Rock for rescuing the manuscript from microbyte limbo; Ethan Ellenberg for his faith and enthusiasm; and Paul McCarthy of Pocket Books for his patience and prodding.

We want to thank our children, Allison Williams and Jonathan Marshall, for understanding why their fathers had to spend so many sunny summer afternoons in "the room where the man that killed his kids lives," instead of at the swimming pool.

Finally, we want to acknowledge a very special debt to Seth Thompson—friend, colleague, and godfather of this book. It would never have been written without him.

B.L.M.   P.H.W.

Several of Nature's People
I know, and they know me—
I feel for them a transport
of cordiality—

But never met this Fellow
Attended, or alone
Without a tighter breathing
And Zero at the Bone—

—Emily Dickinson
from "A Narrow Fellow in the Grass"

Contents

PREFACE
xiii

PROLOGUE
Danse Macabre
December 22, 1987
Murder on Mockingbird Hill
1

PART ONE
Point of No Return
Cloudcroft, New Mexico, 1976–1981
Incest and a Fortress of the Mind
17

PART TWO
Patterns
1940–1976
The Past, Marriage, Life in Uniform
89

PART THREE
The End
Arkansas, 1981–1987
Sheila and the Death of Pain
157

EPILOGUE
Mutatis Mutandis
Lockup, 1988–1990
The Dying of the Light
283

AT HOME FOR THE HOLIDAYS . . . AND MURDER

Gene Simmons: In the military he was a straight-laced sergeant who demanded discipline and order. To his family he was an unpredictable tyrant, driving them into a stranger and stranger existence, until there was nowhere left to go . . .

Becky Simmons: For months Gene's wife had been sleeping in one of the children's rooms. Now Gene came to her in bed with his gun drawn. "Oh, Gene, don't kill me, Gene," she said . . .

Sheila Simmons McNulty: She bore her father's child and lived with the nightmare of his affection. Before he killed her, Gene Simmons would speak gently to his eldest daughter . . .

Dennis McNulty: A bitter enmity burned between Sheila's husband and her father. When the McNulty family showed up for the Christmas holiday, Gene didn't hesitate—he ambushed Dennis from behind a curtain . . .

Loretta Mae Simmons: Gene Simmons told his most sensitive and perceptive daughter that he had a surprise for her. While three other children waited outside, he strangled her with a nylon cord . . .

Little Gene Simmons: A blow to the head with a iron pipe didn't kill him. Instead, he jumped up, ready to fight. His father drew a pistol . . .

Preface

Once the shock and outrage, the horror and the grief began to abate, family, friends, and the press all asked the same question: *why?* What concatenation of forces and events had, in the six days surrounding Christmas 1987, driven Ronald Gene Simmons to the grisly murders of fourteen of his own family and a homicidal spree in a nearby town that left four people wounded and two others dead?

Even when fragmentary details of Simmons's life began to emerge, lay speculations still tended toward simple answers, those that could be accommodated in some inches of print or a sound bite on the evening news, and the psychologists and criminologists who probed Simmons's motives were reluctant or unable to arrive at any sort of revelatory conclusion. The law found Simmons fit for trial. He was eventually convicted in two separate proceedings, twice sentenced to death, and executed on June 25, 1990. But the sordid tale of incest, isolation, and violence that those trials and the investigations of reporters brought to light still begged more questions than they settled, and the bereft families and friends were left to anguish without fully understanding *why*.

In the television footage and press accounts immediately following his arrest, Simmons is a balding, overweight white man in his late forties with a stubble of gray beard, drooping eyes, and a shattered, hangdog air. But that bedraggled image is misleading. Simmons was tired then, emotionally purged and still on the cusp in his transit to cold perfection, his private, rock-walled transcendence. As his trials progressed, Simmons's beard thickened to a spade-shaped flame of gray, then spread in a broad, patriarchal fan, even as his body sloughed flesh and he achieved an ascetic gauntness. His eyes brightened, and his self-control was patent. Aside from one calculated outburst in which he struck the prosecuting attorney, Simmons moved through the legal proceedings with the demeanor of a saint seeking his own martyrdom—or the devil his due.

As immediate interest in Simmons waned, as new horrors replaced the old on the front page and reporters on deadlines concluded against Simmons's stony silence, it became clear that the question was not *why?* but *who?* Who is this Ronald Gene Simmons, and what made him?

Since that day in spring 1988 when we first walked up the rutted, red-clay drive to the house near Dover, Arkansas, where Simmons annihilated his family, our research and our speculations have turned on those two related questions.

The documentary foundation of that research rests largely on Simmons's personal records, letters, notes, and photographs, and those of his children. Additional materials came from press accounts, private correspondence, and public records. For more intimate information we interviewed or queried dozens of Simmons's relatives, in-laws, and acquaintances, as well as human-services workers, prosecutors, attorneys, and others involved with Simmons's legal odyssey. Beyond prepared statements demanding a speedy execution, Simmons himself did not speak for publication. He left no journal or diary, and only one rambling but suggestive note.

Many of the conclusions and assumptions on which we have proceeded represent what must now be considered consensus. In all our broadest beliefs about the character of Ronald Gene Simmons we have met no evidence or opinion in direct contradiction. Some particulars, however, are speculative, and some of the dramatic scenes are re-creations based upon our specific knowledge of Simmons and the dynamics of his family. While being faithful to the established facts, we have, in some cases, also attributed motives and emotions that represent "most likely" assumptions that are consistent with those known facts. We have not attempted to edit reality, but when conflicting information has surfaced we have often elected to ignore that which was clearly rumor, unfounded opinion, faulty recollection, or a likely lie.

By whatever gruesome measure such things are calculated, Ronald Gene Simmons's homicidal rampage ranks among the worst: He murdered more of his family in a shorter period than any killer in American records. By whatever standard we judge others, his crime was heinous, the act of a madman, an embodiment of evil. But evil holds a fascination. When it excites prurience it engenders itself and, in that, triumphs. When it foments vendetta—an eye for an eye—it does the same. It is not banal, and it can never be ignored. The opposite of love is indifference, not hate; the opposite of evil is not good, but compassionate reason and understanding. If our understanding of what boiled forth from Ronald Gene Simmons in any way or to any degree diminishes the odds for another like him to arise unchecked, this book has realized our intent.

Bryce Marshall
Paul Williams

PROLOGUE

DANSE MACABRE

December 22, 1987

MURDER ON MOCKINGBIRD HILL

Idea cold-trails itself in a circle,
Like light bent by the gravity of the gun

—PAUL WILLIAMS
from "A Nocturne"

The low, gray December sky swirling above the southern foothills of the Ozarks belied the joy of that four Simmons children felt as they clambered off the Dover school bus, followed by their classmates' laughter and cries of "Merry Christmas" and "See you next year." Like schoolchildren everywhere they had used this, the day before Christmas break, to steal a march on the holiday, spending more class time in whispers and expectations than with books and lessons. They had exchanged cards and presents with their friends and been treated to free periods by their teachers. Even Loretta, the eldest and, at seventeen, well into that adolescent independence all parents dread and all younger siblings ridicule, was burbling happily about the coming holidays as she, her sisters Marianne and Rebecca Lynn, and her fourteen-year-old brother, Eddy, started up the eroded red-clay drive that wound between bare oaks and dark cedar toward home at the top of the ridge.

In the Simmons family, Christmas had always been the season holding out the annual promise of greatest joy, and this winter in particular the children yearned for it keenly. It was many years since happiness had been an abiding condition in their home, but the past few had been especially fraught with tension, and since March it had been almost palpable. Their father's anger and withdrawal had both intensified, and their mother's anxieties had touched everyone. But this Christmas would have all the family together again—even Sheila and Billy and Gene Jr., who were married and lived away from home—a prospect that seemed to have granted some peace to both of their parents, and the children bent toward the familiar rhythms of the season like battered flowers toward the light. The tree, the house festooned with cards saved from Christmases past, the small extravagances of food and presents were familiar and consoling themes. The slim promise of normalcy filled the four with happy anticipation as they climbed the hill that took them home.

Halfway up the steep and rutted drive their voices fell, their spontaneity momentarily muted by the unexpected figure of their father ambling down the hill to meet them. But they were quickly reassured by Dad's broad grin and their own irrepressible spirits. With book packs and coattails flying they all rushed up to meet him.

Ronald Gene Simmons, wearing the stubble of a nascent beard and a dirty baseball cap that dripped long, thinning wisps of gray hair from beneath its headband, herded his four youngest children into the compass of his arms, only half hearing their excited chatter as, smiling, he urged them up the hill while they competed for his distracted attention, asking questions about their big brother, "Little Gene," and his daughter, Barbara, and prating to their father about the day's events at school.

Loretta, who was eager to see Barbara, skipped along ahead, and Eddy struggled to get into his blue nylon knapsack to show Dad his unopened present from a class Christmas party. "I'm going to put it under the tree and wait until Christmas morning to open it," Eddy said, hoping this self-discipline would please his increasingly demanding father. Marianne took Little Becky's hand to help her up the hill.

To a passerby the smiling father and his four happy children might have resembled an aging hippie and his family. Gene Simmons's old air force field jacket and well-worn combat boots fit the image of a middle-aged refugee from the sixties, one of those holdouts of time and culture who are commonplace in the Ozarks, but Gene would have been indignant, even outraged at the thought. His disdain for the drugs, the social and sexual anarchy he saw represented by the sixties was total and absolute. The site of his home was, in Gene's eyes, well planned and practical, his clothes comfortable remnants of his military career. Any counterculturist would have found cold consolation on Mockingbird Hill, the name Gene had chosen for his thirteen hardscrabble acres, where his benign autocracy and concrete walls sheltered the family from a corrupt and dangerous world.

The children topped the drive that led to their ramshackle mobile home with its cobbled-on additions and ugly chimney flue of concrete blocks, unaware what was the source of their father's disarming smile that had coaxed their high spirits along. For a man consumed by rules, plans, and schedules, the course of his day's work so far had not gone at all well. Most of all it was the noise; he had not thought about the noise or that it would unnerve him. It was not the shots so much—though they were louder than he had dreamed—but that wet flopping against the closet door, that iambic closure still thrumming as a pulse in Gene's ears. No, not all the details had gone as he had rehearsed them in his mind for months, but he could take satisfaction in having found alternatives to suit his larger plan, to cast a perfect circle around his pain.

He stopped the children, and they stood quietly, shivering with excitement in the wind beneath the tall sea-green flame of cedar that blocked the view of the front of the house. The wind spoke sotto voce to Loretta through the stunted pine and skeletal oaks along the top of the ridge: *What's wrong?*

"I have a special Christmas surprise for all of you," Dad told them, "but I want to give it to you one at a time."

With the smile now frozen on his face and eyes stinging bright in the wind, he told the three younger children to wait in the old Chevrolet station wagon parked beneath the cedar and listen to Christmas carols on the radio while he took Loretta inside. "Then," he said, "I'll come back and get each of you for your surprise."

Loretta heard no answer in the wind as she helped Little Becky into the car and walked with her father toward the still house standing in the shadows of the winter trees.

With her father's arm around her shoulders Loretta could smell the perfume of cheap wine and Schlitz that hung on her father like a palpable mist separating them. Loretta had lately been taken with religious fundamentalism and Pentecostal literature, and the contempt and anger she felt toward her father were only deepened by his drinking. She had even told her mother and her friends that she hoped it would kill him. His long, brooding spells spent isolated in his room with bottles of beer or sweet yellow wine had become a fixture of family life, and she could not associate that mist of alcohol with the loving, cheerful father who had greeted them in the drive. She could not escape the question in the wind, even if she thought it silly—like Marianne and Little Becky looking under the beds after watching *Nightmare on Elm Street.* After all, it was Christmas, and Dad had a surprise for her.

"What is it?" she asked her father. "What is it you have for me? Is Barbara asleep?"

Loretta was especially fond of her little niece, who had been staying with the family since September while Little Gene was trying to reconcile with his wife, and all of Barbara's young aunts had delighted in spoiling her. Barbara was fun, and Loretta hoped she wasn't taking a nap with Mom.

Her father ignored the question as he propelled her across the fiberglass-roofed porch, with its litter of fireplace kindling and used auto parts, and through the sliding glass doors into the family room.

The bulbs of the Christmas tree winked brightly in one corner, and the television cast a flickering puddle of light on the brown-carpeted floor. The rest of the house was dark. Its stillness was not right. There was no sign of Mom, Little Gene, or Barbara, although Little Gene's Toyota was parked outside near the cedar where the other children sat waiting.

Loretta laid her books on the sofa, spellbound by her mounting apprehension, unsettled by her dad's urging her into his room, where her surprise was waiting, before she had even taken off her coat.

Dad's bedroom—his sanctuary—was two doors down and on the left in the hallway of the addition to the old mobile home. It was the only door in the house with an inside lock and had always been off-limits to the children. Even Becky, their mother, had been sleeping with the younger girls for more than a year. This was where he kept his boozy counsel among the dozens of boxes and hundreds of files containing the records and documents that defined his life. This was where he kept tinned kippers and sardines and

7

candy to sustain him in the isolation of his dervish thoughts and congealing plans, *immobilis in mobile*. Closed away within the close intimacy of the house, this was where he kept everything that mattered anymore, and this was where he brought Loretta. What better place to hide a Christmas surprise?

Like all else Gene Simmons did that day, his bringing Loretta in first was not arbitrary or accidental. The eldest and, at eighty-nine pounds, physically the largest of the four children, Loretta was also an inquisitive, perceptive girl. Her sensitivity to the world around her had made her one of those who can sense the emotional tenor of a room as soon as she walks into it. The disdain that Gene held for her intelligence had turned to apprehension, fear she might suddenly realize her situation and ruin his surprise.

Loretta stopped when Gene started to shut the door behind them. The silence of the house was deafening, unnatural, and there was nothing like a present in the room that she could see.

"No," she said, turning to go. "I want to see Barbara. You can give it to me later."

"You've told me that for the last time," Gene said. He wedged the door shut with his boot and reached for her.

Something in his tone, something more than the contempt and anger she had grown accustomed to, terrified Loretta.

"Let me go," she said, her voice rising. "Let go of me." She tried to push past him, her hands flailing for the doorknob.

The insolence outraged Gene. He pushed Loretta back, knotted her hair in his left hand, and hit her twice in the face with his fist, splitting her upper and lower lips.

Gene released her hair as she twisted away, put her

8

hands to her face, and fell face down on his bed, mute with shock. Gene whipped the yellow-and-white braided nylon fish stringer from his jacket pocket, wrapped it swiftly around Loretta's neck, crossed his hands, and yanked the loop into a garrote that tangled with the chain of her crucifix. At first Loretta struggled, clawing at the cord. She fought her way onto her back and saw her father's glittering eyes, as years before her sister Sheila had done in different but equally obscene circumstances, linking acts of life and death. Gene put his knee on her chest and tightened the stringer, and by then she was too weak even to tear her own flesh where the noose bit into her neck. The last Loretta saw before the cold found her heart was her father's face, his painted smile and the isinglass patina of his eyes.

Relief and satisfaction were what Gene felt as he watched his daughter die. She had not struggled loudly enough to warn the others. His plans were going well, if not entirely as he had intended. His morning's work, while the four children were enjoying their Christmas parties and presents at school, had convinced Gene that he could not rely on his short-barrel .22 pistol for clean kills with a shot to the head or the heart. But as he unwound the fish stringer from Loretta's neck and lifted her body off the bed he looked on his work and found it good. Things were at last going his way.

He carried the thin, limp body across the hall to the bathroom. With only the shower plumbed, and its use rationed, Gene kept water for face-washing and light hand laundry stored in large plastic trash barrels. Wanting nothing left to chance, Gene lowered Loretta's body headfirst into the barrel of water in the bathroom and held it there until he was certain she was dead.

Satisfied, he carried her into her narrow room next

to the bath. Rock stars and Jesus looked on from their posters as Gene lay Loretta's body on the bed and paused to push the wet hair from her eyes.

But he could not linger; there was still much to be done. Although he knew the children would not usually disobey him, he could not trust their impatience or curiosity.

Gene went back out to the station wagon and saw its windows fogged with the breath of his children. He opened the door to the happy blare of carols and told Eddy that it was time now for his surprise. Just wait a while longer, he told eleven-year-old Marianne and her little sister, Becky; their turns were coming. True to his word, Gene returned to lead each child inside. He did to each of them what he had done to Loretta. He treated each of them equally, fairly. That was important to Gene.

When he was done Gene rested for a while, watching television and sipping from a bottle of Château LaSalle while he went over again what he had to do. The flickering screen and the lights from the tree cast bright, lurid patterns on his face.

Finished with the wine—and it *was* making things easier—Gene took a six-pack of Schlitz from the refrigerator and walked outside to the rear of the house where he kept the scarred wheelbarrow in which he had mixed mortar to build the wall of concrete blocks that ran along the military crest of the ridge. Using a flashlight to cut through the gathering darkness, he carried the children one at a time from the house to the wheelbarrow and trundled them along a well-worn path past their playground, with its clubhouse and swinging tire, and into the woods to a newly dug privy pit where their mother, brother, and niece all lay.

That morning, shortly after the children boarded the Dover school bus, Gene had heard Becky, his wife, walk sleepily back down the hall to the room she and Barbara were sharing with Marianne and Rebecca Lynn. He waited until he heard her door shut before unlocking his own and stepping out. He turned right, into the living room, where he plugged in the Christmas tree lights and switched on the TV, then crossed to the double sliding-glass doors and went out onto the cold porch that was a catchall of broken tools and used parts for pumps and automobiles. Gene rummaged in the shelves and boxes, discarding first a small crowbar and then an ax handle before settling on a two-and-a-half-foot length of one-inch galvanized pipe.

He reentered the living room, wedging a broom pole behind the glass door to lock it from the inside, and sat for a while, transfixed in front of the television, its shifting images as meaningless and profound as the whorls of a mandala. How clear things were for Gene, now that there were events ordained to release him from a world of betrayal and pain, just as a dog that has swallowed a treble hook will rip out its bowels to kill the pain. He lay the pipe on the floor beside him, took a short-barrel .22 revolver from his belt, and made sure it was loaded. His pockets bulged with extra hollow-point ammunition. He picked up the pipe, stood, stuffed the pistol back in the waistband of his trousers, and started down the hall toward Eddy's room, where Little Gene lay sleeping.

Gene's own plan entranced him; he could imagine thinking about himself thinking about himself, could imagine he saw himself gliding noiselessly down the hall. How simple and coherent things were now that he knew what he must do to square the ledger with all those who had trespassed against him, had caused him hurt or disappointment.

He opened the door to Eddy's room, across the hall from where Becky and Barbara lay, and saw

Little Gene lying asleep. Little Gene, the first betrayer, "the one who wouldn't work," his father called him, was curled asleep on his side. Propelled by rage and reverie, there was no moment of indecision as Gene slammed the pipe down on the head and shoulders of his namesake son—the bearded one who looked so like him.

To his father's horror, the blow did not kill Little Gene or even stun him. Bleeding from a lacerated scalp, he sprang from the bed, shocked and confused but prepared to fight. In rising panic Gene dropped the pipe, snatched the little revolver from his pants, and shot his son in the chest from less than three feet away. Still Little Gene would not fall. He screamed and lunged at his father, and Gene shot him again, the bullet striking to the left of his nose. Little Gene would not go down. He lurched forward, trying to cover his wounds as he made for the door. Gene grabbed him and shot his son again in the head. Little Gene fell and lay on the floor with his head in an ell of the wall by the closet door, still clawing at the wall and trying to rise. There Gene held the pistol to his son's skull and fired, rupturing the cranium in a shower of blood and soft tissue. Little Gene's body began to flop loudly in spastic reflex, pounding like timpani on the cheap hollow-core doors of the closet.

Leaving Little Gene in his convulsive death throes on the floor, Gene reloaded his pistol as he stepped across the hall, scattering spent cartridges as he went. He was unnerved, rattled by the ear-rending explosion even a .22 creates in a closed room, and even more by the thumping spasms of his son, sounds that drowned the mantra of procedures echoing in his mind.

His wife looked up at him from the bed where she sat as Gene came into the room. Three-year-old Barbara was sobbing, balled in terror in her grandmother's arms.

"Gene, don't kill me, Gene," Becky pleaded.

Gene could hear his son still thrashing on the floor in the other room. He turned and went back across the hall, saw that Little Gene had not moved, grabbed the pipe he had dropped, and rushed back before Becky could pick up Barbara and run. Without pausing he came in swinging the pipe and hit Becky twice in the head. Stunned but still conscious, she struggled to shield Barbara with her body. Gene dropped the pipe and pulled his pistol and shot her twice in the head, spattering the walls with a fine pointillist mist of blood.

Gene rolled Becky's body away, passed the nylon stringer five times around Barbara's throat, and throttled her on the bed.

At the last hollow sound of Gene Jr.'s throes Gene was left with the ring of gunfire in his ears, the sweet reek of scorched cordite in his nose, and a babble of compulsive injunctions swelling inside his head.

Moving quickly now to outrace his growing panic, Gene reloaded his pistol and hurried down the hall, through the living room where the Christmas tree stood blinking cheerfully, and out into the raw morning. Breathing heavily, he stood and listened and watched to see whether a snooping neighbor or passing driver might have heard the shots. No one came, but still he waited, fearful that a phone call might yet send blue lights flashing up his drive.

Presently Gene calmed his heart. He went back into the house just long enough to open a beer before returning to his vigil at the wall of concrete blocks that looked down on the county highway. The effectiveness of the .22—or its lack—worried him. His plan, patiently evolved over the preceding months, could be jeopardized by it. There was no turning back, however; he would have to think this through carefully. Plans were made to be carried out. Success was found only in seeing them through, step by step, to their ordained conclusion. It had to be done.

Again agitated, Gene returned to the house, improvising feverishly to obey the urgent chatter in his brain. He began tearing doors off cabinets and knocking holes in the walls at random as he turned over the possibility of claiming a maniac had stormed the house, perhaps thus buying him time to complete his plan, if the police should arrive. Eventually he abandoned the idea. He drank another beer.

Several weeks before Christmas, as his plan took final form in Gene Simmons's mind, he had set the children to digging a new privy pit in the woods behind the house, gouging with a pinchbar in the flint-clotted spine of the ridge, worrying out slabs of sandstone as big as tombstones until he had a hole the size of a narrow grave. Using the wheelbarrow, he carried the three bodies from the house to the hole and carefully laid them inside. He soaked them in kerosene and laced barbed wire between the bodies, as he would do with the four children later that same day, to keep them from imagined insects and prowling scavengers. That night, as a final precaution, he would cover the fresh earth with sheets of roofing tin, as he once had with a stray dog he shot for killing his chickens. Gene Simmons loved his family and would do whatever he could to keep their grave undefiled.

With Becky, Barbara, and Little Gene laid in the pit by midmorning—and with no neighbors or police yet on the scene—Gene had regained some of his detached composure. He felt warm and satisfied inside the field jacket that hid the bloodstains on his shirt. He walked back past the children's playground, heedless of the echoes of their laughter that soughed in the scrub oak and cedar. He mounted the three concrete steps to the porch, already amending his plans. The .22 would not do for all he had in mind, certainly not for all he had left to do today. He could not get the sound of the gunshots or Little Gene's convulsions out of his ears.

Gene poured himself a tall glass of Château LaSalle and sat down to watch "Wheel of Fortune." There was no point in cleaning up the blood-raddled bedrooms; he had worked things out that far. All he had to do was wait for the bus that afternoon. Even with the muted, iambic tom-tom of his heart keeping panic cadence, he could be pleased with things so far, with the proof of his integrity. It was happening now, and in a few days it would be done.

Despite the wine and his numbing absorption in the television, Gene could not keep his thoughts from roaming the mindscape of his past, mixing his satisfaction with bitterness and self-pity and his memories of Sheila, his oldest daughter, the one he loved and whose fault it all was. He had given his heart to her in New Mexico, had given her his dreams, and a child, and she had given him all this.

Sheila, he thought, Sheila Marie. My ladybug, my little princess. I loved you, and you destroyed me, destroyed us all. You knew that you were the key. I told you that. And I told you I would see you in hell.

PART ONE

POINT OF NO
RETURN

Cloudcroft, New Mexico,
1976–1981

INCEST AND A FORTESS OF THE MIND

In the mountains, there you feel free.

—T. S. Eliot
from "The Waste Land"

CHAPTER ONE

In south central New Mexico, on the rugged westward slopes of the Sacramento Mountains, U.S. Highway 82 drops more than five thousand feet from the resort village of Cloudcroft to intersect with Highway 70, sixteen miles away, just north of Alamogordo. At nine thousand feet—and on about the same latitude as Nagasaki, Lahore, and Marrakech—Cloudcroft lays claim to being the southernmost ski area in North America, "Playground of the Four Seasons." The town's rural addresses lie in remote, arroyo-like canyons that stretch far back into the surrounding Lincoln National Forest, a steep alpine forest thick with evergreens and thousands of western mule deer. In spring, when hikers and golfers begin to replace the skiers and hunters, mornings are still cold and often overcast, giving way before noon to the bright, crisp mountain days that the local chamber of commerce extols. Cloudcroft's history has been touched by Geronimo and Billy the Kid, as well as by Robert Oppenheimer, whose infatuation with the region helped bring the Manhattan Project to nearby Los Alamos and, through it, the atomic bomb into being. There is a wildness to these southern Rockies that gives scope to dreams of freedom, independence, and unlimited power.

Early on the morning of May 5, 1981, Ronald Gene Simmons hunched over his thick paunch and pulled himself low behind the handlebars of his red 400cc Suzuki motorcycle, trying to hide his nose and ears from the icy bite of the mountain air as he leaned through the curves down U.S. 82. Despite the cold and the low morning clouds, he was in thrall to the moment and, for that moment, master of something more powerful than himself. It was a rare escape for Gene from the thunderheads of fear and anxiety that had been gathering in his life since March, when Sheila had told him she was pregnant. But now, as the blare of his exhaust filled the tunnel bored through the mountain and silenced his uncertainties, Gene felt a swell of optimism, confident that he had the world in command.

At the foot of the grade he turned left into the four-lane flow of commuter traffic on Highway 70 and accelerated into fifth gear, letting the hypnotic drone of the engine carry him through the mild May morning toward Holloman Air Force Base south of Alamogordo. The job he was beginning today, his first since retiring from the air force in 1979, was returning him to the Computer Sciences Division of the air force's 6585th Test Group, the place of his last active-duty assignment. Now, as a GS-4 civil service employee and outside the military pecking order, he would not enjoy the status he did as a noncom nonpareil, but he was happy to have the job and be back within the familiar military order in which he had always excelled. Even with free school lunches for the children and commissary shopping privileges, his retirement benefits and meager savings had been taken to the limit to provide for a growing family of eight, a mortgage, and now payments on the Suzuki that he had to buy. He took further consolation in the job by considering the unambiguous demands of the computers he would operate, the strict procedures of the dark room, and the neat efficiency of numbered matrices superimposed on images of rocket-powered test sleds.

Gene thrived on such narrow regimens, for he was a diligent, exacting, and effective martinet. But his work so defined him that it could never be said that he lost himself in it. Rather, it was the nature of the work—the impersonal precision—that found a void made ready for it in Gene's spirit. Outside the verities of the military chain of command Gene saw a world of moral chaos, riotous with competing egos and emotions, lacking order or discipline, incomprehensible. He longed to hold life static, like a frozen frame of film, and impose on it an order as benevolent as one of his numerical grids.

At home, Gene's security was in the role of paterfamilias, final arbiter of justice and mystery within the temple of his family, and that cloistered family was the center of Gene's universe, one that he held together with the compelling gravity of a black hole, ravenous for respect and affection. Until the past two years his will had been their unquestioned way. Any challenge to his judgment angered and frightened Gene—implying as it did some shortcoming—and of late those challenges had multiplied.

He could never ignore the humiliating possibilities of the law or the lash of public outrage for long, despite his streak of cunning that, though facile and not deep, allowed him to imagine himself a powerfully resourceful man, one capable of sustaining acts of will by intelligence or deception or bluff, however empty or egregious. The new job was a case in point. Happy as he was for the income and to be back on

21

military ground, Gene had convinced himself it was not coincidence that he was hired less than a week after pressure from a state social worker and the threat of prosecution for incest had forced his relations with Sheila into the open and required him to suffer the indignity of discussing them with a psychotherapist. It was, he believed, all part of his design to defuse the intrusive and self-righteous scrutiny of liberal do-gooders, outsiders who had no appreciation of his intelligence, his integrity, or his love for Sheila Marie.

Gene's litany of self-affirmation lifted him out of himself on the motion of his humming tires, opening up his thoughts to better days, although, in the welter of anxieties that he now had to deny, it was hard for him to realize that the beginning and end of those days stood less than a year in the past.

He had left his aging Dodge van at the Avis lot, where he rented a Pontiac Phoenix for the trip he and Sheila were taking alone together to California. It was the end of July 1980 and scorching hot in Alamogordo, and since the van had no air conditioning Gene had a justification beyond the Dodge's high mileage for the expense of the rental—not that anything was ever too good for Sheila, but especially not for this trip.

"Come here, sweetheart," he said to Sheila Marie.

She slid across the front seat into the crook of his arm and laid her head on his shoulder. The cool of the car was delightful after the heat of the town that now fell away behind them, and she could enjoy it and her father entirely alone, without Loretta's hateful looks or the teasing of the little ones. She knew he treated her special, that she got things the others did not, but if Dad wanted that, it must be right. Certainly she felt special when she was around him. She had always been his favorite. And he was different, too, when they were together. He never yelled at her the way he did at Mom or called her the kinds of names that he called Little Gene. She was always ladybug or sweetheart or little princess. She liked that last name best.

Gene ignored the monotonous landscape and drove south in silence, heading for Interstate 10, which would take them west. He felt the contrast between the cool air from the vents and the warmth of Sheila's body against him. He could feel the beating of her heart in time with his own. An open smile was fixed on his face, and he was flushed with anticipation, sexually aroused. He took his hand from around her and cupped the inside of Sheila's denim-clad thigh, drawing her even closer.

Sheila made a satisfied sound and cuddled to him.

"Dad," she said, her voice tiny and immature for almost seventeen, "how long till we get there?"

"Not today, ladybug. Get the map, and I'll show you."

Sheila took the Rand McNally atlas off the dash and opened it on her lap to the facing pages that showed the interstate system and its connecting highways. Gene traced their route with his finger, through Phoenix, across the Mojave Desert, up California's central valley, and over the coastal range to Mill Valley, north of San Francisco Bay, where Gene's stepfather, Dad Griffen, lived. He closed the atlas and let his hand rest at the top of her thigh.

"We'll stay somewhere around Phoenix tonight, little princess," he said, "just you and me. Maybe we can go through your coins one more time."

Sheila drew her feet up on the seat and leaned toward her father again. "Okay," she said.

The coin collection had really been her older brother's, and Little Gene had passed it on to her when he discovered chess. Even this trip all the way to California just to go to a coin show was Dad's idea. Sheila had never understood the attraction of collecting things, except that it gave her something to do, but Dad doted on her for pretending an interest, and he would help her with it for hours, talking about mint marks and proof sets and other things she only half heard. What she did hear in it all, however, was *you're special.* And no one else made her feel that way. She felt dumb and awkward in school; Little Gene and Dad didn't get along, so her older brother avoided her as well; and her sisters were jealous of her. She felt funny when Dad touched her the way he was touching her now, but that made her feel special, too, and it really got Loretta's goat, and *she* was such a little know-it-all, just like Dad said.

Once on the interstate Gene turned down the country station on the radio and said to Sheila, "Little princess, I love you. I really love you. You know, you are really the woman of the family now, just like I'm the man. Do you know what that means?"

Sheila, curled half asleep against his loving strength, dutifully answered, "Yes."

"I mean," Gene went on, "there are things a man needs, things that Mom and I don't share anymore."

"Like what?" Sheila asked.

Gene hesitated before he said, "Well, she doesn't really understand me anymore, sweetheart, not like you do. You know I have plans for our family—good plans—but everyone has to do their part. It's a lot of work, and I don't think Mom can do it anymore. She's not very strong, you know, and things just haven't been the same between us since her . . ." Gene stumbled against the words "tubal ligation" and said instead, "since Little Becky was born."

"Uh-huh," Sheila said innocently, expectantly.

"There's a lot that Mom used to do that you have to do for me now. You are so important to me, to all of us, really. You're the only one I can count on, the only one who can make me happy. Don't you think I ought to be happy, ladybug?"

"You do everything for us," Sheila said, echoing one of her father's favorite phrases.

"That's right," Gene said, "and I always will, especially for you. You are my sunshine, Sheila Marie, my little princess. As long as I know you love me, everything is going to work out just fine. And you do love me, don't you?"

Sheila drew as close as she could and laid one hand on his chest. "I love my daddy," she said.

Gene let his hand slip from her shoulder and beneath her arm to her breast. He held her breast and his own breath but did not move his hand. He went rigid, flushed and palpitating.

Gene Simmons was in love.

Gene spoke to Sheila of many things between Alamogordo and Phoenix, growing animated and boyish as he explained them to her: incomprehensible details of his finances, the dream he had of returning to Arkansas, where the family would live happily ever after in a big house in the country, and Sheila would be the woman of that house, and he would be the man.

Never dreaming what he meant, Sheila acquiesced to everything, infatuated with the importance her father lent her.

At a motel outside Phoenix that night Gene rented them a single room and took Sheila out to a McDonald's for hamburgers. When they returned to their room he told her to shower and get ready for bed; they had an early start the next morning.

Sheila came out of the bathroom wearing only her panties and one of her father's old T-shirts that she often slept in and found him sitting on the edge of one of the two double beds, wrapped in a short bathrobe. He had turned the lights down low.

"Come over here," he said. "They will charge us extra if we use both the beds."

Tugging at the hem of the shirt, Sheila crossed the small room and started to the other side of the bed.

"Come here and sit by me, sweetheart," Gene said, patting the place beside him and ignoring the discomfort that was evident on Sheila's face.

She sat by him, stared at the carpet, and held her hands between her legs.

Gene put one arm around her and took her hands in his free hand. "Little princess," he said, "you are so beautiful, and there is so much you need to know, so much I need to teach you, to keep you safe."

He kissed her on the mouth in a way he never had before, and Sheila did not know how to respond to the thrill of embarrassment and pleasure it caused in her. She knew only that she could not tell him not to do it, did not want to tell him not to, despite the panicky racing of her heart and her father's violent trembling. She let him move her hands aside and touch her bare leg and her panties between her legs. She let him draw her back onto the bed.

Fear compounded the desperate longing of Gene's every fumbling word and deed.

"Don't be afraid," he said into her ear. "I won't hurt you. I love you."

He pushed up her T-shirt and nuzzled her small, young breasts, kissing her and saying, "Oh, Sheila, my little princess, you make me so happy" as he tugged at her panties and parted the flaps of his robe.

"Quiet now. Don't be afraid. This is what people do when they're in love. I love you. I won't hurt you."

But he did. When he entered her, feverish and hurried, Sheila felt a wrenching pain and something like a sickness in her stomach. She felt the strangeness of his flesh within her flesh, felt his crushing weight, his chest against her face. She felt she was being smothered and tried to cry out, but he only held her tighter as she beat the bed with her fists and pummeled it with her heels. And then there was a final pain, a final, bucking lunge against her, and it was over.

Gene lay upon his daughter, gasping and sobbing about his love, blessing her and telling her how happy they could be. He raised up on his elbows and looked down at her, but she would not meet his gaze. Small tears squeezed through her clenched lids.

Gene rolled aside, pulled back the spread, and helped Sheila between the sheets.

"You're a woman now, little princess," he told her. "You can make all my dreams come true."

The realization and frustration of all Gene's dreams had begun four years before, when he first came to the Sacramento Mountains as a thirty-five-year-old career air force NCO, fresh from a three-year tour in England. He felt on top of the world that April in 1976. He was proud of the master sergeant's stripe he had earned the previous October and basked in the status that his assignment to the Space and Missile Systems Organization observatory carried with it.

In April at that altitude a light sifting of snow still lay on the ground, but the air was dry, and the sun warm. It was good country, Gene thought, and the duty station itself suited his nature nearly perfectly. Located on a solitary bench of the mountains about three miles northeast of Cloudcroft, the SAMSO Electro-Optical Observatory focused its telescope on air force communications satellites and the electro-optical detectors on high-flying aircraft. The year before Gene arrived it had also become part of an air force project to study space-laser communication.

Gene had a fascination with computers and high-technology electronic equipment that stood in curious counterpoint to his deep longing for a primitive farmstead. He also cherished the idea of himself as part of America's space effort, as a warrior on the cutting edge of technological efficiency, and the job at SAMSO appealed to his stern sense of patriotism by uniting duty with the prestige of exotic, highly secretive work.

The observatory was thirty-two miles from Holloman AFB and, manned by a single officer and seven enlisted men, maintained semiautonomy from the air base in the valley. For Gene, the observatory was a space-age recapitulation of the military outposts of the Old West, and Ronald Gene Simmons, master sergeant, USAF, would now be second-in-command—and acting site commander during the captain's absence. Much of the work at SAMSO was classified top secret or higher, and Gene had full discretion over all of it, a distinction he had earned through a career that his superiors often cited as exemplary.

Captain Lyon, the site commander, had no reservations about his new topkick. He had seen MSgt Simmons's Service Record Book, and it read like a tribute to the ideal administrative NCO. More than spotless, Gene's record included distinguished service in Vietnam, where he won the Bronze Star, and a dozen awards and citations for efficiency. Several of Gene's performance reports during his career had characterized him as "head and shoulders above his peers," and none was ever less than glowing, bejeweled with superlatives attesting to his zeal and ability to operate an office "under minimum supervision."

Behind a desk, with papers to process and procedures to follow, he was a wizard of efficiency. As Captain Lyon would soon discover, Gene made his superiors look good. He kept their lives free of the red tape and paper-shuffling that would keep them away from the officers' club and the golf course. Like a dogged technocrat in the hive of a Japanese corporation, Gene worked long hours without complaint, voluntarily added to his duties, and studied the requirements of his job on his own time, memorizing reams of orders and regulations. Lyon, like all his previous commanders, doted on him.

Despite forewarning from the NCO he was replacing that off-base housing was scarce in both Alamogordo and Cloudcroft, Gene spent more time scouting the canyons around Cloudcroft in his blue-and-white '71 Dodge Sportsman van than he did scouring the real-estate pages of the *Alamogordo Daily News*. Longing for a rural retreat in which to raise his family, Gene explored outlying towns and villages such as Mayhill and La Luz, photographing houses that appealed to him, especially those girded with stone fences or walls of concrete block. With his family due to fly in from England in late May, he at last put down a hasty deposit on a house at 901 Cedar in Alamogordo, the only vacant rental that he could afford. But the house was intended to be temporary. For Gene's desires, it was too suburban, too hemmed in by neighbors, and its low redwood privacy fence did too little to define his piece of the earth.

Two days after renting the house Gene had a surprise visit from his half-brother, Pete Griffen, who was in New Mexico from California to look at an antique car he had found in a magazine advertisement. Having heard from his father that Gene had just arrived there, Pete decided to pay an unexpected call.

Gene was in a temporary office at Holloman, waiting to be processed through to SAMSO, when Pete showed up. Gene and Pete had never been close, but as adults they had cultivated a stiff civility, and Gene's reaction to Pete's visit was subdued, distracted, slightly formal—all the social graces that he knew. Without showing much interest in why Pete was there or how things were with him, Gene toured his brother around Holloman, drove him to the observatory, and took him to see the house on Cedar Street.

To Pete, Gene seemed more at peace than he had been since the earliest years of his marriage. He was less voluble about petty complaints, less prone to be prickly, defensive, or self-righteous, until Pete pointed out the dog ravages at 901 Cedar and brought out Gene's sensitivity to implied criticism.

Forced to acknowledge the clawed flower beds and piles of dog droppings in the yard, Gene said, "Look, it's not yours to worry about. I know how to take care of my family, Pete. I've already talked to the real estate company," he lied, "and they're going to make an adjustment, believe me."

Retreating to neutral ground, Pete asked about Gene's family, especially his wife, Becky, who sometimes wrote to him.

"They're doing fine," Gene said, warming to the change of subject. "You ought to see Sheila Marie. Ladybug is a real beauty. And she's still Daddy's girl, of course. The only thing is that I have to worry so much about her. You know how boys are, and her time for that is coming. I'm not going to let her get caught up with all these perverts and dopeheads. She's the sweetest thing you've ever seen."

On May 18 Gene flew back to England to rejoin his wife, Becky, and their five children, who had been awaiting him in the Bedfordshire hamlet of Honeydon. Once he had overseen the packing the air force took over, leaving Gene and Becky and the kids free to go to London, where they spent the night of May 25 at the Heathrow Airport Holiday Inn before flying over the pole to San Francisco the following day.

They landed in San Francisco the afternoon of May 26, and after a thirty-six-hour visit with his stepfather, William Davenport Griffen, in nearby Mill Valley, Gene rented a car and took his family on a welcome-home tour down the California coast. They drove through the twisted pines along Monterey Bay, saw Seal Rock and the mission at Carmel, then continued down Highway 1 past Big Sur, Hearst Castle, and Santa Barbara.

They spent the night in Anaheim and on the twenty-ninth went to Disneyland. Gene bought balloons and T-shirts for the children and took their pictures with Goofy and Minnie and Mickey. The next day they moved on to Sea World in San Diego before turning east on I-8 toward New Mexico.

Becky looked forward to the trip with special anticipation as a kind of homecoming. She had been born in New Mexico, the fifth child of Jose Manuel Ulibarri, a driver for the Condon Coal Company, and Lidia Mae Barnum Ulibarri (later Novak), both native New Mexicans. When her mother remarried after Jose had abandoned the family, and her stepfather moved them to a ranch near Walsenburg, Colorado, Becky maintained a nostalgic yearning for the state of her birth as a place of good memories. Deep down she held the hope that it would recreate some of her recalled happiness with Gene, make him less abusive and demanding, make him quit hitting her.

CHAPTER TWO

Becky was still youthful-looking in 1976, and in certain angles of light, quite pretty. At five feet one inch and her high school weight of one hundred eight, Becky's figure was still trim, petite, yielding little to five pregnancies. Her Anglo-Mediterranean and American Indian ancestors had blessed her with resilient olive skin and high cheekbones, large eyes and dark, straight hair. Her daughters would develop into amazing lookalikes, and to a lesser extent her genes would cast an *indio* stamp on her sons as well.

The years and Becky's cooking had been less kind to Gene's figure. Deskbound at his job and fond of beer and snacks, Gene had gained fifty pounds in the years since his marriage and bloused at the middle. But in Becky's eyes, when he arrived in Honeydon after almost two months of separation, he was still "my Gene," for despite Gene's growing moodiness and violent turns she was still devoted to him, dependent on him in every way.

Gene, too, was happy to be reunited with his family. He had missed them during the separation, missed their support and the sense of purpose they inspired in him, for they were in need of his protection and guidance. Gene saw his family as a beloved burden, certain, however, that his attention to the smallest details of their lives would someday be rewarded with the inner peace of a farmstead, a few hens, and a garden. Sometimes it was just more than he could do to shelter them outside that imagined Eden.

If his own sense of self needed them at his side, it also required that he provide for them in a manner that no one, least of all his sniveling half-brother, Pete, could fault. So on June 3, once the family was all together again in New Mexico, Gene took a small spiral notebook in hand and made his official inspection of 901 Cedar in Alamogordo.

Followed by Becky and the children, who voiced occasional discoveries of their own, Gene proceeded through the house and yard, documenting the shortcomings in a list he later transcribed into a militarily terse, typewritten summary of demerits: "Large hole in wall under telephone; soap dish broken in shower; many straight pins under chair cushions; large water stains on ceiling; animal hair on all beds, floors, and furniture; windows dirty; yard full of dog droppings . . ." Gene's final indictment of the house filled four pages. On June 4 he demanded that Shyne Realtors include his report on "the condition of the quarters" in his rental file, "so that at the time I vacate, I will not be inadvertently or erroneously charged for damage that was incurred prior to my occupancy."

Lists of all sorts were an article of faith for Gene, who saw nothing more useful than enumerated facts. The facts that he had dealt with for most of his military career existed, for him, only on paper. The act of recording them made them real. In numbers and things that could be numbered he saw the most sublime utility, the existence nearest to perfection, for numbers ionized facts, separating them from their emotional charge. Only when rendered neutral, stripped of their emotional content and conventional value, could facts be accurately assayed. In this morally depthless field facts assumed whatever specific gravity Gene assigned them, imposed a basis for order, some hope of clarity, even finality, in the confusion of wills and competing emotions that revealed the disorder of the world. Gene sent one copy of the disclaimer to Shyne and filed three others in different folders among his hoard of records that had just arrived in their boxes from England.

Gene did not just keep records; he collected them in a way as thorough and thoroughly eccentric as that of a Victorian philatelist for whom the act of collecting became an end in itself, making sheer numbers a virtue. He kept hundreds of Christmas cards and letters, triplicates of military orders and citations, quires of blank requisition forms, as well as contracts, titles, pamphlets, magazine stories, news items—a blizzard of papers that he felt were important, and usually in multiple copies—and added to the accumulation with lists of everything, including cans and cans of file cards detailing family finances. Gene could, if he chose, find Becky's grocery bill from the second week of July 1973 or chart the rising cost of Kraft mayonnaise since 1971. He needed an entire footlocker for Polaroid photos, color slides, and 8mm home movies alone, each dated in his curious quasi-military notation—year, month, and day written together as a single six-digit number.

After the air force had delivered the family's clothes, furniture, and housewares to 901 Cedar, and the family had taken a couple of weeks to set up housekeeping, Gene requested an additional week of leave and on June 23 piled Becky and the kids in the Dodge van for a trip to Walsenburg and a visit with her mother, Mae Novak, on the ranch where Becky had never felt at home. They stopped once along the way to take Polaroids of themselves among the snow-bright dunes of White Sands before pushing on to Colorado, heading for higher ground.

The house at 901 Cedar was still a sore point with Gene, and he couldn't shake his irritation at Pete for pointing out the chewed toys and dog turds in the yard. It had brought him face to face with the sense of inadequacy and self-doubt that he so scrupulously denied, even to believing that three years in green and pleasant England had put that terror behind him.

Gene felt better with Sheila sitting beside him as they bumped along the unpaved road to the Novak place outside Walsenburg. Becky rode in the back with the rest of the children, keeping them still while Gene held forth about the ranch, identifying livestock, dwelling on how to build a barbed-wire fence and how he would do it differently, as though he, not Becky, were the one with roots there. He moved Sheila onto the console between the seats and put his arm around her.

"There's a heifer," he said, drawing her close.

That was how Mae Novak saw them when she came out of the house to greet the van. She hugged Becky warmly but stiffly and mussed her grandchildren's hair, but she kept her eyes on Gene, who waited with Sheila until the other children had gone inside.

He helped Sheila out through his door, and with the van between him and his wife and mother-in-law Gene tucked in Sheila's shirt, running his hand across her belly and bottom inside her slacks. He came around the side of the van with his arm across her shoulders.

"Go give Grandma Novak a hug, ladybug," he said to Sheila, and she did as she was told.

Later, when they were alone, Mae Novak said to

Becky, "How come you weren't sitting with your husband?"

Always awkward and abashed before her mother, Becky stammered. "I—I had to get the kids' shoes on," she said.

"Well, what was he doing with your little girl up there?" her mother asked.

"There just wasn't room in the back, Mom," said Becky.

"Well, it should have been Little Gene, then. It just doesn't look right."

Gene had brought with him the .22 caliber Ruger pistol that had been in storage while he was in England, and he was eager to test his aim. While Mae was quizzing Becky, he and Abe Ulibarri, Becky's brother, went out plinking. They took turns picking targets for each other—a limb, a can, bleached cow skulls in the ranch's boneyard, where diseased stock was burned and limed—and it took Gene only a few rounds to find his sights. Soon he was hitting everything that Abe pointed out.

Abe said, "Damn, you haven't lost your eye."

"Once you learn to do something right," Gene said, "you never forget how."

Gene felt that Abe admired and envied him, and, ignorant of her suspicions, he believed that Mae Novak, despite her bluff manner, thought he was a good enough husband, better than Becky should have hoped for. He was less comfortable with Edith, Becky's half-sister.

Edith was as opinionated as Gene and equally outspoken. Moreover, she had never let Becky forget the mean straits in which Gene had left her and the children while he was in Vietnam, when Becky lived in a tiny trailer in the pasture with a pittance of an allotment from his monthly pay.

"You're just his slave," Edith would tell her. "I don't know how you can stand him."

Becky protested. "He's a good husband," she said. "A good provider."

"Oh, yes," Edith said. "I've seen how he provides for you. I just don't know how you can let him do that to your children."

And when Becky took the hurt to Gene he said, "She's your bitch-sister. Somebody ought to shut her up good, if you can't. I don't even want to talk to her."

Whatever he may have felt, the hearty atmosphere on Ma Novak's working ranch acted like a tonic on Gene. He liked the log and barnboard outbuildings, the post-and-rail corral, the milk that came warm from the pail. There were cattle, horses, dogs, cats, and chickens, of which Gene was especially fond, admiring their utility and ability to live on shit. The children gamboled on Ma Novak's bearskin rug and mugged for the camera beside its embalmed smile. They ate meals at a large table with a rotating host of Becky's extended family—brothers, half-sisters, in-laws, cousins—and everyone pitched in on the chores. They rode horses, with Gene setting the younger children across the pommel in front of him. He had Becky take a Polaroid of him in the saddle clutching six-year old Loretta, his second daughter, and in the other hand holding the Buntline-barreled single-action revolver in profile for the camera. Gene is looking directly at the lens, showing his teeth, radiating enthusiasm, his eyes hidden behind the black disks of his sunglasses.

The happy trip to Walsenburg, combined with his dissatisfaction over the house in Alamogordo, strengthened Gene's resolve to find a place in the mountains for himself and his family. Just two years before his posting to England Gene had missed the chance to buy his boyhood home near Hector, Arkansas, a carpenter's-Gothic house in a valley of the Ozarks that held mythical significance for him. It had been the place of Gene's happiest years, from six to ten, and had fixed forever in his mind a child's notion of paradise, one that included trackless acres of forest, a dirt road, a pitcher pump outside the kitchen, and a privy in the trees. Gene had long had his heart set on returning to Arkansas, but the Sacramento Mountains were good country, too; he could make his family happy here. He would be eligible for retirement in three years, and this would probably be his last duty station. Through hard work and careful planning a place here in New Mexico would appreciate in value, be an investment to finance the longed-for return to Arkansas.

Always methodical, Gene was capable of prodigious concentration, and now he was determined to be in a mountain aerie before winter, and preferably before school started in September. He began with Geologic Survey topographic maps, marking the roads and canyons around Cloudcroft that he wanted to explore. He had Becky and the children look through the "for sale" notices on bulletin boards in grocery stores and laundromats, and in the evening he pored over the real estate classifieds in the *Alamogordo Daily News*. On weekends and in the long summer afternoons after he got off at the observatory, Gene combed the roads marked on his topo maps, looking at properties and building his castle in the air.

Even raising five children on an air force sergeant's pay, Gene had combined parsimony with his mother's life insurance benefits to put aside almost fifteen thousand dollars in cash and savings bonds. His base pay as an E-7 of one thousand thirty-two dollars a month was the family's sole income, but he was confident it would be enough for what he wanted.

He found it on July 17, in Wills Canyon, eleven miles southeast of Cloudcroft.

The Wills Canyon place lay to the west of Cox Canyon Road, a two-lane blacktop limned by a thin strip of private acreage through the ponderosa pine and Douglas fir of the Lincoln National Forest. The forest closed in on the house site, a raw cut bulldozed in the wall of the canyon slope, gullied by erosion. The rock from the excavation had been pushed into two more or less concentric arcs facing the road. A circle drive passed through a carport on the back of the house, and a single set of stone steps led from the road to the front door.

The clapboard house had three bedrooms, two of them cramped beneath the eaves upstairs, and one bathroom. In the living room a hearth and fireplace of native stone took up most of one wall. The three acres also had two outbuildings, access to a spring, and an asking price Gene could afford.

Negotiations with the owners were almost pro forma. Gene was eager to move, and he believed he was getting a bargain, for there was little private land in the area, and developers were beginning to buy up much of it. On August 5 he and Becky signed an agreement to purchase the place for twenty-four thousand dollars—ten thousand down and the balance financed for five years. Almost the exact day that the final payment was due—July 27, 1981—Gene would leave Wills Canyon, at last headed for Arkansas, not as a pilgrim but as a fugitive.

Despite the dispatch with which he found and bought the Wills Canyon place, Gene saw nothing hasty or haphazard in his decision. The dream of retiring from the air force to a life of rural independence and self-sufficiency was one that he had held for years. He had collected and read hundreds of magazines on gardening and back-to-the-land survival, written for pamphlets on crops and animal husbandry from the Department of Agriculture and local extension agents, and had an encyclopedic collection of fix-it books from Time-Life. Along with these he kept a growing file, dating back to his return from Vietnam in 1968, of *Air Force Times* clippings and other government publications about retirement benefits. Extensive preparations and plans, however foiled by his execution of them, were characteristic of Gene. All his life he had been a transient longing for a place to homestead. Now the time had arrived, and Gene wanted to believe that he had left nothing to chance.

A part of Gene's stated motive for moving to the backcountry was concern for his children. He believed that simplicity and isolation would allow them a more wholesome upbringing than they could have if exposed to the dangers and perversions that exist in cities. To him, cities represented drug dealers, racial blurring, decadence, moral and environmental pollution. Gene equated the clean mountain air and the uncluttered beauty of the national forest around Cloudcroft with purity of soul. But other, more practical considerations also spurred his urgency to move. In saying good-bye to Becky in England he had left her pregnant with their sixth child, Marianne Michelle, who would arrive on December 17. His family just needed more room to grow. And remembering his own awkwardness and difficulty in changing schools frequently as a teenager, while forgetting his own fractiousness, Gene wanted his children to be able to start and finish high school in the right sort of place, and Cloudcroft boasted one of the best school systems in the state.

Gene felt about his children much as he did about his records: Just having them gave him a sense of security, and more was always better. He was simultaneously able to treat them as ciphers and smother them with love. They were his treasury, his capital, and he valued them in many ways. They affirmed and defined his manhood, his virility. They were a sure source of love, affection, and admiration. They were extensions of himself, truly flesh of his flesh, in whose best qualities he saw intimations of himself. And they were the labor that would transform the wilderness into a garden.

Little Gene, just turned fifteen, felt the burden of his father's expectations most of all. Because Gene had to report for duty every day and there was no air force assistance for the move to Cloudcroft, he made his son second in command. And found fault in everything he did.

"Do you think you're too good to work?" Gene demanded. He had left Little Gene an exact list of what to load in the U-Haul trailer, and when Gene came home from the base one day, barely half of it was done. "You're a damn sissy—you know that? You expect your mother and sisters to do everything. Get your butt busy."

Gene's anxious anticipation of the move had made him edgy, but his febrile ambitions for the place in Wills Canyon, plans that rang with confidence, also blocked out his son's surliness. That confidence had even been able to convince his skeptical stepfather of the soundness of the purchase and wheedle a no-interest loan from him. Things were going just as Gene had envisioned. To celebrate, as he often did when he felt things were going right, Gene bought himself a present.

In a fawning letter to Dad Griffen he justified the six hundred dollars he spent on the red Honda 90 trail bike by pleading Becky's need for the van now that there were no neighbors near enough for her to borrow a phone in an emergency. Gene would not have a telephone in his house. It opened up too much of the world, allowed strangers into your home, and tempted children to frivolity.

By October, however, the first hint of Cloudcroft's annual eighty-nine inches of snowfall gave Gene second thoughts about the Honda. He needed a serious vehicle for the serious work of self-sufficiency. The best he could manage was a ten-year-old International Scout four-wheel drive, which he bought for $1,129 cash.

Gene saw a lot that needed to be done on the Wills Canyon place before cold weather hit. Even before Becky had the curtains hung, Gene, dressed in his homesteader's uniform of denim bib overalls and a cowboy hat, had organized the children into work crews. He had them clearing and stacking rocks, mixing mortar and carrying concrete blocks for a retaining wall at the rear of the house, cutting brush, and grubbing out stumps. And the more Gene looked, the more he saw to do. Projects multiplied in his mind like the rabbits he intended to buy, and each child's list of weekly chores—in addition to the coolie work—grew accordingly. The folder marked "Home Improvement, Wills Canyon" fattened with receipts for tools and building materials.

Even without the endless round of labor, the move spelled a difficult adjustment for the children. Tiny as Honeydon had been, there had been other children their age, and dances and outings organized by the Methodist chapel for them all. Here, their only contact outside the family was during the school day. None of them did well academically that first year at Cloudcroft. They came home on the bus immediately after school and worked late, often under lights, to keep pace with Gene's demands. What little social life they had once enjoyed was compressed to nothing.

Gene continued to believe that things were going just fine, that he at last had his life and his family in harmony with his dreams, working with a well-tuned efficiency. It was not Arkansas, but it was a place in the woods. His job gave him security, status, and an unusual degree of independence. What's more, he had another child on the way. It was the life he had always hoped for, and it started coming apart almost at once.

It did not take Gene or his family long to realize that his ambitions for their new home taxed the limits of their time and energy. But even at that, if Gene had been better able to cope with uncertainty, he might have muddled through his frustration, diminished his bounding expectations, and eventually come to terms with the realities of building a farmstead. But he was not, and by November an ominous possibility arose that threw Gene's efforts into further confusion.

Since he had first arrived at the SAMSO observatory there had been persistent rumors of its possible closing, and in November it became official. The air force announced that the facility would be placed on "a caretaker status as soon as feasible," and its activities taken over by a smaller, less expensive mobile unit. It struck at the very root of what Gene had worked for.

But Gene was not alone in wanting to protect his plum assignment. Captain Lyon urged his staff to do all they could to cut costs and improve efficiency, in hope that the Pentagon might relent. Gene responded with the tireless efficiency of an automaton. He spent longer hours at the observatory, constantly assuming more and more of the duties, eventually allowing Lyon to transfer all other staff NCOs from the site. His herculean efforts did preserve his job for a few months longer, but they also cast an ever larger part of the burden of improvements at Wills Canyon on Becky and the children.

The Simmons family celebrated birthdays and other holidays with great enthusiasm, and Christmas was the high feast of their calendar. But Christmas 1976 arrived as a mixed season for Gene. All the trappings of the family tradition were undercut by his anxiety over mounting bills and the observatory's closing. The hundreds of Christmas cards they had received over the years were unpacked and strung in fading festoons from the window frames and mantelpiece. The tree, a native cedar, was trimmed with an overabundance of ornaments and extra cards. And despite the bills, Gene saw to it that there were brightly wrapped presents beneath the tree for everyone, including a chess set for Little Gene, his first, a gift that was perhaps the best his father ever gave him, for it eventually gave him an interest and a life beyond the family. For himself, Gene had a new child, Marianne Michelle, born one week before Christmas Eve.

As winter closed in, shrinking the small rooms of the house, family recreation centered around the television and elaborate game tournaments—in checkers, dominoes, and cards—all with seedings and double-elimination brackets. Little Gene's name appears as the winner in nearly every one, giving Gene a flush of resentment that he tried to mask as pride. And Sheila Marie was maturing fetchingly into a shy, nubile adolescent.

CHAPTER THREE

The fate of the SAMSO observatory weighed heavily on Gene's mind. Losing his assignment there threatened to do more than inconvenience him, for now that he was financially and emotionally committed to his plans for Wills Canyon, the job was essential to them. Gene was a creative paper shuffler, frequently cited by his superiors for originality, but he was less flexible when it came to plans he made for himself and his family. He saw the job as integral to the shaky gestalt he had forged and critical to its survival. Losing the assignment with SAMSO could mean a permanent transfer, forcing him to sell the property under pressure and risk a financial loss that could further delay any hope of rural independence, any dream of Arkansas.

Despite this, Gene continued to chart a course of improvements at Wills Canyon and kept the children busy moving them forward, but he was becoming increasingly eccentric and obsessive in his concerns.

A series of air force directives to test the water from the wells supplying the observatory awakened Gene to the threat of water pollution, and he had a fastidious aversion to pollutants. Although allergy tests failed to reveal any physical sensitivity, he gagged in the presence of tobacco smoke and was a militant nonsmoker. Now water as well as smoke would be included among his manias, and pure water would take on a symbolic, almost sacramental meaning for him, one reminiscent of General Jack Ripper's soliloquy on the subject in *Dr. Strangelove*. His "Water" file bulged with articles about contaminants, testing, and purification.

Gene's worries that winter were not all hollow, however, especially those to do with money. Cars, motorcycles, new children, and mortgages are heavy drains on even the most disciplined budgets, and Gene's penchant for impulse purchases of big-ticket items—such as the Honda and the International Scout—did nothing to stanch the leaks. The income-tax return that he filed in 1977 records his total air force salary and some interest earned on savings as eleven thousand three hundred forty-six dollars. It was a meager income to hang his ambitions on, and rising inflation in the next two years would stretch it to a thread.

In spite of the announced plans to mothball the observatory, Captain Lyon sent Gene to SAMSO headquarters in Los Angeles, California, on February 1, 1977, to attend a four-day program reviewing the organization's projects, hoping that his superlatively efficient chief NCO might influence SAMSO's decision about the Cloudcroft facility. Gene prepared the trip authorization himself and manipulated vouchers and reimbursements for his travel by commercial air liner to allow him to pocket the difference between the first-class ticket routinely provided by the air force form 626 and the economy-class seat that he actually took.

The obedience of Gene's family was so complete

that despite his frequent absence the work at Wills Canyon went on. Little Gene and Billy were learning the intricacies of using the pinchbar to remove rocks, and even Eddy, hardly more than a toddler, was pressed into service to police up the scattered debris and building scrap. The concrete-block retaining wall along the back side of the house site, where the bulldozer had left a crumbling face of loose, eroding scree, was stalled by cold weather and Gene's hectic schedule at the observatory, but the walls of coursed rubble between the house and Cox Canyon Road grew from the daily exertions of the children. Gene proudly photographed them bent over their work, moving in a gang across the stony patch of ground. They truly were his coolies—*ku li*, the bitter strength.

In late winter Gene started a subscription to the Russellville, Arkansas, *Courier-Democrat,* from which he clipped and saved dozens of real estate listings. But he also filed stories from the police beat, feature articles, human interest stories, and photographs of people he did not know, as though he could become part of the community vicariously. His earlier failure to buy the old home place at Hector had fueled rather than dampened his yearning for the Ozarks. As he had done when house hunting around Cloudcroft, Gene ordered every map he could of the southern Ozarks, where the national forest ends and the plateau shears off into the Arkansas River valley.

Secure in the stern regimen he had established at home, Gene became his other self at work—politic and amiable. One of the most startling contrasts in Gene's behavior was this disparity between his private and public faces. TSgt Jacobsen—the NCO whom Gene was replacing—warmed to him, and Gene took enough interest in Jacobsen to keep a complete copy of his Service Record Book in his files at home, in clear violation of law and policy. Jacobsen was about

Gene's age, married, with children, and, like Gene, originally from the Midwest. These objective facts did more to smooth their relationship than anything in Jacobsen's character or demeanor, for that was how Gene felt he best knew things and people, and he put a lot of stock in family and regional background. But Gene was a crafty and efficient administrator, not above using others to further his own career. Knowing that the observatory's records were not up to par, he saw to it that Jacobsen's name, not his own, appeared on the annual inspection conducted in April 1977.

Gene was still the senior NCO, however, and he used that position for all the perks it was worth. In May he made another trip to California to transport a military vehicle back to Cloudcroft, and again he manipulated the authorization forms to allow him to cash in on the difference between a first-class and an economy-class ticket.

Gene's children also had quite different lives away from the family home. Although their father's demands caused their grades to suffer, they made friends, and Loretta, the second daughter, was positively outgoing, while Little Gene's dark good looks made him a hit with the girls. Warmer weather and the end of school did not mean a vacation for the Simmons children; their chores and work details lengthened with the afternoons, and the rubble walls rose thick and uniform along the Simmons perimeter. When Gene arrived back in Cloudcroft, following a whirlwind trip to Arkansas to look at some property just before his thirty-seventh birthday on July 15, the storage shed at the rear of the house was almost complete, and the poultry pen needed only to be wrapped in chicken wire.

Including his enlistment in the navy from 1957 to 1961, Gene would have twenty years of combined military service in September and be eligible for retirement, and that presented him with a knotty decision. If he retired as a master sergeant before he had completed the improvements at Wills Canyon, his retirement income would be about six hundred dollars a month, little more than half his base pay. He had worked hard to insure that his performance at the observatory would single him out for promotion and, therefore, a larger retirement. But if the observatory did close, and he had already reenlisted, the prospect of his being transferred became almost a certainty. He especially feared, as he wrote in a letter to Dad Griffen, being "sent to Korea" or someplace else where he could not have his family with him. That fear seemed to outweigh the financial burden of early retirement. Gene's resolution of the impasse was to keep his sights set on Arkansas while redoubling his efforts in Wills Canyon.

With the electro-optical observatory in limbo and no new projects being assigned to it, Jake Jacobsen's lingering presence allowed Gene to excel at his duties while also spending more than his usual off-hours attending to business at Wills Canyon. Using a system of batter boards and string, he laid out line and level for the boys to follow in building the walls. He finished enclosing the shed behind the house and populated the poultry yard with a few hens, a red rooster, three mallards, and two enormous white turkeys. Each evening one of the girls—Sheila Marie or Loretta—had to shoo the birds back into their pen after they had spent the day roaming and pecking at will across the two and one-quarter barren acres, in Gene's belief—inspired by a Department of Agriculture brochure—that foraging poultry would lay waste to ticks and other insects. But the luxury of two senior NCOs on a staff of fewer than a half dozen men came to an end in August when, more than a year after

Gene had arrived to replace him, Jake Jacobsen finally received his marching orders. Captain Lyon then officially transferred all of Jacobsen's duties to Gene, who would eventually be the one to turn out the lights at the observatory.

Like so much in Gene's life, the new duties existed only on paper and in imagination. With but three enlisted men remaining on site there was little to do beyond routine administrative work and the cheerless task of completing the last phases of the space laser observations. Gene and Captain Lyon had been reduced to a desultory routine of signing and countersigning orders and authorizations for each other when, in November, the air force issued the official call for deactivation of the observatory, to be effected in June 1978.

The rumors being replaced by a written order did release Gene from one horn of his many-pronged dilemma, narrowing his options. With cutbacks at Holloman also underway, it was unlikely that he could expect to be assigned there permanently, especially in conjunction with a promotion. Moving up would necessarily mean moving on. Unless he could be assured his choice of station, Gene was resigned to staying in only until events forced the issue, and then to retire. He was counting every penny that a few extra months would bring to his retirement benefits.

Money was not long at Christmas that year, but no one would have known it by the gaiety of the Simmons household. The tree was a whimsical, spindly pine, its thin branches sagging beneath the weight of glass balls, blinking lights, wads of tinsel, and plaster-of-paris ornaments the younger children made in school. The collection of cards was unpacked and strung, and Becky played Christmas carols on the stereo while she worked in the kitchen, cooking a country feast for her Gene. Still, it was a Christmas of mostly new clothes and inexpensive board games for the children.

Sheila was Gene's exception.

Little Gene had had enough spankings when he was younger not to openly defy his father, despite his growing rebelliousness. He kept his anger bottled and his thoughts to himself. Not so with Loretta, who, although only nine, was quick to cry out against inequities in the way Gene treated his children.

"How come Sheila gets to go and I don't?" she would ask; or "How come Sheila doesn't have to do any chores?"

Gene's response was to grab Becky by the arm, sling her into the bedroom, and scream at her for allowing Loretta to be disrespectful.

"I'm sorry, Gene," Becky said through her sobs, praying he would not hit her. "Please don't be mad at me. I'll try harder."

Becky had long accepted and usually encouraged Gene's attention toward Sheila. Her own father had abandoned her family, and she and her stepfather had never gotten along, so she thought Sheila lucky to know a father's love. But in the past two years she had also seen how this favoritism was causing resentments and jealousies among her other children, especially Loretta and Little Gene. This Christmas she cautiously mentioned it to Gene.

He was indignant. "That's ridiculous," he told her. "I love all my children. But ladybug loves me more than the others."

Despite the hot denial, Gene did see to it that Sheila and Loretta had almost identical new outfits— blue jumpers and frilly blouses with stock collars— but he also gave Sheila the gift of a ring with a green stone, the color of Loretta's envy.

With the observatory closing, Gene had to put in a request for reassignment. He listed only two duty stations in his preferences—Holloman and Little Rock AFB in Arkansas—effectively putting his decision on whether to retire in the hands of the air force. A permanent assignment to Little Rock, his first choice, would put him in a position to extend his enlistment, take advantage of the certain promotion that would go with it, and use the prolonged security to realize his hopes of returning to the place of his childhood happiness. Assignment to Holloman could not be permanent and would leave him marking time until early retirement. In February he received orders transferring him to the 6585th Test Group at Holloman, with a reporting date of July 31.

That same month Gene saw an opportunity to capitalize on his position at the observatory and on his supply of cheap labor at home. Under the rubric Simmons and Sons Janitorial Services, Gene finagled a subcontract to "clean and maintain the U.S. Air Laser Communications Ground Station." Fully familiar with the wiles of civilian contractors, Gene tapped the air force for one thousand three hundred seventy-five dollars, more than a month's salary, but Little Gene and Billy—the "Sons" of Simmons and Sons—never saw more than pocket change from the late-night work.

In nineteen months Gene had worked wonders at home and at the observatory. His rock wall, by design or coincidence, stood about chest high, the same as a rifleman's parapet, and ran straight and level between two metal farm gates hung from stout pine posts at either entrance to the circle drive, forming with it a flattened D shape pressed against the side of the mountain. His strings and batter boards had done the job. It did not occur to him to credit the children for doing what he believed they ought.

Even though retirement loomed more likely than reenlistment and promotion, Gene was peacock proud of the work he had done at the SAMSO facility. Since Jake Jacobsen had left the previous August, Gene had put his stamp on the administrative functions of the place, and his superiors thought it the imprimatur of near genius. However gnarled his personal finances and familial relations, Gene had always been able to perform at peak efficiency on the job, and that was never more true than in 1978. The magnitude of his ability and the charm of his professional, public personality were never clearer than in the performance report he received that spring.

In the report, Captain Lyon writes: "Master Sergeant Simmons has demonstrated outstanding performance in . . . administrative and financial duties. . . . Sergeant Simmons's inputs to the deactivation plan were thorough and precise and *accepted by both our headquarters and HQ Air Force Systems Command* [emphasis added]. Sergeant Simmons is a loyal, mature, and conscientious NCO. . . . I recommend that he be promoted to Senior Master Sergeant well ahead of his contemporaries."

Lyon's recommendation was seconded by officers at every echelon of SAMSO, including its commanding general.

With all this beckoning a bright career, Gene still burned with his vision of Arkansas. Less than a week after the glowing performance report, Gene received a letter from Mrs. W. T. Wortham, an elderly family friend who lived near Hector, Arkansas, and whom Gene had called on during his trip there the previous July.

"Dear friends," she wrote, "Just a few lines. You wanted me to let you know if I heard of any place for sale. Luther Lee has a sign up to sell. You might write him. There are a number of places for sale around Scottsville, but . . . I imagine they are all wanting a big price."

Rationalizing that it would enhance the value of his homesite, Gene made an offer and put down five hundred dollars earnest money for eleven acres adjoining his property. And if the additional burden of yet another mortgage were not enough, Gene also bought a new Subaru Brat four-wheel-drive sport truck, draining twelve hundred dollars from his savings and adding to his monthly bills. In addition to his bank loans, Gene was making interest payments to his stepfather on a personal loan that he would never fully repay.

Gene was getting into deep financial waters. In one of his infrequent letters to Dad Griffen, written on April 30, Gene mentions the purchase of the Subaru but carefully justifies it as necessary for his forty-five-mile round trip each day to Holloman and further demonstrates both his devotion as a husband and his economic savvy by pointing out the lady's Bulova watch he received from the Subaru dealer as an incentive. Gene knew that his stepfather viewed him and his financial acumen with some skepticism, and he was at pains to keep Dad Griffen well disposed.

Turning to the topics of land, privacy, and water, Gene wrote, "Since most of the land here in the mountains is [national] forest land there is little private property. Most of the private property is being subdivided. *To keep other people out from around our place* [emphasis added] and to give us more room for more animals, we are trying to get the 11 acres across the road from our house. One of the acres contains the spring which is the source for our water, and on another acre is our water tank [i.e., pond] and pump house. I could see possible legal problems in the future if the land was owned and developed by someone else."

This hint, and the hope that Dad Griffen would take it without Gene's actually having to ask for more money, had been prompted by his loan application for the property being refused at Alamogordo Federal Savings and Loan. The implication that he had miscalculated and was in no financial condition to take on another thirty-four-thousand-dollar responsibility was at least as bitter to Gene as the idea of strangers encroaching on him. A second offer of twenty-six thousand dollars for three of the four tracts was likewise turned down for a loan. It was like the first whiff of blinky milk about to sour—not bad yet, but not to get any better.

Stymied in his attempts to secure his flanks at Wills Canyon, Gene looked again to Arkansas. In June he took a twelve-day leave and drove the Subaru to Hector for a look at the property Mrs. Wortham had mentioned in her March letter. The neat white farm house he found there sat well back from the road, shaded by large oaks and fronted by a clipped privet hedge. Gene did not bother to inquire about the price, recognizing that the manicured and well-maintained farm was beyond his means, even with the sale of the Wills Canyon place. He returned to New Mexico, frustrated and disappointed. After his heady successes with the wall and at the observatory, things were just going to hell.

Gene's mood remained dark that summer, his anger never far from the surface, and the intimidation he used to manipulate his family turned especially cruel.

Little Gene, who would be a high-school senior that fall, became singled out for much of his father's wrath. "You're a lazy little ingrate," Gene said when Little Gene complained about not being allowed to see his friends. "You eat my food and sleep under my roof, and you think it's too much to do a little work."

But things did not come to a head until one night when Becky meekly suggested that perhaps the children *were* being worked too hard.

"Gene," she said one evening after the children had been out working until well after dark, "they're just babies. Can't they have a little time to be kids?"

"Well," he said, "they're going to be grownups someday, and it's time they started learning what that is all about. I can't do everything around here."

"I know, Gene, but . . ."

"But what? Are you turning against me, too? Turning them all against me? Don't I do everything for all of you? Where would you be without me? Married to some drunken coal miner like Andy Novak? This is my home, and I will have the respect I deserve. I won't listen to this in my own home."

And then he slapped her.

Becky tried to turn away, but Gene grabbed her and said, "Don't you ever turn from me. By God, if you love me, you will show me some respect." His fist knocked her across the roomful of terrified children.

The children knew that this had happened before, but never in front of them.

"Stop it, you bastard," Little Gene screamed, and he leapt to his mother's defense. Gene whirled and hit him. Little Gene tried to fight, but he was no match for the much larger man. Gene beat his son to the floor, smashing his fists into his face and body until Becky and Loretta and even Sheila begged him to stop. Finally he did.

Two days later Little Gene was gone. At first Gene affected indifference, assuming his son had gone to stay with a friend from school and would soon be back, penitent. But when there was no word from him after three nights, and Becky was imploring her husband to do something, Gene became concerned. On the following day, however, Gene received a call at work from Becky's mother, Ma Novak, who told him that Little Gene had arrived in Walsenburg the day before, having hitchhiked from New Mexico.

Through her Gene convinced his son to come home and drove to Walsenburg to get him, but there was no forgiveness in it, especially when Gene had to defend himself to his mother-in-law against Little Gene's accusations of abuse, isolation, and overwork.

The ride back to Cloudcroft was knotted in silent hostility. Gene's antipathy toward his oldest son would never abate, and he kept a hard eye on Little Gene for the rest of the time he lived in his father's home.

Sheila, too, claimed more and more of Gene's attention that year, for that was the summer she blossomed. The progression of photos of Sheila for the year show her going from footed pajamas to tight blue jeans. Bit by bit, as the year progressed, Gene's camera lens slid down her body, cropping more and more of her head to focus on her breasts and hips. Sometimes he prompted her to strike a sexy pose—shooting one hip or boosting her breasts tight against her shirt with her forearm. From the summer of 1978 until the end of her life a little more than nine years later, Sheila would be at the center of every photo in which she was included and never far from the core of Gene's every thought.

Although Gene left most matters of schooling to Becky, he had some concern for Sheila's academic trouble. In England her teachers had complained that she would go for weeks without completing an assignment, spinning out excuse after excuse. The F's and D's continued through her first year at Cloudcroft and improved only slightly during the next two. In October 1978 the results of her Armed Services Vocational Aptitude Battery placed her in the eleventh percentile in verbal skills and in the thirtieth in overall academic aptitude. Then her grades soared dramatically to A's and B's when she was a senior, the same year she came out of her shell and was elected to a class office, the same year her father raped her.

With the exception of Loretta, none of the Simmons children did consistently well in school. Little Gene was bright but erratic, although he did excel at chess and started the chess club at school. William moped along for twelve years with grades just barely passing, and Eddy, like most of his brothers and sisters, struggled with reading and math. Gene's response to poor report cards and notes from their teachers was to scold the kids and let his threats ride on the promise of Becky's displeasure.

Gene reported as ordered to the 6585th Test Group at Holloman on July 31 and immediately requested another five days' leave to return to Arkansas. Although Arkansas's usury laws had kept interest rates down, the inflation of the Carter years was pushing home prices up even in the rural South. In some cases they had more than doubled just since Gene's trip to Arkansas in 1977. The situation for him was, if not grim, at least dispiriting.

In this gloomy frame of mind Gene returned to Holloman and installed himself in his new office at the 6585th, still in a quandary over his future. Having to work on the congested air base, in contrast to his New Frontier outpost in the mountains, was offset by the unique status Gene enjoyed there. Had he been a civilian, he might have been called a consultant. He described his position as that of "resources advisor" on "matters of policy and financial management . . . [I] established procedures for the preparation and timely flow of financial/procurement/supply documents." Gene was the resident expert, the top gun of desk jockeys.

Financial management was no consideration, however, when it came to things that brought Gene pleasure, and nothing brought him greater esteem in his own eyes than a new child. At Gene's urging Becky had ceased using her IUD, and by September she was pregnant. Becky's first six children had all been small at birth, with Sheila not quite five pounds, and the doctors at the clinic were concerned enough about this pregnancy to perform an amniocentesis in December and advise her against having any children after this one.

There were a lot of new clothes at Christmas again that year, including sweatshirts stenciled with "Cloudcroft Bears"—the high school mascot—for everyone. For the younger children there was also a stake-bed Radio Flyer wagon, a red one, suitable to hauling rock. Little Gene, his beard and sideburns shaved since his return to school, looks mature and self-assured in the family photos, tending toward the handsome. Sheila is winsome, her face and figure filling out in a woman's proportions, her hair falling almost to her waist. There are no pictures of Becky that season.

Gene was approaching the pinnacle of his career, where his reward would be retirement at half pay. Despite all his anxiety over the future, all his debts, and his failure to move events in favor of Arkansas, he would never be this well off again. Still wrapped in the regimented security of the air force, he could not foresee how the uncertainties of life outside it would undo him in the coming years, could not admit the possibility that there were dark urges percolating through capillary cracks in his levee of sanity, through the obsessive backfill of recorded facts, all the retaining walls of stone and self-deceit.

CHAPTER FOUR

He could not keep his eyes off Sheila Marie. All during that close, enclosed winter of 1978–79 the snow and low clouds and rock parapets compressed the family circle at Wills Canyon, and Sheila was everywhere Gene looked. With the six children in two small bedrooms and only one bathroom for eight people, privacy was not even a pretense. Within that constricting space Becky's pregnancy, nearly certain to be her last, seemed vast to Gene, in size and in portent. At times he felt disgust for her distending belly, especially when he marked the contrast between it and Sheila's smooth legs, her young breasts beneath the T-shirt she wore for a nightgown. Procreation, self-replication, was a compelling force in Gene's psyche—a family the size of a Mormon patriarch's was central to his rural paradise—and the thought of Becky's losing that capacity struck at something deep within him, boding another threat to the perfect future he was working so hard to create. If Gene saw any end to the succession or number of his children, he gave no one any clue. And if he gave any realistic consideration to how he would support them all in any estate much above penury, he kept it to himself.

Without knowing at all what to make of it, Sheila became at once uncomfortable and infatuated with her dad's attentions. Sensitive and sheltered, she was as modest as any adolescent, but without an older sister or intimate friends her own age she was emotionally years younger than going-on-sixteen. And Becky was as reticent about discussing sex with her daughter as she was ignorant of its varieties, for Gene was the only man she had ever known.

Sheila knew she was her father's favorite, and she placed him at the center of her world as well. Given the limits of her life up until then, anything else would have been surprising. But the ways he asked her to pose, his attempts to photograph her in the bathtub—as he did all the children, roaring with laughter at their modesty—caused her to feel an embarrassment that shaded into guilt, as though she were somehow responsible not only for the way he behaved but for the way he made her feel. He hugged her closer now and leaned in cheek-to-cheek when they had their pictures taken together, often letting his hand slide up the leg of her shorts. Sometimes she could smell beer on his breath or the onions he put on his burritos. Those were good smells to Sheila, ones she associated with her father as the loving, omnipotent protector he wanted the family to believe him to be, the smells of his good-night kiss. But they were mixed lately with that abashed sense that she was changing her father, causing him to act in disturbing ways, though that guilt was not enough to overcome Sheila's still infantile adoration of her dad.

Beginning in the early 1970s, and increasingly since Sheila Marie had entered puberty, Gene had logged dozens of newspaper clippings on the pitfalls of sex and drugs. His favorites came from the moralizing pens of Ann Landers and Dear Abby, especially those columns with enumerated lists of dos and don'ts for raising children, tips on counseling them about sex, and those containing cautionary tales on the perils of immorality. Illegitimate pregnancies, venereal disease, rape, abandonment, and indelible social stigma were all likely ends for a young girl not protected by a strong and loving father, especially a girl as glowing with fecund possibility as Sheila Marie. As his concern grew and the file thickened Gene saw clearly that it fell to him and him alone to instruct and protect Sheila. He convinced himself that his yearnings and cloying attention were in fact the natural instincts of a father.

Little Gene's rebellion the year before had permanently alienated father and son and made Gene acutely sensitive to challenges to his authority. When Becky's child, Rebecca Lynn, was born in June, Gene had to grapple with another reality that flew in the face of his inflexible will. The doctors had all but ordered Becky to have her tubes tied following the birth, but the procedure also required Gene's consent, and he was adamant in his objection.

With Becky lying in the hospital bed, still exhausted from the labor, Gene spoke in a clenched whisper. "No," he said. "No, I won't hear of it. What do they know anyway? We're healthy country people with seven healthy kids. What if we want to have another one? What then?"

"Gene," Becky said, "the doctor said I shouldn't. I can't even have an IUD in there."

"Well, okay," he said. "I can wear one of those things. A rubber."

But Becky knew better. He never had—had refused to, in fact. She began to cry. "Gene, please don't," she said. "I could die, Gene. The doctor said it could kill me."

Begrudgingly, Gene relented, but he would never forgive her.

The end to Gene's uncertainty about his military future came in August with a call to appear before the promotion board. With a transfer to Turkey imminent in the promotion, he declined the interview, simply penciling on the promotion application, "Plan to retire."

The decision to retire and raise a burgeoning family on half pay and a stony patch of unproductive acreage was a watershed in Gene's life, for in doing so he committed himself to a life for which he was woefully unsuited. When it came to the brass tacks of living off the land, Gene was at least two removes from reality, a vicarious dilettante. Until he purchased the place in Wills Canyon, Gene's only experience of rural life was in his childhood memories and the several visits, over many years, to Ma Novak's ranch. Becky, who had lived on the ranch, was probably better fit for the practical matters of gardening and husbandry than he, but Gene held no regard for the abilities of a woman. Instead he relied on what he read, and he read widely. *Mother Earth News,* despite its largely left-leaning, proto-hippie appeal, was one of his constant sources of inspiration, as were the booklets and brochures from the Department of Agriculture. He studied *Popular Mechanics* and kept his Time-Life series in a bookcase by the bed. Gene had some jack-leg skills as a carpenter and mason, but he had no concrete, realistic grasp of the dynamics of a farmstead, and least of all of how to make it pay. Like an opium smoker's dreams, Gene's imaginings were always superior to and unmoved by reality.

The recurring affronts to his plans and authority were driving Gene deeper into quasi-military regimentation. Gene was an airman in an era when careerism was rampant in the air force, and his work was principally clerical, making him a military man but not necessarily a martial one. Still, the military was all he really knew, and even an airman would not have been ignorant of the three things any army must be able to do: move, shoot, and communicate. Gene had the transportation in his Subaru Brat, the aging Dodge, and the decrepit Scout; he had a deer rifle and the long-barreled .22 revolver; but he wouldn't have a telephone. So, the military model supplied an answer: CB radio.

The radio had several appeals to Gene. It was more impersonal than a telephone, requiring the use of strict, established procedures. He had only contempt for the CB cowboys who polluted the airwaves with their truck-driver jargon and endless nattering. And because it broadcast in the clear but could be turned off or on, the CB was both more and less private than a phone. He did not have to respond to any calls he didn't want to take and could monitor any made by Becky or the children.

Work at Wills Canyon was going on at a route-step pace that summer as Gene found an endless list of things that would be better done before his retirement. One gnarled stump in the eroding face of the mountain took a full week to gouge out before Gene could begin the rude carpentry of yet another outbuilding, a small woodshed with a useless loft where the children liked to hide and play. But there was little enough play, for Gene had passed beyond being merely stern with his children. As he sensed reality impinging on his dreams he redoubled his efforts to transform it, as though denying facts could change them, as though forcing the children to work harder would make them happy. No amount of raw labor would ever have turned the Wills Canyon property into anything but a scatter of rocks, yet Gene insisted on seeing a garden in the waste of stone, one made to flourish by his hand, the flesh of his flesh. It was to him as though he had done all the work himself.

As Gene went through the motions leading to retirement Little Gene was making plans of his own, plans that would help him break free from the oppressive circle of his family. There would be no running away and shameful return this time, however. Earlier that year Little Gene had taken his college aptitude tests and scored very high in science and social science, and above average in business, though low in creative arts. Along with administering the ACT college-aptitude test, the high school assisted Little Gene in getting information from three schools: New Mexico State University, NMSU at Alamogordo, and Arkansas Polytechnic University in Russellville. In August 1979 Little Gene applied to NMSU-Alamogordo, indicating an interest in physical science and "communications in general," although he would declare a major in journalism before the fall semester actually began.

With his discharge set for December 1, Gene requested four days' leave, to begin September 4. He was now turning his attention exclusively to his family, his finances, and the realization of his dreams. Increasingly short-tempered as a chaos of unstructured details raged in his head, Gene reviewed his lists, added to them, and tongue-lashed the children for what was left undone. Then he pencil-whipped his bankbook. Regardless of how he tortured the figures, they proved more intractable than his cowed family. Every way he turned them, they came up short. On September 9 he resolved to borrow his way out of debt and applied for a ten-thousand dollar loan at Security Bank & Trust of Alamogordo, dropping his small equity deeper into the maw of mortgage.

In his financial statement accompanying the loan

application Gene claimed a net worth of nearly twenty-seven thousand dollars, a monthly air force income of more than fifteen hundred dollars, and eight hundred sixty-seven dollars in total monthly expenses. He made no mention of retirement to the loan officer.

Becky dreaded Gene's retirement. As it approached, his behavior had become more erratic and abusive, his demands more impossible. Since having her tubes tied Becky had received less and less of Gene's affection and more and more of his ill temper. She took what joy she could in her children and kept up a regular correspondence with both her family and Gene's, although Gene read every word she wrote and opened letters sent to her before he brought them home from the post office. His attentions toward Sheila were unsettling, but Becky would not allow herself to see them for what they were. Small wonder, for she was suffocating on her own. Deprived of "my Gene's" love, she began always referring to him as "Dad," in part in solidarity with the children and in part as a reflection of her own reduced place in the family. She was torn by fear, loyalty, fatigue, and a feeling of utter helplessness. Gene and her devotion to him had defined her life until now. They had shared the same dreams; he was her rock. Now, as she saw that rock crumbling beneath those dreams, her mute desperation was without any buffer of security, physical or financial.

Gene was not ignorant either of the possible consequences of retirement, the toll it can exact. For most of a decade he had been collecting news clippings about servicemen who had gone mad or fallen into suicidal fugues after leaving the military. Among them he had one series of articles from a Fairfield, California, newspaper, dating from his assignment to Travis AFB in the early 1970s, about a recently retired lieutenant colonel who, "despondent over his . . . retirement from the air force," shot his wife and sixteen-year-old son while they slept, then turned the gun on himself. It was a scene that, eight years later, Gene would recall and, in part, repeat. After his discharge in December 1979 Gene began adding to the file again with accounts of murders at family gatherings.

Whatever Gene feared or felt about his retirement, it was worse for Becky and the kids. At home all day now, Gene began working himself tirelessly and pushing the children to tears. There were always more rocks to be moved, clumsy attempts to terrace the thin, stony soil for a garden, and an infinity of other projects that leapt to Gene's mind. In detail, the place was a clutter of building materials, five-gallon buckets, and half-finished jobs—unmortared concrete-block stopgaps to erosion that fell over, scrounged wooden pallets that lay everywhere only half salvaged, jerry-built sheds that leaned in unpainted dereliction. Seen from across the deep wash that parallels Cox Canyon Road, however, the place had an impact. It was imposing, primitive, stark. The rude and even tiers of stone marched up the hill to the house like the steps to a neolithic altar, mysterious as the plinths of Stonehenge, pregnant with opaque symbolism.

Everett Bannister, the principal at Cloudcroft High School, witnessed the transformations in the Simmons place almost daily as he drove past it going to and from his own home about a mile down Cox Canyon Road. He had never exchanged more than a passing hello with either Becky or Gene—they did not belong to the PTA and never came to open house at the school—but he had gathered from the talk around the small high school that the children lived in semi-isolation under the strict yoke of their father. The children all seemed friendly enough with other stu-

dents, and his impression from his brief greetings
with the parents was that Becky was also a nice
woman. But something about Gene Simmons always
struck Bannister as strange. Often when he would
drive by, and the children were working on the rocks,
they would stop and wave at him. But not when Gene
was there. Then they would stay bent over their work,
except for the youngest ones, who would run to hide
behind the collection of old cars.

Bannister did his best to shrug it off. He knew that
the oldest Simmons boy had been something of a class
leader and continued to coach the chess club even
after his graduation. The others were undistinguished
students, but Bannister reasoned that bright kids like
Little Gene didn't come from miserable homes.

Fat, pushing forty, and losing his hair, Gene marked
his retirement by beginning to grow a beard. As with
all important acts of life, he kept a file to document it.
He was vain about the resemblance it gave him to the
actor Pernell Roberts, and he filed away two *TV Guide*
covers featuring Roberts, along with dated Polaroid
photos of the beard's progress. But as it grew, the
two streaks of gray that radiated from his chin gave
Gene the look of a Svengali. The beard, in fact, did
become a compulsory concern of the family, as Gene
allowed different children the honor of measuring it
and encouraged them to draw pictures of it. The
beard was emblematic of his new life, of his escape
into a world wholly of his creating.

Gene was doing more, though, than simply trying
to make his retirement dreams come true. He was
attempting to create a self, for despite his beard,
denim overalls, and straw hat, Gene was incomplete.
But his search for inner resources was all outside
himself. He was lost beyond the defining procedures
of military life, and no degree of order or compulsive

perfection was proof against a gnawing sense of inadequacy.

That Christmas was the poorest yet for the Simmons family since they had come to Cloudcroft. It was the only one of the decade not recorded in pictures. Gene was strapped for cash, overwhelmed by the proliferation of demands his imagination placed on his resources. However much confidence he may have drawn from self-deception, Gene needed his family more than ever, needed their unwavering love and obedience and the sense of identity he leeched from them. As the season revolved into winter Gene found himself with a baby on his knee and his eye on Sheila Marie.

The new year turned toward spring, and Gene's economies became draconian. He cut Becky's allowance for food and enrolled the children in the free lunch program at school to supplement their diet of corn flakes, beans, Velveeta, and tortillas. If he were ever to get to Arkansas, he needed every cent. And if he were ever to complete the improvements at Wills Canyon, he needed every minute, with none to spare for a job until they were complete.

The children felt the pinch. They were not the only students at Cloudcroft schools relying on public support, but it did set them apart, make them feel different without distinction. This, added to the crippling dependency and puny self-esteem that Gene's browbeating and isolation had bequeathed them, made Sheila, Billy, Loretta, and Eddy—the four Simmons children then in schools at Cloudcroft—even less secure in their social station, more self-conscious of things that made their family different from others.

In 1980 Sheila Marie was in full, shy bloom, and that sense of being different compounded her social awkwardness. Her grades hovered around passing. She was not involved in any school clubs or activities. She had never had a date or been kissed on the lips by a boy. At sweet sixteen, in almost any ordinary family, this would have been her year, for youth lent her its beauty. Small-boned like her mother, Sheila carried a hint of plumpness that softened the sharp angles of her face. She had the beguiling, coltish qualities of a girl just becoming a woman, just becoming comfortable with hips and breasts. She had reached the age all fathers dread.

For Gene, dread and desire became one.

The previous year Gene had read and saved a long article from the Russellville, Arkansas, newspaper about a woman in New England who had shot and killed her own daughter to keep her from becoming a prostitute in Boston. Although it was the mother who shot the girl, sobbing to her daughter, ''I can't let you go,'' it was the father who was painted as the villain of the piece, through his failure to love and counsel his child.

This and similar stories that he collected deepened Gene's conviction that he had a special duty to Sheila Marie.

But Sheila was not the only woman in Gene's family who caused him worry and concern. As much as he enjoyed having the baby, Rebecca Lynn, on his knee, she also represented those growing bills, as well as Becky's fall from grace. Becky's tubal ligation brought on an early menopause that sent her into abject depressions. Gene made some attempt to understand —he read and filed pamphlets on the physical and psychological effects of menopause—but he could not overcome a hollow sense of futility, waste, and surrender in filling Becky's barren womb with seed. She had failed him, failed to continue providing him with children, and because of that he could take no comfort with her in sex. She, who had once been a bulwark to all his dreams, was now another that he had to prop up. He had no patience for or understanding of her frequent mood swings. "What the hell are you crying about this time?" he would say. "Don't I have enough on my mind? How the hell am I supposed to do everything I have to do if you're going to be like that? Tell me, just tell me." And Becky would say, "I don't know, Gene. I don't. Please don't be mad at me. I'll do better. I'll try to cheer up. I just feel so god-awful some days." "*You* feel god-awful. What about me? Don't I have to listen to it all the damn time? Go ahead, get sick, cost me more money. You don't give a damn about anything or anybody but yourself."

And Becky would run from the room in tears to sleep another night with one of her girls.

More than ever Gene knew that this weak vessel could never be left responsible for preparing Sheila Marie for the ways of the world. What, after all, could a barren woman understand of a man's needs? Of a young girl's desires?

Sheila, too, was suffering from a confusion of emotions and a special kind of isolation. Like her more rebellious brother, Little Gene, Sheila was beginning to recognize how different her family was, how much more full and carefree were the lives of her friends at school, and that self-consciousness intensified her natural shyness. If not for the fact that many of her classmates found Little Gene attractive, Sheila would have had few girlfriends, although Gene's restrictions left her little time for them anyway. Adolescence, her mother's neurasthenia, and being her father's pet were isolating her within the family as well, leaving her lonely, frightened, and desperate for affection.

Loretta Mae, seven years younger and a keenly perceptive girl, harbored a deep resentment of Sheila and her father. Little Gene, the moody and restive older brother, had moved out of the house the previous fall and was too absorbed in chess and college and girls to provide Sheila any support. Her mother was an emotional wreck—fretful, frightened, more in need of comfort than able to give it. Billy, the brother nearest Sheila's age, was a willow. He could bend with the wind of his father's mercurial temper, but he was no support. It was only Gene who took an interest in her.

Paralleling the flux of relationships within the family, the farmstead also began to fall deeper into disorder, for Gene, an accomplished scrounger, devoted not a little of his new freedom to collecting all manner of things for the Wills Canyon place that might be useful to have "just in case." The sprawl of clutter around the house and outbuildings swelled to include salvaged sheet-iron and tin roofing, poultry feeders, pipes, fittings, spare engine parts, tools with cracked handles, used structural steel, and a hodgepodge of wrenches, pliers, screwdrivers, hammers, saws, and wrecking bars. And the money was going faster than Gene had anticipated. The four thousand dollars in his bank account remaining from the loan he had taken out the year before could not possibly make up the shortfall in his retirement income for the sixteen or eighteen months he had planned to spend on improvements before looking for a full-time job. But Gene was unable to admit it into his equation.

The only one of the Simmons family who did seem to have things going his way that year was Little Gene. Supporting himself on part-time jobs and chronically short of money, Little Gene was nevertheless discovering the delights of college coeds and the challenges of college courses. But it was in chess that he made his mark. Even after graduation Little Gene remained active in the high school chess club he had started, serving now as team coach. In April, 1980, his own tournament play won him the co–Junior Chess Championship of New Mexico, and coincidentally on the same day, the 29th, he received word that as "alternate winner" he would be eligible for a five-hundred-dollar Kiwanis Club scholarship if the winner defaulted. He came to Wills Canyon seldom now, and only to see his mother. His father, trying to postpone his own employment with money borrowed from Dad Griffen and the bank, began to refer to Little Gene as "the one who won't work."

On those rare Sundays when Little Gene was at home Becky's joy at having him there was soured by the tension between him and his father and by Gene's flagrant doting on Sheila, as though he were taunting Little Gene, saying to him, "See, this is what you get if you love me." Becky knew Gene's eyes and could sometimes see in them not only that contempt for Little Gene but a bedroom glint that was not meant for her. She turned away in horror and self-recrimination from the thought, the same thought whose horror was, for Gene, becoming its own justification. He had convinced himself of the duty of his desire.

Gene knew that he was contemplating incest, for he had clipped and saved more than a half dozen newspaper and magazine articles on the subject over the years, including one that described the dynastic intermarriages of Egypt and the Hapsburg Empire. His reason and his sense of decency, however, were obscured by his overwhelming desire to possess Sheila—emotionally, spiritually, and physically. Especially since Becky had become repulsive to him, sex began to lurk like a footpad in every cranny of Gene's thoughts, and he found his compulsive masturbation humiliating. His own desires and his conviction that it was for Sheila's good formed his resolve.

Having convinced himself of the obligation to "teach Sheila about sex"—the glibbest lie every incestuous father will tell—Gene could also submit to his psychosexual need to replace Becky in his static vision, and Sheila was practically her clone. Gene saw the confused dependence that he had created in Sheila—and was soon to take advantage of—as a sexual overture to him. He was sick at the thought of anyone else possessing that sexuality and exposing Sheila to all the shame and degradation he had read of so often in Ann Landers. Like the commander in Vietnam who said it was necessary to destroy a village in order to save it, Gene saw no alternative but to introduce Sheila to sex in order to protect her from it.

Once he had justified himself to himself, the narrow mores and suffocating hypocrisies of the world outside Wills Canyon fell away, and all things again seemed possible. His nagging financial worries and Little Gene's lèse majesté evaporated. He could rebuild his dream and with his own flesh close the breach Becky had left in it. It was to be a new beginning.

Gene's mind spun. Stepping irrevocably over those lines of law and decency, turning wholly inward for ratification of his acts, was itself the source of his hubris. Like Raskolnikov in *Crime and Punishment* or André Gide's Lafcadio, who believed that their very crimes proved them exalted above common morality, Gene was convinced that he had achieved some new level of understanding, a higher consciousness where conventional standards did not apply. He was filled with an ardor for slicing through a knot of difficulties in a single, defiant act, to reveal a world in which everything is simple, coherent, and possible. Gene's logic was like Occam's razor in the hands of Procrustes, reducing vast problems to a single, violent solution.

Between May 5 and July 21, living in a welter of emotions, Gene collected four traffic citations for speeding and reckless driving. As a release and an emblematic act in defiance of convention, speed was irresistible to Gene. His Honda 90 was not a motorcycle worthy of the name, but the sporty (if increasingly unreliable) Subaru Brat injected him with a fresh vitality. He shaved the patriarchal beard, leaving only a raffish Zapata mustache, and tore around the twisting canyons and steep grades of the Sacramentos like a dashing hell of a fellow, furious to overtake his fixed idea. Nothing could stop him now.

CHAPTER FIVE

Using Sheila's enforced coin hobby as an excuse, Gene announced that he was taking her to a numismatic show in California as part of a special visit to see Dad Griffen, then beginning to suffer the first phases of Alzheimer's disease. Becky was disappointed, relieved, and disturbed by the plan. She had always felt close to Dad Griffen, had kept up most of the family's correspondence with him over the years, and she would have liked to see him. She also wondered, although she did not dare say so, how Gene could justify the expense, since practically all that she heard from him nowadays was about money and how she had to be more frugal. Moreover, the family hadn't been on a vacation together in nearly four years, and now they were missing their first chance. Her sole consolation was in having Gene gone and being alone with her children, and her one misgiving was in knowing that he was alone with Sheila.

Gene and Sheila returned to Wills Canyon on August 8, bringing with them pictures they had taken at Dad Griffen's. In the photograph he had Sheila take of him and his stepfather Gene seems to be leering at her through the lens, his smile as innocent and inane as a moonstruck teenager's. In the shot of Sheila with Dad Griffen her smile shows signs of strain, and her hands are knotted anxiously at the fly of her jeans.

Becky saw the wet affection with which Gene now approached Sheila, and she tried to put it down to doting, the kind of generosity that, from time to time in the past, Gene had shown toward all his children. But during August and September she had a sick sense that something was grotesquely wrong.

First there were the gifts. Three times before school started Gene disappeared from Wills Canyon for an afternoon and returned with bright clothes for his little princess—western boots and gingham shirts, a white braided belt and a red blouse with pointed collars, a striking Navajo vest of real wool. And after school began Becky could no longer deny her apprehensions. Every afternoon Gene would drive into Cloudcroft to pick Sheila up from school and leave the other children standing at the curb, waiting for their bus. It was sometimes hours after the school bus had dropped them off that Gene and Sheila returned home, with her snuggled in the crook of his arm. For weeks Gene followed Sheila everywhere with his Polaroid.

Twice during September Gene had sex with Sheila in the back of the Dodge van. But despite his professions of love and her meek submission, the magic wasn't there. Gene knew he had not really won her, that she did not yet understand his depth of feeling and could not share it. When he asked her she said it didn't feel right, and for a while the incest ceased.

Winter passed; Gene grew back his beard, and it was March before Sheila knew she was pregnant.

It had been another tense, cash-poor Christmas, with little cheer to welcome the new year and ease the bleak weeks from January to spring. Sheila, disoriented and frightened, found a sea anchor in school. Her grades improved dramatically her senior year. She won a mathematics award and was elected to a class office. She tried to bury the memory of her experience with her father, to deny it even to herself, and the concentration she turned to her studies was part of that process, taking her outside herself. The wound might, in some grotesque way, have knitted a stronger patch on her personality had Gene not continued his unabashed courtship for her affection.

Gene made no effort to disguise his infatuation with his daughter. He would have her in his room alone and talk to her in ways he spoke to no one else.

"Ladybug," he would say, holding her unresponsive body to him, "I love you so very, very much. You are the world to me, little princess. What we have done together is not wrong, no matter what anyone tells you. I did it to protect you, so no one can ever take advantage of you. It is our secret, though. Do you understand?"

"Yes," Sheila would say, hoping he wouldn't touch her there again, but not really caring if he did.

"I want to teach you everything I know about the world. I want to protect you and make sure that no one ever hurts you. You are so important to this family now, little princess, and it's so important that you be happy. All you have to do is tell me what you want."

But Sheila was silent.

Sheila had not seen a doctor to confirm her pregnancy before telling Gene, and he did not take her to one before telling Becky and Billy, but the announcement hit the parapeted stronghold in Wills Canyon like a siege engine, shattering Becky and widening the breach between Gene and his children. Gene nevertheless took some satisfaction in the vague symbolism of revealing the news to his family on the day of Sheila's senior prom, March 21, 1981.

Sheila did not have a date for the prom and would have preferred not to go, but Gene had insisted. He bought her a new dress of pale robin's-egg blue with white lace trim and a high, loose waist to smooth the small rise of her belly. She brushed her hair again and again and replaced the barrettes. She was in no hurry to go, but her dad kept calling upstairs, "Are you ready yet? Come on, I want to take your picture." So she was dressed and waiting long enough to regret it.

Gene had told her that he was going to explain things to Becky, and Sheila felt more anxious and uncomfortable than ever. When she came down the steep stairs in her odd-fitting clothes she felt all angles and clumsiness.

"Oh, look at this," Gene said, calling Becky and the other children to him. "Isn't she pretty, Mom? A real princess. Stand up straight, ladybug."

But the cut of her clothes made Sheila feel that she looked more pregnant than she did, and she hunched forward while she posed for the Polaroid, crossing her hands in front of her, gripping two fingers tightly with her other hand.

Gene drove Sheila to the prom, all the way reassuring her that things would be all right, that Becky would understand, that there was nothing to worry about. He loved her and would take care of her. A new baby, he told her, was always a joy.

When he returned home Gene called Becky and Billy together and sat them on the sofa in front of the stone hearth. He peeled his face and voice of all expression, paced the floor, stared into the corners of the ceiling, and began to speak.

"Now listen to me, both of you," he said, "and don't say anything until I've finished. Sheila Marie is going to have a baby."

Becky gasped and began to speak.

"Shut up," Gene snapped. "Now, this is our baby, and we have to do everything we can for Sheila. She needs us all. No one else needs to know anything about it, not Dad or Ma Novak or anyone. There will be no blaming, not one doubt that this is a child we all love. Understand? We will raise this child just like any of our others, and I want you to let Sheila know that. She needs us now, and we've got to stand beside her. That's all. We can talk about it more tomorrow."

Billy looked away in confusion and embarrassment, but Becky was struck dumb. She burned with cold shock and incredulity, as though the world had collapsed upon her.

"Billy," she said numbly, "go to bed now." Then she went herself to tuck in the little ones. She did not even have to ask whose child it was, and Billy was not long reaching the same conclusion.

Later, when Gene brought Sheila home from the dance, the house was quiet except for her mother's gasping sobs coming from the corner of the room she shared that night with the girls. When Gene and Sheila brought Becky her breakfast in bed the next morning she wore the blasted look of a concentration-camp survivor. All day she called her children to her and would not get out of bed. Even Gene spent more than an hour alone with her, lecturing her on how she ought to feel, himself brimming with confidence that his admonitions had set things right.

In a parody of concern and practicality Gene supplied Sheila with literature on adoption and abortion, each of the booklets emphasizing the terrible emotional toll of either course. In fact, he had made up his mind as soon as he knew Sheila was pregnant that they would keep the child and raise it in the family. Now that he again saw a woman growing heavy with his child, even though the woman was his child, Gene was filled with a fresh enthusiasm. He enrolled Sheila under his Civilian Health and Medical Program and on April 7 took her to Thunderbird Obstetrics and Gynecology in Alamogordo for the first of a half dozen visits. He bought books on baby names and breast-feeding. Gene could not have explained his joy, and it would, at any rate, be short-lived.

Gene was not so dissociated from reality that he did not recognize the trouble he might face over Sheila if the facts leaked out. He warned Becky repeatedly that he could be arrested, she could lose the children, and they might have to sell their property.

Becky did, however, tell Little Gene what had happened, and he was appalled. His personal sense of right and wrong and his grudge against his father's rages called Little Gene to act, but the strong bonds of family and his mother's pleas for him to be quiet on the matter tied his hands. Tossed on this dilemma, Little Gene confided in Sheila Hiller, a former classmate and friend, who urged him to contact the police or the New Mexico Department of Social Services. Little Gene vacillated for several days until April 17, when he made a call to the Otero County office of Social Services, telling them about Sheila Marie and his father. Then, fearing the consequences for himself and his mother, he drew a red herring across his trail with two anonymous calls to Social Services on April 18 and 20, the days before and after Easter. But by then he had spoken to others as well, and the rumors about Gene and Sheila were spreading.

Abe DeLeon, director of the Otero County office, ordered an immediate investigation and the following week notified the office of the district attorney, Steven Sanders.

The name Simmons rang a bell with Sanders. Just days before getting the message from Social Services he had received a call from a furious constituent demanding to know the source of rumors that he was the father of his pregnant, unwed daughter's child. The man said it was an outrage that he should be falsely accused when it was common knowledge that Gene Simmons really was the father of his child's child. Sanders naturally had taken no action on angry hearsay, but it stuck in his mind, looking in hindsight like a portent.

On April 20, Beth Simpson, a case worker in the Otero County office of Social Services, went to Cloudcroft to investigate the rumors.

She spoke first with Everett Bannister at Cloudcroft High School, who confirmed that he had heard the stories and allowed Simpson to meet privately with Sheila in his office.

To Simpson's surprise, Sheila readily told her that, yes, she had had sex with her father and was now pregnant by him. She told Simpson about the trip to California and the two times in September after they came back. She answered willingly, softly, never looking at the case worker.

Simpson then drove to Wills Canyon, where she confronted Gene with Sheila's testimony about the incest and her pregnancy.

"Yes," Gene said, "that's right," as though they were only matters of fact without moral or legal gravity. He said that he had told Becky, who was sitting there with them, and that the two oldest children, Billy and Little Gene, also knew.

"How do you think this will affect them?" Simpson asked.

Gene blandly dismissed the notion that there might be any problems in his marriage or his family.

"Besides," he told Simpson, "that's all over with. I'm sure you understand that I had to do it so she could learn about those things, to protect her. Sheila is very naïve and trusting, and it was my duty as her father. We've already discussed all this among ourselves, and we've decided that the child should be raised as part of this family, and when it is old enough we will tell it about its heritage. We know what we are doing," Gene concluded, "and we really don't need any help."

Like police officers and emergency-room physicians, case workers have to develop a very hard bark to deal with the human suffering that their job addresses. The Simmons incest was not the worst case Beth Simpson had encountered, but something in Gene's arrogance and obvious domination of his wife and children moved her to act with more than usual dispatch. The day after her initial interview with the Simmonses she made a verbal report to an assistant prosecutor in Sanders's office. Social Services, however, did not request immediate legal action. Rather, using the threat of it as a stick, they developed and got Gene to agree to a program of psychological counseling that would include Becky, Sheila, and the younger children. On May 1, Gene and Sheila went to the Holloman Air Force Base Mental Health Clinic for their initial psychological profile tests. After seeing the results Simpson was even more disturbed. In her subsequent report to the district attorney's office she noted that "Sheila's emotional immaturity [and] lack of ability to express her feelings" were largely as a result of living in what Simpson termed a "dysfunctional family."

Dysfunctional families come in many guises, but they have in common a single afflicted individual— usually a parent suffering from alcoholism, manic-depression, or some other psychosocial ill—who manipulates or dominates the family so completely that the emotional stability and healthy dynamics of it are deformed. Perceptions and behaviors are grotesquely altered to accommodate and protect the one at the expense of the many, exactly as had happened in the Simmons family, who bent their will, their very construct of reality, to Gene's.

In the whorl of events and revelations connected to the incest and Sheila's pregnancy Gene maintained an almost stoic poise and reacted to the events with charades of normalcy. He relaxed his labor demands and hauled the entire family off on cold, dreary picnics to affirm its solidarity. He reverted to the overalls and straw hat that had been his uniform when Wills Canyon was new to him, all potential and optimism. A united front would, he thought, impress the intrusive social workers with the stability of his family. The family would go along for the sake of survival, and Gene had so distorted the emotional space around him that survival meant perpetuating the warp.

Gene also felt a peculiar relief by being caught up in the system, a feeling, at least, that he was on familiar ground. He had worked the system well while in uniform, and psychological evaluations were nothing new to him. He knew the demeanor that would elicit confidence without engendering envy or fear; he knew how to give the right answers to standardized questions. But the kinds of inwardly directed exercises he encountered in counseling didn't sit well. Throughout the five weeks of family therapy with Becky, Gene continued to deny, even in the face of his own admissions, that there were any problems in his marriage or family, insisting that Sheila would remain at home, have the child, and let the family raise it. Gene treated the counseling not as therapy but as a negotiation, a pro forma accommodation to regulations.

In part out of necessity and in part to satisfy the appearances he thought might soothe the concerns of Social Services, Gene took a civilian position with the 6585th Test Group at Holloman. He would later contend that a filing error in the Holloman Civilian Personnel Office delayed his being employed there any earlier. His confidence that he could successfully work the system again was running high. He was feeling celebratory when he bought the powerful red Suzuki motorcycle, cheerfully ignoring the fact that his license had been suspended the previous October for the spate of tickets he received during his anxious waiting for a chance to rape his daughter. He looked on Sheila's belly with pride.

But Gene was not just bluffing or hoping to slip passively through the legal consequences of what he had done. The issues of child molestation and incest were more than in the air; they were in the local papers and the courts. And Gene was not oblivious to the possibility of a legal battle with Social Services. He contacted the Hebard and Hebard law firm, tried to plead indigency—thereby getting the state to underwrite his action against it—but was scotched by Simpson's report to the attorneys that he had both a salary and a retirement income. He did learn, however, that any admission of criminal activity made in counseling could come out in court. Feeling tricked, Gene immediately stopped all contact between his family and both the counseling center and Social Services.

Beth Simpson was convinced that the situation in the Simmons home was ominously askew, and, frustrated with the closed-ranks denial of a problem by Gene and Becky, she filed a seven-page request with the district attorney for a consent decree that would remove Sheila, Loretta, and Marianne from the home, place Gene on pre-prosecution probation, and require continued counseling for him and Becky. Among other considerations, Simpson insightfully noted that "Normally a young person of Sheila's age has begun the separation process, but *due to the symbiotic relation-*

ship between Sheila and her father [emphasis added], Sheila has not been allowed to become involved in the normal social activities outside the home that are required for social maturity and independence."

Gene was ignorant of the request for a court order, but his brief swell of confidence would crash into a trough of panic toward the end of June.

By now the gossip-sketched story of Gene and Sheila was well advanced, and Sheila's pregnancy could no longer be concealed. She would not attend school, but Everett Bannister arranged to deliver and pick up her assignments and allow her to graduate. Because he knew Social Services and the D.A. were already involved, however, he never discussed the situation with Sheila or her parents. Among faculty and students at Cloudcroft High School, and among all the parents who knew, Gene was already a pariah.

Beth Simpson filed her request with Sanders's office on June 8, and nine days later Sheila delivered her child at the same hospital where her baby sister, Rebecca, had been born two years before. Sheila's daughter was christened Sylvia Gail, the only one of Gene's children not to bear family names.

On July 20, the day after Sheila and Sylvia Gail came home from the hospital, Otero County Deputy Sheriff Jeff Farmer, responding to a request from the district attorney's office, drove to Wills Canyon to question Sheila. Gene was at work, and Farmer spoke with Sheila in Becky's presence, but neither of them would answer his questions, not even when he told them he knew they had been working with Social Services and that his investigation was, in part, at the agency's request.

"Sheila refused to make any statement or comment," Farmer wrote in his incident report. "No further details."

If Farmer's visit caused Gene anxiety, the next few days intensified it. One of the lead stories in the Alamogordo papers for that summer was the trial of former Alamogordo mayor and city commissioner Frank Carr, Jr., charged with five counts of sex crimes against minors. On June 26 the paper reported Carr's conviction and possible sentence of up to sixty years in prison and forty-five thousand dollars in fines. District Attorney Sanders was a crusader for juveniles, active in local and state child-welfare projects, including the statewide task force on child abuse. He put crimes against children high on his docket, and police and prosecutors alike breathed that air. Immediately after the Fourth of July holiday Deputy Farmer was back in Cloudcroft continuing his investigation, questioning neighbors, teachers, and schoolmates of the children.

Criminal consequences he had never foreseen were looming large for Gene. He could not go anywhere outside his property without feeling the opprobrium of his neighbors in Cloudcroft, where people would turn away from him, and he could hear his name whispered in conversations on the street when he passed by. Even at work he sensed a chilly distance between himself and his co-workers. Hearing of Farmer's renewed investigation, Gene leapt into a panicky reordering of his plans.

Misrepresenting his financial situation once again by claiming his employment at the 6585th as a permanent job, Gene went back to Security Bank & Trust for a refinancing of his first mortgage and on July 28 was granted a one-year balloon loan of fourteen thousand dollars against a lien on the property in Wills Canyon. At the top of the agreement was noted "moving expenses for family." During the next week Gene would mount a logistical exercise that in its multitude of details rivaled a battlefield redeployment.

With the exception of clothes and personal articles, he inventoried practically every item at Wills Canyon, every scrap of loose tin and every broken hoe, listed them according to priority, and calculated how much of what would go in each vehicle they were taking north. At his dictation Becky recorded a list of more than two dozen last-minute things to do, what to leave and what to take, and contingency plans for all sorts of highway problems. He was leaving it up to Becky and Little Gene to actually pack and move, for Gene was headed to Arkansas, taking the younger girls with him to insure he would not end up there alone.

On August 6, Gene rented a house in the postage-stamp community of Ward, Arkansas. Little Gene, who would make two trips with a U-Haul to move his family, was remaining in New Mexico and would see to the sale of the house and land in Wills Canyon. Becky would return once with Billy to move a truckful of tools and salvaged building materials. Gene would never see New Mexico again.

When Jeff Farmer arrived at the Simmons home in Wills Canyon with an arrest warrant on August 10 he found the house deserted.

PART TWO

PATTERNS

1940–1976

THE PAST, MARRIAGE, LIFE IN UNIFORM

Over the gulfs of dream
Flew a tremendous bird
Further and further away
Into a moonless black,
Deep in the brain, far back.

—THEODORE ROETHKE
from ''Night Crow''

CHAPTER SIX

The heritage that Ronald Gene Simmons was born into at the Chicago Lying-in Hospital on July 15, 1940, was to haunt his life with uncertainty. He had no grandparents, a mother who was sickly and undemonstrative, and a father whom he never knew.

Eva Loretta Richardson, Gene's mother, had herself been orphaned at age ten, was adopted by her mother's sister, Nancy Ellen, and her husband, Joseph Port Quinn, in October 1919, and changed her legal name to Loretta Richardson Quinn. Throughout her life Loretta would be obsessed with ancestry, family trees, and the research of mail-order genealogists, forever seeking herself in records.

Loretta was a bright, sensitive, talented, even gifted girl, and the Quinns themselves were childless, so Loretta passed from being one of nearly a dozen minor siblings to being an adored and cozened only child. She spent her childhood in Rock Island, Illinois, where she studied piano and voice at home and enjoyed an active teenage social life as a member of Rainbow Girls and Kings' Daughters. High school president of both the Poetry Department and the

French Club, a member of the Short Story Department and the Junior English Council, as well as a staff writer for the English department magazine and the school newspaper, Loretta was an exceptional student. In 1926 she won first place in the silent reading section of the National French Achievement Tests and published an essay in *Magazine World,* a periodical for high school students sponsored by *Atlantic Monthly.* She was also both a member of the Rock Island Trinity Episcopal Church and, at her aunt and uncle's reluctant sufferance, a regular in Sunday school at the First Church of Christ Scientist. For much of Loretta's young adulthood, regardless of her registered church membership, Christian Science would appeal to her need to believe in the miracle of self-regeneration, the mystical link between will and reality.

Following graduation from high school in 1926, Loretta enrolled at Augustana College in Rock Island, and the next year she entered Iowa State Teacher's College at Ames, Iowa. Prior to what would have been her junior year Loretta was elected to the Sigma Tau Delta honorary English society. But she had no opportunity to accept the honor, for the Great Depression came early to the Quinns.

Loretta and her family were among the first hit by the Depression, although not among the worst. Still, Loretta's slim fraction of an inheritance and Ellen and Joe's nest egg were suddenly worth only cents on the dollar, and Loretta had to leave Iowa at once and return to Rock Island.

Loretta genuinely loved her adoptive parents, and they her, but the year away had left Loretta with an urge toward independence for which Ellen and Joe— and, in fact, Loretta herself—were not prepared. Intelligent, naïve, refined, and humiliated by the reverse in her life, neither Loretta nor her aunt and uncle wanted her to take a common job in an office or a ladies' store. In the convention of genteel poverty she joined the Rock Island Fine Arts Club, wore darned gloves to the meetings, and took in private students for French and piano lessons. But things did improve for the Quinns, and in 1929 Loretta enrolled in the School of Nursing at the Michigan Children's Hospital in Detroit, an experience that was to shatter her nerves and expose her fragility, her crying need for approval, acceptance, and the sense of belonging to a family, a need that would wear down her ambition and recur in her second son.

Loretta was eternally tired and constantly falling short of what she thought was expected of her by the teachers and nurses at Children's Hospital. Feeling out of step and isolated, Loretta began to suffer the fears of abandonment and isolation so common among orphans and foster children.

"You promised you'd come [to visit] after I'd been here a week or two," she chided her aunt in one letter. "I don't think you want to come. I dreamed last nite that I went home for my vacation and you didn't want me at all and told me to go right back. Was that nice?"

By late March Loretta was racked by her competing desires and loyalties. Still overwhelmed by the hospital's demanding routine, which she detailed in her letters, Loretta maintained an image of herself as the outsider, the more refined one, the one least suited to the physical demands of nursing, and before the spring semester was done, the pressures of school and the tension of her anxieties had driven Loretta to a nervous collapse.

In April she left Children's Hospital and returned to Rock Island, where she remained under a doctor's care for several weeks. In September she resumed giving private lessons in French and piano, living at home with her aunt and uncle, but in 1932–33 she did complete a one-year course at a local business college just across the Mississippi River in Davenport, Iowa. The following year, on May 9, 1934, when she was twenty-five, Loretta married William Henry Simmons.

William Simmons was a coarse, lantern-jawed man who had worked himself up to the position of industrial inspector with the International Harvester Company. Ellen and Joe thought he was an unlikely mate for Loretta, and she soon felt the same way. But she was pregnant within a month of her marriage and delivered her first son, Robert William, on March 5, 1935. She stayed with William Simmons until the following year, when she divorced him and returned to finish her degree at Augustana College, where she graduated in 1937, summa cum laude.

If the divorce was shocking, Loretta's remarriage to William in 1939 was well-nigh scandalous, but the attractions of a family of her own were greater for Loretta than the allure of being a single mother in the abyss of the lingering economic depression.

William's job took them to Chicago, where Ronald Gene Simmons was born in July 1940, almost six weeks premature.

Born to a mother already marked by instability and driven to define her life in ways that ever defeated her, Gene may also have had the circumstances of that birth to account for something that, in him, never was. Some psychologists argue that the event of birth is the seminal rite of passage, one echoed in the perithantic (near-death) experiences recounted by hundreds of people over thousands of years, in which they emerge into the clean, gauzily lit presence of the godhead after passing through the crush of a dark and terrifying corridor. Absent this experience, the theorists maintain, premature babies, whose nervous systems are not well enough developed to record the experience, may never know, even in religious ecstasy or drug hallucination, the sense of rebirth that is a common element in psychological theories of individuation and spiritual teachings alike, and is, in fact, a recapitulation of that definitive, nearly universal human experience, being born. Gene began life deprived both of living roots and of those initial creases in his brain.

Gene was often ill during the first years of his life, and his older brother, Robert, was now beginning school, leaving Gene the sole object of Loretta's day. Less than two years later, however, on February 4, 1942, Loretta bore a daughter, christened Nancy Ellen, and less than one year after her birth William Simmons dropped dead on the job, felled by a massive "coronary thrombosis."

At thirty-four, the mother of three, and in need of a job, Loretta joined the growing number of young widows the war would create, took her children back to Rock Island, and found clerical work at an office of the War Department in neighboring Moline.

While working at the War Department Loretta met William Davenport Griffen, a civil engineer fifteen years her senior, and in October 1943 she married him.

Griffen was a better match for Loretta than her first husband had been, for he was well educated and an enthusiastic painter. Slight of build and with regular, unprepossessing features, Dad Griffen, as Gene would later call him, was diligent, decent, and fastidious. He was not a man to inspire grand passion, but he was steady, sober, and affectionate, and Loretta's marriage to him lasted twenty-seven years, until her death in 1970.

Peter Ira Griffen was born to the couple in May 1945, and Loretta was pregnant again before Thanksgiving. In May 1946 she delivered twin boys prematurely, and both died within hours of birth.

Following the death of the twins William Griffen, now employed by the Army Corps of Engineers, requested and received a transfer to Little Rock, Arkansas. In October 1946 Dad Griffen settled his family more than seventy miles from Little Rock, near the tiny town of Hector, in a rustic, rural home surrounded by the Ozark forests, a far cry from the smokestacks and prairie winters of Moline.

For Gene, who was beginning second grade when the family moved to Hector, and for his half-brother Pete, that house would come to symbolize home. As adults, each would try to buy it and fail. As the crow flies, it is about ten miles from the Griffen home in Hector to the burned remains of the house in Dover, on Mockingbird Hill.

The isolated household at Hector, twenty miles from the nearest paved road, was not entirely conventional. There was nothing out of the ordinary about using a hand pump or a privy, but Dad Griffen was gone from home four nights a week. On Monday mornings, early, he took the steam train to Little Rock, where he stayed and worked until Friday evening, when he caught the train back to Hector, leaving Loretta essentially alone to raise the children. Gene rode the bus to the Hector school and had a whole forest for his playground. Having been coddled through his infancy, Gene was now the middle child, equally jealous of the privileges his older brother enjoyed and the attention Loretta gave to the babies. The colicky fits he had suffered as an infant became tantrums for recognition. Still, those years at Hector would remain in Gene's memory as the happiest of his life.

In September 1950 Dad Griffen moved his family to Little Rock, to an area in transition from countryside to suburb called Landmark. The principal at Landmark School, where Gene was a wholly undistinguished student, recognized that he was a troubled boy and became his confidant and counselor, but Gene made no friends his own age. Outside the family he was solitary, and inside it he was an increasing problem.

In 1952, at age seventeen, Gene's older brother Robert left home to join the navy, and Gene assumed the prerogatives of oldest boy with a will. His teasing of Pete took on a meaner cast, physically and emotionally. Now he bullied and threatened the smaller boy, poking, pinching, and slapping him when no one was around to see. More subtle were the tricks Gene played on Pete, urging him to climb a forbidden fence or pee off the porch, then telling on him for doing it. Gene didn't lie so much as manipulate events and the way they were recounted.

Once Gene coerced Pete into getting on a bicycle that Pete was too small to ride. The resulting crash left Pete scraped and shaken, and he ran home in tears to tell his mother. Gene got on the bike and beat his brother there. When Pete stumbled up the steps Gene had already rattled out his case against his little brother, accusing him of taking the bicycle when he had been told not to and of bending the spokes that Gene had kicked in to support his story.

Knowing her sons, Loretta was inclined to believe Pete, but Gene bellowed in protest, stomped the porch, and fell into a screaming fit until his mother was ready to pass over laying blame.

As Pete has recalled, "He just couldn't stand to be questioned. He had to be right, had to be boss. He'd throw a really big fit if you crossed him on that. Things just had to be his way."

Soon this fractiousness spread to his relations with his parents as well. His grades were abysmal. He refused to do what he was told. He screamed at his mother and stomped the floor in frustration, denying that he was in the wrong—about anything. In frustration, Dad Griffen resorted to spankings to control Gene and once whipped him with a length of garden hose. But nothing worked. Realizing that Dad Griffen would not do him any real harm, Gene began to taunt his stepfather.

It was more than Dad Griffen and Loretta could deal with. Neither of them was given to emotional outbursts, and Loretta's health was already beginning to fail her. In the fall of 1953 they enrolled Gene in the Morris Academy in Searcy, Arkansas, about fifty miles north of Little Rock, a Catholic boarding school that often worked with problem boys.

By Thanksgiving, however, his parents relented, and Gene was back at home, enrolled in Fuller Junior High School in the Sweet Home community, southeast of Little Rock. Humbled by the discipline of the good fathers at the Morris Academy, Gene made some efforts to accommodate a world he had not made. To demonstrate his responsibility, and to have the spending money denied him as a punishment by Dad Griffen, Gene took on a paper route. But that, too, came to a bad end.

Between the Griffen home and Fuller Junior High there was an all-black neighborhood that Gene and Pete had to walk through and where Gene threw his papers. One day he came in shaking with fright. He had been threatened, he said, by a group of black kids along his paper route. He begged Pete, then only eight, to go with him to face the other boys. Pete refused, and Gene quit the paper route, shamed by his cowardice and by revealing it to little Pete, whom he blamed for the humiliation.

In 1954 Dad Griffen, now fifty-five, was beginning to suffer significantly from allergies and asthma, and

Loretta was contending with a host of ills that in time would include arthritis, cervical cancer, colitis, angina pectoris, and hardening of the arteries. Gene's behavior did nothing to lessen their complaints. Surlier and no better able to control his tantrums, Gene was the source of much distress for all those around him. Already larger than either of his parents, he began to threaten them and balked at all forms of discipline.

"You hit me again, and I'll knock your head off," he once told Dad Griffen.

In September 1955, when he was fifteen, Gene was sent again to the Morris Academy, this time for the year.

Meanwhile, health was becoming an overriding concern in the Griffen household. Nearly debilitated by his asthma and allergies in the pollen-rich air of Arkansas, Dad Griffen requested a transfer to Albuquerque, New Mexico, where he moved the family in December, leaving Gene to complete the spring term at Morris Academy.

Gene rejoined the family in June 1956, and to everyone's relief, things went smoothly at first.

Gene was subdued and polite when he returned, so much so that the family felt the academy had worked wonders. But within a month he began to slough his veneer of contrition.

"No," he would tell his mother when she asked him to do anything he did not want to do. "You can't make me. Just get away from me. Don't touch me. None of you cares anything about me. I hate all of you."

Gene found fault with everything and barked at everyone. He refused to study, made no friends, and spent hours on end alone in his room. But the mounting medical bills would not allow his parents to send him away again. The stress made Dad Griffen gag on

his asthma and caused Loretta palpitations and short-
ness of breath.

In the throat-chapping aridity of Albuquerque and
among a family full of bronchial preoccupations, Gene
developed his lifelong antipathy toward smoke and
the nervous habit of clearing his throat, as though in
perpetual fear of choking.

In February 1957, one month into Gene's second
semester at Highland High in Albuquerque, Dad Griffen
was transferred to Berkeley, California, where Gene
enrolled at the Berkeley High School. But within the
month Dad Griffen had moved them yet again, this
time to suburban Mill Valley, north of the bay, where
Gene entered his third school that year, Tamalpais
Union High. He completed the semester at Tamalpais
but did not graduate.

Already, at age seventeen, Gene was dreaming of a
return to the idyllic Ozarks and having a big family
tucked away in the hills. It was a dream he often
harped on when disparaging Albuquerque or Mill Valley or any place that wasn't Arkansas.

Gene was an outcast within his own home, and all
events seemed to push him further from the circle of
love. His mother's cervical cancer was diagnosed that
year, and once her radiation treatment began she
needed more support than she could offer. Pete and
Nancy gravitated to Dad Griffen and demonstrated
sympathy for Loretta. Nothing Gene could do could
make him the center of attention or claim his mother
as an ally. He tempered his outbursts of anger and
know-it-all posturings around the house, but Gene
was deeply unhappy, desperate for some sort of recognition, to have others hold him in the same high
regard he held himself.

What Gene found when he took his search outside
the family, however, was humiliation.

In the summer of 1957 Gene found a job at a local

golf club working as a waiter and busboy. The family was pleased to have him doing something, and Gene seemed initially content to be earning a little money and slowly inching himself out of the nest. But it came to a sudden and disgracing end.

Gene came in one evening from the club restaurant covered in garbage—orange peels, coffee grounds, bones, bread, gristle, and grease. He refused to tell anyone what had happened, refused to discuss it at all, preferring to stand on his surly dignity. He did not return to the club again, even to pick up his last check.

On September 5, with Dad Griffen's and Loretta's grateful permission, Gene enlisted in the United States Navy, seeking a sea change in his frustrations.

CHAPTER SEVEN

Like the whale hunter Ishmael or Conrad's Lord Jim, Gene took to sea with a troubled spirit, a restive anxiety, a sense of alienation. He was, like Melville's narrator, "of a mind to knock people's hats off in the street." For Gene, enlisting was exorcism, rite of passage, and adventure all in one. But in navy boot camp at San Diego he also found a disciplined environment in which he could lose himself, cease to be who he was, and recreate himself as what he could do, and do very well, as he discovered.

Following boot camp, in November 1957 Gene was assigned as a clerk with the AFDL-21 Ship Repair Facility in Guam, where he would spend the next nineteen months. On Guam he enrolled in GED preparatory courses, and in May 1958 easily passed the series of tests necessary to earn his equivalency diploma. He also completed, during the following year, military courses in photography, personnel administration, typing, and "navy mail."

Gene was not a malcontent but followed orders promptly and efficiently. He was eager to please those in authority, and as a clerk/typist he had at last found something he was really good at—far better, in fact, than most others around him—and it gained him the recognition and regard that he had, by his quarrelsomeness, forfeited all claim to in his family. During his more than one and a half years on Guam, however, Gene left the island only once, on a seven-day leave to Hong Kong, where he flew on a military hop on March 9, 1959 and returned to Guam on March 16 as ballast on the USS *Orca.* Adventure was not an itch he was ready to scratch on his own.

Gene sailed stateside on July 1, 1959, with orders to report on board the USS *Missouri,* then berthed with the Pacific Reserve Fleet at Bremerton, Washington. He was now a Yeoman Third Class, making one hundred thirteen dollars a month, and with enough saved to buy himself a 1954 Ford sedan.

Gene had grown an inch while on Guam and filled out in his chest and shoulders; his uniform looked good on him, and he wore his hat at a rakish angle. He was the sort of sailor the navy thought good for its image, and he was drafted for duty to appear in photos of navy personnel doing good works and giving checks to charity.

Despite this dashing appearance, Gene was socially awkward. He had never dated while bouncing between the all-boys Morris Academy and a different public school every other year, and, with his intact idealism about wives and mothers and his fastidious aversions to sickness and miscegenation, he returned to the States sexually no wiser than the yarns and scuttlebutt of his shipmates could make him. But he did like girls. More specifically, his dream included a wife and children, and he set about finding one with single-minded intent.

Gene had also learned to like beer, but he was no one's drinking buddy. In fact, throughout his life he had no close male friends. He wasn't one to prowl the bars or haunt the enlisted men's club with a pal, looking for girls and leering over the foam of a three-two beer. Instead he became a regular at the USO dances held at the Bremerton YMCA.

Gene was too self-conscious ever to take to the floor, but the USO did have girls, lots of them—wholesome, wide-eyed volunteers who delighted in dancing three dances with a fellow and making bright small talk. Among them was a slight, dark eighteen-year-old from Colorado named Rebecca Ulibarri who would let Gene bring her punch and chat with him while they sat one out, and she struck a spark of possibility in Gene.

He had had his eye on her for weeks before he found a chance he liked to meet her. One evening of a dance he noticed that she was not on the floor. But while milling around with some other sailors outside the gymnasium where the dancing was going on, Gene saw her in the glass-fronted office next to it, typing up the USO schedule for the coming month.

"Boy, she can really fly," said one of the other fellows about Becky's typing.

Gene snorted. "I can do better than that," he said.

"Oh, yeah? Prove it," said the other sailor.

"I don't need to prove it," Gene said. "I know I can."

"Yeah, you're afraid to," the other sailor said. "C'mon, let's go ask her."

Gene agreed, if the other fellow would do the talking.

Becky blushed at the challenge—she had noticed Gene, too—but acted cocky and accepted.

With the other sailor timing them, Gene and Becky took turns hammering out the mimeograph master on the old manual typewriter. He won handily.

"Now," he said to her, "you've got to come have some punch with me."

He told her he was from Arkansas and planned

someday to return there and buy back his family home, where he would raise a family in the pastoral solitude of the hills. He told her she was beautiful. She told him that she loved children. Becky had never met a man so attentive and self-assured, so eager to share his dreams with her.

Becky had graduated that spring from high school in Walsenburg, Colorado, and come to Bremerton to be with her older sister, Viola O'Shields—whose husband, Roger, was also in the navy at Bremerton—during the last weeks of Vi's second pregnancy. Prim and pretty, bubbly and gregarious, Becky also carried a burden of uncertainty north with her from the erosion-etched family ranch.

Bersabe Rebecca Ulibarri was born in New Mexico, the youngest of five, and until the eighth grade lived in the small town of Raton. Her father had abandoned the family when Becky was young, and her mother, Mae Barnum Ulibarri, eventually remarried to Andy Novak, who moved them all to an arid four-hundred-acre spread fourteen miles from Walsenburg, where he worked intermittently as a coal miner. Soon Andy and Mae had another daughter, Edith, and three years later a son, John. Andy Novak made a keen and often cutting distinction between "his" family and the Ulibarri-surnamed children. It was tacitly but generally understood that when the Ulibarri children finished high school they could have the interest on their life insurance, but there was nothing else for them in the Novak home. As the youngest and last Ulibarri child left in the house, Becky passed her high school years under this cloud of uncertainty.

Becky's mother, Mae, was a tough, savvy woman who built the ranch's cattle herd calf by calf, raised poultry, pigs, and a garden, and generally made life possible throughout the frequent strikes and layoffs that kept Andy out of the mines. Becky, on the other hand, never felt the ranch was home, never felt she had a place there. She had chores, of course, but she hoed her weeds in pedal pushers and black flats and never wore cowboy boots. She was girlish and pin-neat, always insisting that her cuffs and collar be buttoned and no loose threads hang from her hem.

Becky was popular in high school but did not stand out among the forty-five students in her senior class, who all assumed that Becky's future was in marriage —to someone. It seemed to be what she was reaching for. She often went dancing with her favorite brother, Abe, and loved the flaccid, sentimental rock 'n' roll of the late 1950s, especially "Teenager in Love," by Dion and the Belmonts. She was also a great corre-spondent, writing frequently to many cousins and friends and one pen pal in England, escaping through the mail from the parched, dreary acres of the ranch to other towns, happier families, and a distant world where the TV was called a telly and two weeks were a fortnight.

Following graduation, Becky was rescued from limbo by Viola's invitation to come to Bremerton. She was gone like a shot, arriving in Washington about the same time as Gene, in the summer of 1959.

After helping Vi around the house all day Becky had plenty of free time when Roger came home in the evening. He and Vi encouraged her to volunteer at the USO as a good, chaperoned way to make friends and, perhaps, meet a fellow or two. And she did. She went out on dates with several of the young servicemen she met at the YMCA dances and brought them home to meet her favorite sister and brother-in-law. But never Gene.

In November Roger O'Shields was transferred to the Great Lakes Naval Training Center in North Chicago, Illinois, and Becky moved with them, to help the O'Shieldses get settled. Then she went to Minnesota, where another sister, Tilly, also had a new baby and was in need of a hand. After the first of the year Becky migrated south to stay with relatives in Texas. Throughout the winter and spring of 1959–60 Becky and Gene kept up a steady and ardent correspondence. Although they had known each other for less than a month when Becky left Bremerton, they had fallen for each other with all the emotional tonnage of their mutual needs. For Gene it was a need to be the center of someone's world, to be loved, respected, even adored, and this Becky did, because her need was to know the love and strength of a good man. She had never known it from her stepfather and as a small child had often blamed her natural father's abandonment on herself, believing he hated her because she was thin, ugly, and dark. She mistook Gene's authoritarian vanity for strength and thought his obsession with being in charge was his way of taking care of her, for Becky basked in the love love has for itself.

Happiness was plain on both their faces when in July 1960, at the end of their postal courtship, Gene and Becky were married at Raton, New Mexico, in the small Spanish-language church that Becky had once attended. Gene's periwinkle-blue eyes shone, and Becky's dazzling smile lit the entire ceremony. Afterward they held hands and kissed and posed for pictures beside Gene's Ford, Becky in a white cocktail-length dress and Gene in his dress blues.

The marriage surprised Gene's family, who had not met Becky, and when he arrived with her in Mill Valley the week after the ceremony they were amazed at the changes in him. Confident in Becky's love, Gene was affable and outgoing, affectionate with everyone, and bursting with plans for the future. Dad Griffen liked Becky at once, and Loretta, while reserving a mother-in-law's judgment, was pleased at what she saw in Gene.

In January 1961 Gene offered to extend his tour of duty for one year if he could stay at Bremerton. Becky was pregnant by this time, due to deliver in July, and Gene was torn between wanting to remain in the security of the service and not wanting to go back to sea and be separated from his wife and new child. In May he offered to reenlist if he could continue in "my present career field." With his commanding officer's endorsement for admittance to an advanced training program for office personnel, Gene reneged on his reenlistment, instead opting for the year's extension, expecting the advanced school to keep him off sea duty. But it didn't work out that way. On July 24, ten days after he had extended and nine days after the birth of his son, Ronald Gene, Jr., his request for school was denied, and Gene found himself tangled in the paperwork web he had spun.

On August 10 Gene received orders to report on board the USS *Henrico* at San Diego for maneuvers in the Pacific beginning September 6. He took Becky and Little Gene to Walsenburg, where they would stay while he was at sea.

The task force returned to San Diego in May, and on May 6 Gene took a fifteen-day leave to go to Walsenburg for Becky and Little Gene. Gene was a short-timer again, with less than two months left to serve, and the navy just wasn't working out. His efforts to secure special schools and promotion had backfired and sent him back to sea. And however secure those navy checks, they weren't much. Bolstered by some particular office skills and a greater self-confidence, Gene thought there might be a financial shortcut back to the land in civilian life. On July 13, two days before his and his son's birthday, Gene was released from the navy, and in August he found a job at the Bank of America in San Francisco.

Gene's job was to verify deposits from armored cars, and he handled it with accuracy and integrity. He was making nearly nine thousand dollars a year, more than six times his navy pay, and was fantasizing about becoming a banker himself. He enrolled that fall at Marin College in Kentfield, California, making a D in business English, and a B in consumer economics. But something was not right. Despite his veneer of self-confidence, Gene still felt the awkwardness of being an outsider. The social skills he had honed in the forecastle didn't sort well with the buttoned-down ambiance of the bank, and the uncertainty of advancement, the lack of objective, emotionally neutral criteria, such as ratings tests, placed Gene in a situation of being judged for who he was, not what he could do.

The navy had been good for Gene, and he had liked it, but he had no relish for being separated from Becky. Her admiration and the very fact of his son made him feel more important than he ever had, gave him a kind of definition greater than being a superior clerk/typist out to sea. So in January 1963, despite having to enter at a reduced rank, Gene enlisted in the United States Air Force, where he would remain for more than sixteen years, separated from his family for only the thirteen months he would spend in Vietnam.

Gene reported for duty at Langley AFB in the Norfolk-Newport News area of coastal Virginia on March 15, 1963, and was assigned to the Services Squadron of the 4500 Air Base Wing. His job was CQ (charge-of-quarters) of the base Visiting Officer Quarters, not unlike a combination of batman and night manager at a motel. Becky was now pregnant again, expecting in October.

Becky was proving adaptable to the itinerant life of a military wife, but this move was especially easy, even longed-for, because Roger and Viola were stationed just across the bay in Norfolk. With Roger frequently at sea, Viola saw a lot of Becky and Gene during the more than four years they were at Langley, especially of Becky, and the two families socialized regularly when Roger was in port, getting together for picnics and cookouts or just to spend a Saturday afternoon "visiting." This was the first time the O'Shieldses had met Gene, and they found him an odd but not wholly objectionable duck. Being generous people, in fact, Vi and Roger looked for things to like in their brother-in-law.

He had none of the common vices, drank beer in moderation, and had a strong aversion to tobacco smoke that appeared comically prudish in those days before the Surgeon General's report. He was industrious and seemed to take a genuine interest in his children, especially in whoever the youngest might be. By objective measure, there was little they would find to fault in Gene.

Gene also had an active mind that became engrossed in information, facts. He listened to the radio, watched television news, and read newspapers and "informational" literature of all sorts, compiling an autodidact's canon of knowledge the way flies accumulate on a gummed strip.

When he was ashore Roger O'Shields made a conscious effort to get to know Gene. Gene, however, did not make that easy. Calling on his potpourri of undigested facts, Gene liked to hold forth on whatever he had most recently memorized. And Roger soon discovered that this was not for the sake of argument, for Gene became irritable and flustered if Roger brought anything to light that Gene didn't know or that was in contradiction of him. His tactic then was to retreat into forms of sarcasm and one-upsmanship. Roger eventually recognized that this starchy vanity ran to the very core of his brother-in-law.

One afternoon Roger and his oldest son stopped by the Simmons home in Hampton and found Gene tinkering with his Mercury Comet, one of the two or three old cars he always had around. Gene liked to flatter himself with the notion that he was handy, and he was changing the spark plugs when Roger made a comment about the cost of a tune-up he had had done at a garage.

"Little Gene, come here," Gene said to his son, who was playing nearby. Gene threw a greasy hand across his son's shoulders and grinned fatuously at Roger. "*We* do our own tune-ups, don't we, son?" he said.

Roger was not stung by the remark, but without knowing exactly why, he found the gratuitous sarcasm disturbing.

At home Gene was settling into patterns that would darken throughout his life. He controlled the mail through a post office box and had no telephone. Becky did not know how to drive, and Gene liked having her dependent on him. Living in town, with Viola so nearby, neither did it put him out. The Becky he desired, perpetuated, and helped to create was wife, mother, and child to him all at once. Gene held complete discretion over money and usually made the family budget without consulting his wife, expecting her to make do on a stipend that always left out children's clothes or Kotex or something for the movies. He began to berate her in public if the money wasn't enough and took pleasure in correcting her country grammar in front of others. The scoldings over money happened so frequently that Vi began to suspect that he kept Becky intentionally short of cash so she would have to come to him and beg for it just to feed the children.

But Becky was, in the conventional sense, a good wife. She kept Gene's house, raised the children with love, and crowed his accomplishments, however modest. He was "my Gene," and there was little else Becky saw as hers.

Gene's job at Langley was even cushier than being a navy mail clerk, but Gene was not complacent about his career. In August 1963 he completed the air force's Records Management and Training Course and signed up for math and political science classes at the Newport News branch of the College of William and Mary, although he quickly dropped the political science course and did not complete freshman math. He was, however, doing double duty to provide a good income. In October he took an evening job as a security guard in the area GEX (Government Employees Exchange), knowing he would need the money when his oldest daughter, Sheila Marie, was born later that month.

Gene's initiative on the job began to pay off as he was steadily elevated to positions of increasing responsibility within the Base Housing hierarchy. He continued to impress his superiors in all areas save one: The only category of Gene's performance reports in which he did not receive the highest mark was in answer to the question, "How well does he get along with others?" Gene was as correct as a butler and almost as much fun. In May 1964 he was promoted to Airman First Class (E-4).

From the beginning it was clear to everyone who saw them that Sheila Marie was Gene's favorite. Becky, who had never known this sort of fatherly love, was delighted for her daughter, reluctant ever to come between Sheila and Gene. One of Gene's favorite sports with his children was to toss them in the air and save them in a swooping catch. Little Gene howled in terror when Gene did this, but Sheila screamed with delight, and Gene loved her for it. Girls were always Gene's favorites, the ones he had sit on his lap, the ones he teased and talked to. Gene's relations with women, however, were pulled between his need of their good opinion and his aloofness from the entire sex. But always Gene had to demonstrate his superiority to them, often with puerile displays of machismo.

Gene made a special effort to curry favor with Viola, because she frequently invited his family to her Mexican-American buffets, which both pleased his tastes and saved him money. One evening, while at the table with Vi, Becky, and his sister Nancy, who was in town on a visit, Gene accidentally emptied an entire bottle of peppers on his burrito. When the women all urged him to dump them off and fill another tortilla Gene protested that this was just the way he liked it and wolfed down the sodden mess of chili sauce, beans, and jalapeños. His face flushed, his throat constricted, and his nose and eyes began to run, but Gene would only snort, sling away the tears, and smile.

"He just had to show he was better than three women," Viola later said to Nancy, "especially with two of us pregnant."

William Henry Simmons, Gene's second son, the one they called Billy, was born on January 25, 1965 at the air force hospital at Langley. Billy was a sweet baby, and he grew to be a quiet, industrious, unassuming young man.

In July Gene took a full thirty-day leave and headed west with his family to visit grandparents in Colorado and California, who had yet to see Sheila Marie or Billy. Little had changed at Walsenburg. Mae was still busy holding the ranch together; Andy was no happier to see Becky than when she had lived at home, and there was a chilly distance between Becky and her half-sister Edith. In Mill Valley, where Dad Griffen had recently retired, things were also less than happy. Gene's mother was growing progressively more infirm, and Dad Griffen was becoming fixated, as Gene would later, on the cost of food and the importance of pure water. He thought the price of eggs too high and the tap water poisonous. Gene and his family returned to Langley four days early.

Gene's advancement up the rungs of Base Housing reached the top for his rank in 1965, but he had an ambition to be more than a glorified desk clerk. Gene's inflated sense of his own rectitude seemed to him better suited for duty in the Office of Special Investigations, the security and criminal investigation arm of the air force.

Gene received his transfer to OSI and almost at once, in January 1966, was promoted to Staff Sergeant (E-5). With Roger and Viola now transferred, Becky had to brag about "my Gene" by mail, and she could not have sounded happier if the honor had been hers when she wrote to Vi about the year-long NCO school Gene was then beginning.

Despite the promotion and raise, Gene's economies were increasingly obsessive. Not only did his allowance to Becky not increase, Gene moved his family into the base trailer park, to save fifty dollars a year on rent, and before he left base housing he helped himself to everything from odd dishes to a cornucopia of sheets, pillows, towels, and the thick terry cloth robes provided for visiting generals. He had leave time on the books, money in the bank, and a monthly savings-bond allotment. He had a nest egg of children, including a daughter who adored him, and a dutiful, fecund wife. He had status, prospects, a place in life—and that future in Arkansas, perhaps even at the old home place near Hector, seemed hugely possible.

Although it was to the air force's profit, it was no benefit to Gene for him to find something he could, in fact, do to perfection, or nearly so. In time he would come to believe that the absolute precision he could achieve with paperwork was possible in everything he did, and that it was necessary. Already he was charting the cost of certain family staples—processed cheese and mayonnaise among them—comparing prices at various stores and computing the gasoline used driving to each. Under the discipline of his budget Becky had been reduced to hoarding pennies to buy treats for the children, except when Gene brought home pillow mints from the VIP quarters or a bag of hard candy that he would dole out a piece at a time.

At this point in her marriage Becky saw nothing about which to complain. If she wished they had more money, more friends, a telephone, she still had faith that it was for the best, that Gene knew best, and that she had best make do. She and the children were not living in privation or real want, and her love for and devotion to Gene were still unshakable, so she could believe. Certainly her children never lacked for love, and Little Gene, who began kindergarten in the fall of 1965, showed all the signs of being well adjusted.

All Gene's scrimping was not for nothing, however. In 1966 he bought his first new car, a Dodge Sportsman van, the most expensive thing Gene had ever owned. He could hardly wait to drive the family back to Colorado that summer and show off the van at Ma Novak's, where Gene felt more at home than Becky, whose greatest reward was seeing the envy in Edith's eyes for her prosperity with Gene.

Vietnam was becoming the focus of nearly every serviceman's attention in 1966. Da Nang, Chu Lai, and Pleiku were already familiar points on the map, and the number of American troops in Vietnam was soaring. The contingent that the air force actually had "in country" was relatively small compared to the other services, and most of the pilots and airmen were in the problematic safety of Saigon. In this situation, most of the things that could happen to an air force administrative specialist in the war zone were good—decorations, commendations, promotions. "Combat time" was something not every air force NCO would have in his Service Record Book, and it could prove decisive in advancing a career. What's more, Gene's patriotism was adamant, jingoistic, and unexamined.

In August 1966 Gene wrote a letter to his commanding officer in which he offered to reenlist and volunteer for Vietnam if, and only if, he were guaranteed a billet with OSI in Saigon. In October Gene got that confirmation, to be effective in August 1967.

In January 1967 Gene reenlisted and collected a bonus of almost twelve hundred dollars. In March he completed his NCO course, with a certification to become an "administrative supervisor," and was transferred to the Personnel Investigations Division of OSI. Assigned an entirely new range of duties, Gene mastered them in phenomenal time. An almost incredulous Major John Harrington, Gene's division commander, remarked that "within two weeks after his assignment to this Division, Sgt. Simmons was typing a quality ROI [Report of Investigation] from agents' notes with the competence . . . expected from a far more experienced person. . . . His value to this Division is further enhanced by the manner in which he keeps current with the many changes within the Personnel Investigations field. . . . Sgt. Simmons is an excellent team member."

Gene bought a twenty-foot Serro Scotty travel trailer

and towed it to Walsenburg behind the Dodge van in June 1967. He parked the trailer in the pasture near the Novak house, jacked up the van, removed the wheels, and put it on blocks, insuring that no one else could drive it while he was gone. This, the cold charity of Andy Novak, and an allotment of less than forty dollars a month were how Gene provided for his family's comfort. During the year he spent in Vietnam Gene would continue to control the exchequer even from Saigon, making all their monthly payments by mail.

On August 1 he flew by military air transport from Travis AFB to Tan Son Nhut airport outside Saigon, Republic of Vietnam, where he landed on the morning of August 2 as the sun came up like thunder over the China Sea.

CHAPTER EIGHT

Becky was lost without Gene. Isolated on the ranch and cramped in the tiny trailer with her three children, her only consolation and deepest despair were in thoughts of him. Becky felt helpless without Gene's strength to guide her and shelter her, and she was stunned by the difficulties he had engineered in her life, leaving her here marooned. The crisis of confidence she suffered when Gene jacked up the van and deposited her on the ranch had left her feeling helpless to face the tasks of being a mother. She had never felt so lonely and impotent.

Her loneliness was made worse because she was surrounded by what should have been her family. But she knew how welcome she was in Andy Novak's home. She knew, too, that worse yet would come with winter, when she would have to move them all into the house. Andy would be out of work at the mines a lot, as he was much of every winter, and Andy was his same begrudging, sarcastic self. Her mother stayed busy and had already let Becky know that she felt put upon. Edith, Becky's half-sister, either ignored her or lectured her about how shabbily she was being treated by Gene, about how to raise her children, about how lucky she was to be able to come back.

Becky left the ranch only once during that first month, to go to a rodeo where one of her cousins was riding. That night, after she put the kids to bed in the bunks of the trailer, she sat beneath the gas lantern in the dining nook where she slept and wrote in her daybook about the rodeo and her prayers for Gene, "my Darling husband. . . . I sure miss my Darling so much."

The OSI Headquarters building at 161B Chi Lang Street in Saigon was a three-story concrete box with a square facade beetling from the upper two stories, divided into four symmetrical balconies. A low stone wall, reinforced with sandbags and concertina wire, separated the building from the street, and a "grenade net" of steel pipes and hurricane fencing covered the lower two floors on the side facing Chi Lang. A barred gate in the wall opened onto a small courtyard beside the building. Inside, the headquarters commanded an array of sophisticated security, cryptography, and communications systems, as well as the central files on OSI activities. From this compound the air force OSI directed its efforts against espionage, the black market, and drug trafficking in South Vietnam.

Gene was assigned to the Operations Division, whose responsibility it was to plan and coordinate the various OSI investigations and background screenings for security clearances. Gene's own secret clearance was renewed, but he would routinely handle material at all levels of classification, whatever passed his desk. He was also issued a special curfew pass, one that would be honored by Vietnamese police and allow him twenty-four-hour freedom of movement within Saigon, including the infamous Cholon District, a hive of conspiracy and black-market trade.

Gene's self-image had never been so buoyed as it was by this assignment, and he threw himself into it with monomaniacal concentration, working double shifts in order to read and commit to memory the details of OSI's past investigations and get to know the standing orders and operational procedures. During the few off hours he spent in his quarters Gene would grill the other two NCOs who shared the apartment about ongoing operations. He was ravenous to know all he could in order to feel himself part of a unit that he saw as a moral hub. The delineation of right and wrong, good and bad, was so clear to Gene at OSI, the orders so unambiguous, that he craved to be at the very center, integral and indispensable to the side of the angels.

Gene's rectitude was beyond question, and he now became even more demanding of adherence to orders in others and in the code of behavior he prescribed for himself. His reports on background screenings were bland, stilted, and severe, sprinkled with judgments such as "possible security risk" and "not emotionally qualified." He took special pride in, as he put it, "insuring the highest moral caliber of [air force] personnel."

What the air force insured for Gene in Saigon was the highest living he had known. The civilian quarters he shared had maid service, a cook, laundry delivered at the door. He had a jeep to drive and, through his role at OSI, enjoyed an officer's commissary privileges.

Becky could not have driven herself to the store even if the van were not up on blocks. She had never learned how. When she did go in with her mother or Edith she suffered doubly from being dependent on them and having to endure their silent—or not so silent—censure for the cheap food she had to buy with the forty dollars Gene allotted to her each month. Worse, she could not go to the post office regularly, and Gene's letters were all she lived for. For the sake of her children Becky tried to be strong and put on a happy face. She took them hunting for arrowheads and introduced them to the farm animals, but mostly she fretted: "Wish we could go to the PO. . . . We all miss Daddy so much. Received two letters from my Darling. . . . I sure do worry. He is our future."

But Sheila took it even harder. Her terrible twos were made worse by her father's absence. Overcome by a sadness she could not name, Sheila would cry inconsolably for hours.

"Sheila misses her Daddy so much," Becky wrote in her daybook. "She crys so easy. I have to show my love more."

Among larger OSI investigations in 1967–68 was one focusing on the black-market trade in commissary goods and privileges. Saigon was the most open of markets in 1967, with barter and back-channel deals underwritten by theft and murder. The illicit trade in cigarettes, liquor, and drugs, in conjunction with prostitution and free-lance espionage, was beyond the control of even the most efficient police, and few ever accused the Vietnamese national police or the Saigon constabulary of efficiency. They were part of the payoff system, and U.S. efforts, such as those of OSI, were ill-equipped and undermanned to influence events on the Vietnamese side of the trade. Dockside thefts, servicemen who supplied their Vietnamese mistresses with commissary merchandise to resell, and GIs who themselves trafficked in contraband had combined to create a horn of plenty to supply the black market with American goods. Especially notorious were the commissary branches in Cholon and Long Binh.

In a characteristically broad, Procrustean stroke, Gene proposed to stem the flow of goods by suspending all individual commissary privileges, and the suggestion finally reached Air Force Headquarters in Washington, D.C., before it was rejected. When in 1969, more than six months after Gene had returned from Vietnam, an identical policy was adopted for American troops in Vietnam, he clipped the vindicating article from *Air Force Times* and saved it in his files.

Gene's good opinion of himself, already conflated with the sense of power and importance he attached to the activities at OSI, was further swelled as he quickly began to spot gaps and inconsistencies in the paper trails and testimonies assembled by the investigators.

Gene's first coup came when he was assigned to review the OSI file on the illegal currency exchange. By plotting locations of arrests cross-referenced with confessions, rumors, and sworn testimony, he was able to pinpoint not only the money changers but several other black-market enterprises as well. Soon he was listening to the accounts of OSI agents and MPs who, acting on Gene's estimates, had kicked down the doors, shot it out with the profiteers, and hauled them off from Cholon in irons. For Gene it was as good as being there. By relentless work and ingratiation he had moved to the heart of the wheel, motion without movement. This was Gene's kind of war. One citation in his records reads, in part, "SSgt Simmons, through his alertness, insight, and attention to details, frequently discovered ambiguities and discrepancies in investigative matters. . . . His special assistance to case reviewers not only resulted in identifying numerous black market operations of international implications and eliminating illicit [money] exchange centers, but greatly contributed to a revision of currency control . . . throughout the Republic [of South Vietnam]."

Gene was in the high summer of his career.

Although it was only autumn on the calendar, the hawk of winter was already on the southern Colorado wind. More and more often Becky and her children had to sleep in the house, all together in a single room. Becky did her best to get along, never rising to Edith's scorn or her mother's complaints and always doing her share of the chores, but she felt terribly alone. She took what comfort she could in small events—a trip to see her grandmother in Raton or going to the rodeo. When there was nothing else to do and the weather was mild she would roam the ranch on foot collecting flints.

"I miss my Gene," she wrote in her daybook that fall. "I [am] so lonely and depressed. I wish my Gene didn't have to go." Each letter she received from Gene was numbered in order, as were those she sent to him. In the first three months that he was in Vietnam Becky received seventeen letters and sent forty-one. She pined for him, thought he was the only man who could ever love her, and struggled against their separation. In it all, she did begin to find her strength. One day when she was alone at the ranch with her children and had spent hours playing with them, she found herself feeling happy. "No one came over," the mother of three thought that night, "but I'm finally growing up."

In October Becky received a letter from Gene that sent her into raptures. Gene had a great notion of taking his R&R in Hawaii, where she could meet him. Becky was ecstatic. Feeling demeaned by her dependence on Andy Novak and by Edith's constant sniping, Becky was quick to let the family know how much her man loved her, how he thought of her even in the middle of a war. She wrote Gene a gushing letter full of thanks and adoration, describing her satisfaction at the look on her half-sister's face.

Gene was furious. Whether his original suggestion to meet in Hawaii was genuine or not, he quickly reversed himself. It was too expensive, out of the question, and now Becky had humiliated him by telling others that it was already planned. Becky's hopes of a respite from the winter-bound harshness of Walsenburg were dashed.

"Abe, Johnny, Andy went deer hunting," she wrote in her daybook for October 28, 1967. "They caught [sic] a deer. Got a letter from my Gene. . . . He is sore at me for telling about going to Hawaii. It[']s hard for me to please."

Gene spent his long hours at OSI poring over the records and reports of investigations, keen to spot a clue he could pass on to the field agents, with whom he identified. He read *Stars and Stripes* and the *Air Force Times* and any news magazines he could get, keeping a hodgepodge of articles from them about happenings in Vietnam. With no duties outside the office Gene could have had plenty of time for strolling the boulevards of Saigon, but he spent his few free hours in his comfortable quarters, where he would write letters and make tapes while lounging in his skivvies, drinking beer, and trying to look tough for photographs, despite his Chaplinesque mustache and the premature paunch he carried at twenty-seven, the one that Becky fed with candy and cakes she shipped to him.

Many people believed that the war was all but won by 1968, so Gene passed the holiday season occupied proudly with his duty and secure in the easy living of Saigon.

For Becky the season was one with little joy. She fretted over making her allotment check stretch to include gifts for the children, did some baking for Gene, and felt an increasing friction with her stepfather. Whenever the mines were open she would write in her book, "I sure hate Andy. I'm glad he was gone [today]."

The snow came and began to drift against the fences, completely covering the trailer that Becky now had to abandon until spring. She longed for Gene, for "the feel of you and my hands on you," and her hopes hung on every trip to the post office. In January all the children were sick with flu, and Becky was stricken with terror by what she saw on the evening news: "The VC attacked Saigon. I am sick worried."

It was worth her worry. The Tet Offensive of 1968, launched during the traditional cease-fire of the lunar new year, came as a crippling blow to U.S. confidence. Despite the eventual military victory by U.S. and South Vietnamese forces, the psychological and propaganda effects of the nationwide assault left many people, inside and outside the military, questioning America's role in Southeast Asia, its ability to win the war, and the reliability of U.S. intelligence assets. Any complacency that Gene and the other men at OSI may have felt about their rear-echelon security was shattered by the mortars and Katyusha rockets that ripped into Saigon followed by suicidal cadres of young Viet Cong who stormed through the streets, spreading firefights like sparks among dry leaves.

Gene was already dressed when the telephone rang in his apartment. Always a light sleeper, he had awakened with the first distant concussions of rockets slamming into Tan Son Nhut and the ragged rattle of small-arms fire closer by. A jeep from headquarters picked him up and roared through the confused streets of Saigon as explosions from rockets and sappers' satchel charges lit the night skyline. Gene's throat was thick with adrenaline, his hands sweaty on the unfamiliar plastic grips of his M-16. Stray mortar rounds fell in the side streets off Chi Lang. As sirens and counter-battery fire screamed through the night, and a battle that was much akin to gang warfare ebbed and flowed around them, the other officers and men took up rifles and fighting positions in the headquarters building while Gene manned the phones and relayed messages, sweat standing on his forehead, his bowels constricted, a determination not to disgrace himself knitted in his scowl. He was ashamed of the relief he felt when OSI did not come under assault.

There were probably no more than four thousand Viet Cong involved in the Tet attack on Saigon, and most of the individual actions were of platoon size or smaller, but the men there could never feel as safe as they once had. Gene, however, was specifically cited by his commander for his "coolness" under pressure and his exemplary military conduct. Things soon returned to a semblance of normalcy in Saigon—as normal as things could be in a city racked by corruption and war, where American foreign service staff had fought pistol duels with Viet Cong in the stairwells of the embassy and the chief of police summarily executed prisoners on worldwide television—and Gene resumed his loyal, dogged attention to the shortcomings of his comrades in arms. He unraveled the paper clew that led to two stolen air compressors valued at ten thousand dollars, created flowcharts that resulted in soaring efficiency for this OSI Division, and imagined what he would have done if the Viet Cong had hit OSI.

*   *   *

While Gene was mythologizing his gallantry, Becky's anxiety could not have been greater. She sat in front of the television, quaking with fear and the flu, as images from hell flickered before her.

"The VC are still in Saigon," she wrote on both January 31 and February 1. "Everything there looks so sickening. I am so scared, but I must pray for my Gene's safety. We are still so sick." Four days later she received a letter from Gene saying that he was okay. She thanked the Lord, swore to be a better wife, and threw up in the toilet.

After Tet Becky fell deeper into her winter cafard, a funk relieved only by letters from Gene and the reopening of the mines where Andy Novak worked on the days when they were not all snowbound. The best of her days that winter came with a necklace Gene sent her and the news that he was being assigned to San Francisco when his tour in Vietnam was done. The orders made the end seem real to her. "I sure love my Gene," she wrote time after time in her daybook.

In May 1968 Becky moved back into her trailer, and Gene decided to take his R&R—in Australia. The long Colorado winter spent cooped up in the house had worn Becky thin, physically and emotionally, and she longed for Gene to come home. "I miss my Gene oh so very much," she wrote. "Just 3 months [until he comes home]. Wish it would go by faster."

A true soldier's wife, Becky never wrote Gene about her own problems. She confined her letters to news about the children and syrupy professions of love and concern. Gene, on the other hand, ignored what he knew her life on the ranch must be like and did little to ease her days. Even from half a world away he would reprimand Becky and correct her behavior, once scolding her harshly for failing to seal a stack of snapshots the way she had been told. Then a present would arrive in the mail—another necklace or a bolt of fabric—and Becky would write to herself, "I want to make him happy, not do anything wrong. I love him so much."

Gene had only two months left in his tour of duty when he returned from his Australian R&R, and he set to work immediately to get his orders cut and his recommendations for awards and decorations on file. Gene's unstinting devotion to his job was rewarded with a Bronze Star for meritorious service, the highest decoration a serviceman can receive for anything other than heroism. Gene composed the first draft of the Bronze Star citation, characterizing himself in phrases that do not appear in the final recommendation: ". . . truly professional . . . uncanny ability . . . exceptional knowledge . . . vast responsibilities . . ."

The war had done all for Gene's career that he could have hoped. He had distinguished himself, won the Bronze Star, and had his whiff of powder. He spent his last weeks in Vietnam training his replacement and feeling good. He was a veteran; he'd had his ticket punched, and now he was going home from the war.

Impatient to be reunited with her Gene and swept away from Walsenburg, Becky found strength in the prospect and began to bristle at Edith and her mother. On the first of July, while shopping with Edith in Walsenburg for Mae's birthday present, Becky exploded on the street. She could not later recall what it had been about, except that she was sick of Edith's always telling her what to do. Mae, however, would hear no excuses when Edith reported the scene and her embarrassment. "[It] made Mom mad," Becky confided to herself. "I told her I was sick & tired of being blamed that she hasn't gone anywhere because of me. She makes me sick." And when Edith left for two weeks, Becky summarized her feelings about life in the Novak home: "Good to have her gone, wished they would all go."

Driven deeper into the conviction that her family was all with Gene, Becky would accept his every criticism and obey his every wish, even to destroying his precious letters: "I burned the rest of my Gene's letters, even though my heart wasn't in it." The mentions of him and the children are the only bright spots in her daybook for June and July. "I cut paper dolls for my little ladybug [Sheila]." "My Gene leaves Vietnam tomorrow [July 26], I sure pray he does, he works real hard. I'll be so glad when he is home. . . . I can't believe our time is so near."

Gene arrived at Travis Air Force Base in California at ten o'clock on the morning of July 26 and reported to the OSI detachment in San Francisco, more than fifty miles away. At two minutes after midnight, as soon as his leave was effective, he was on the road for Walsenburg. After getting the Dodge van back on its feet and saying good-bye to the Novaks, Gene and his family drove to California towing the Serro Scotty trailer. Gene had ordered their larger trailer shipped to a mobile-home park in Vacaville, just outside Travis AFB, where Becky set up housekeeping, and Gene assumed his post at the San Francisco office of OSI in August 1968.

San Francisco in the late 1960s was everything Gene loathed. The Summer of Love had passed, and "hippie" had been declared dead by the Diggers commune, but Haight-Ashbury was still the mecca of thousands of dropouts, LSD gurus, and a menagerie of long-haired counterculturists. The sweet reek of marijuana smoke lay in strata above the flower folk lolling on blankets in Golden Gate Park on Saturday afternoons, and antiwar, antimilitary sentiments ran high around the bay from Palo Alto to North Beach. Drugs and disenchantment had been commonplace among many troops in Vietnam, especially those rear-echelon personnel mocked by the infantry as "Saigon Rangers," but not in OSI, and certainly not with Gene's knowledge. Narrow-minded, judgmental, and moralistic, Gene took a self-affirming satisfaction in being part of investigations into drug use and un–American activities, and he soon proved his mettle in support of an investigation into the GIs for Peace movement.

Suspicious by nature and defensively contemptuous of others in general, Gene took a stern glee in matching the names of servicemen with those on antiwar petitions. He gleaned names, dates, and meeting places of the GIs for Peace from the *Berkeley Barb* and *San Francisco Free Press* and sifted from them and agents' reports the air force personnel in the movement. He monitored the progress of each investigation and wrote a series of reports that his district commander lauded as "outstanding . . . allowing me to keep the Secretary of the Air Force, the Chief of Staff, and other . . . senior Air Staff . . . aware of developments. . . ."

Gene at this time was also beginning to take an interest in guns. His experience during Tet had shaped many imaginary battles and firefights in Gene's fancy, and he liked the feel of a loaded weapon in his hand. He went to the firing range, shot "expert" with the M-16 rifle, and bought himself two guns, a long-barrel Ruger .22 revolver and a Winchester .243 rifle, a high-velocity flat-trajectory weapon capable of tumbling an antelope a quarter mile away. Gene was never a hunter—the Winchester was still in its original box in 1987—but he was a crack shot with the pistol. Becky's brother Abe Ulibarri, an accomplished hunter and shooter, would marvel at Gene's accuracy with the pistol when the two of them went plinking for tin cans. Gene could hit a man in the eye at twenty paces with a pistol, and one day he would prove it.

Little Gene and Sheila were both in school now, and alone during the day with only Billy to care for, Becky was again enthusiastic about life. Naturally friendly—neighborly, country folk would say—Becky quickly made acquaintances among the other young service wives at the trailer park. But they were her friends, not Gene's. He did not like having other people in his house when he was at home, so Becky did not ask them. Her day life was quite different from what Gene saw or what visiting relatives would see. And with Gene commuting by bus more than fifty miles each way to work, as well as putting in his usual workaholic overtime, Becky had most of each day to herself and the kids. Deeply alienated from her own family after the tense winter she had just passed, she now happily adopted Gene's mother and stepfather, living in nearby Mill Valley, although her relations with Loretta Griffen were never cozy. Becky was intimidated by Loretta's disciplined intelligence and distant manner, and there may have been some sense of rivalry for Gene's affection, but in either case the two women found little in common. Years later, when her love for Gene had soured, Becky would say of his mother, "She may have been smart, but that didn't help her to raise a son." Becky was closer to Dad Griffen, to whom she continued to write throughout his life. Feeling a part of an extended family made Becky happy and secure.

Gene was less pleased with their new circumstances. He hated having to commute from Vacaville, but it was impossible to find affordable housing around San Francisco. There were no trailer parks in or near the city that would accept children, and OSI's San Francisco office had no base and, therefore, no base housing. Gene was forced to commute two hours each way by bus. Next came a notice that he had to convert his trailer from oil to natural gas or pay another fifty dollars per month for his space. In all, neither the job nor his living arrangements were working out. On February 5 Gene filed a request for transfer to the Travis AFB branch of OSI, justifying it as an administrative change only, one that would require no moving of dependents or household goods, and in March it was granted.

Before the transfer was completed, however, Gene took an opportunity to exorcise an old ghost. Despite the cordial relations he had formed with his family since marrying Becky, Gene remained haunted by the image he knew he had left in their home. But regardless of his need for their good opinion, he would demand and not beg it.

Temporarily attached to the Mill Valley Air Force Station to assist in a narcotics investigation, Gene became, for the only time in his life, part of the actual investigative team.

Armed with a list of particulars that included names, ranks, and service numbers of suspects, as well as detailed information on evidence, vehicles to be searched, and quarters to be inspected, he stood at the agents' right hand, supplying them with facts and figures. The airmen arrested were turned over to Gene while they awaited interrogation. He kept them seated at attention in hardback chairs and would not allow them to smoke or talk. When he took them in to be questioned he read the charges and particulars with the solemnity of a bailiff reading a sentence, impassive in his contempt for the subjects of the investigation.

Dressed in his class-As and girded with a white pistol belt, his fruitcake of decorations topped by the Bronze Star, Gene was not ignorant of the figure he cut when he called on his mother and Dad Griffen the day that the investigation concluded. Ever careful of whom he bragged to, Gene enjoyed his parents' searching questions about the investigation, especially those that he could answer, "Sorry. That's classified." Gene could see that they were genuinely interested in his work, that there was no condescension in their questions, no doubt in his answers.

"We're proud of you, Gene," Dad Griffen said, and that was all he needed to hear. After this, Gene would command his stepfather's goodwill by holding it in disdain, as he did all those whom he had mastered. To compliment Gene was to admit one's own inferiority.

On March 1 Gene was one of twenty staff sergeants in OSI selected for promotion to technical sergeant (E-6). At the end of March his transfer to Travis was complete, and he sold the troublesome trailer and moved the family into base housing, where they would remain for nearly four years, until his transfer to England in 1973. For Becky and the kids it would be the last good place.

CHAPTER NINE

Following his transfer to Travis AFB Gene was named District OJT Supervisor for the 19th OSI, and he soon became a well-known figure in the Bay Area's Special Investigations network, spreading his reputation for rectitude and efficiency. He was neither feared nor loved by the officers and men of OSI—he was all business, all the time—but they marveled at his capacious memory for orders and regulations, his ability to absorb them almost at a glance.

Characteristically, Gene worked long hours and weekends and frequently brought the office home with him, where he would press Becky into typing duty when his sight began to blur and his temples began to pound, as they did nowadays after long hours of concentration or reading. Gene was running fast on the hard path of rules and routine. At home these included fixed schedules for meals, baths, laundry, even the use of the toilet and how many squares of tissue to use, and it was Becky's job to see that they were enforced.

To the children he was remote and omnipotent, a seldom-seen figure whose affection they longed for

MSgt. Ronald Gene Simmons, senior NCO, SAMSO
observatory, Cloudcroft, New Mexico, 1976.

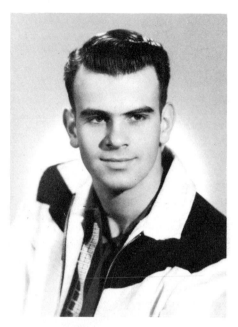

Gene in 1960, age 20. The handsome sailor who swept Becky off her feet.

Sheila Marie, age 12, in England, 1975. One year later, she was all Gene could talk about.

Gene's children in 1978.
Back row (l. to r.):
Billy, 13; Sheila, 15;
Little Gene, 17.
Front row (l. to r.):
Loretta, 8; Eddy, 5;
Marianne, 2.

Gene with Sheila in September 1980, one month
after the incest began.

Gene as patriarch on Sheila Marie's prom night, March
21, 1981, just hours before Gene told Becky and Billy
that Sheila was pregnant. Becky is holding her last child,
Rebecca Lynn; Sheila is to Gene's left. Below are
Loretta, Eddy, and Marianne.

The morning after Gene revealed his relations with
Sheila, March 22, 1981, Becky wore the blasted look of
a concentration camp survivor.

June 6, 1981. Eight months pregnant, Sheila had dropped out of high school and assumed the role of second wife, the pride of Gene's life.

July 7, 1982. One year after fleeing New Mexico, struggling for an appearance of normalcy in the small Arkansas town of Ward, Gene is seen here with (l. to r.) Marianne, Sylvia Gail (his child by Sheila), Rebecca Lynn, and Eddy. The trikes were purchased secondhand for the picture.

Even after the terror and humiliation she had suffered, Becky could still find moments of happiness with Gene, as she did here at Christmas 1982 in Ward.

"Forget me not," Gene pleaded on the icing of the last birthday cake Sheila would eat in her father's home, 1984.

Sheila and her husband, Dennis McNulty, c. 1986. Their romance shattered Gene's fortress of control.

The shattered, exhausted image that Gene presented at the time of his arrest belied the deliverance he had found in death. [W. L. (Pat) Patterson, *Arkansas Gazette*]

Ronald Gene Simmons, 1940–1990.
[Tony Pitts, *Arkansas Gazette*]

with trepidation, sensing something hollow in the words of love that Gene would prate to the younger children, telling them how much he cared and how much he did for them—which Becky would second—but he never encouraged them to talk to him, tell him about what they were doing, thinking, or feeling, unless it was to express their love. Having fathered the children and provided a living for them, he now doubted his own conviction that they would to love him for it, and he demanded a thousand small reassurances. Becky already knew enough not to burden her overworked Gene with her own petty cares, and so a stilted, paramilitary etiquette suffused the family circle, with all consideration and command conferred on Gene.

In September 1969 Gene requested a four-year extension of his assignment to OSI. More than the opportunity to achieve near-perfection as a clerk or office manager, the moral and legal high ground that OSI occupied satisfied his hunger for authority and control and a stamp of superiority, something that he could never achieve beyond the pale of the military garrison or the limits of his family. His vision of morality, however, was sterile, a moral code as opposed to an ethical system, rigid, implacable, and absolute. Ironically, his lifelong ambivalence toward religion sprang from this devotion to prescribed moral behavior. As a powerful moral engine, religion appealed to Gene, but because it, too, was absolute and often absolutely prohibitive, it challenged the self-serving principles that he embraced to underwrite his acts.

Despite his uneasiness with religion, Gene continued to allow Little Gene to receive religious instruction, in deference to his mother, Loretta, who was in rapidly declining health and took an especially keen interest in religion during her last year. She pressed her concern on her son, and Gene would have done almost anything to keep her approval and a place in her will. In February 1970 Loretta suffered a heart attack and almost died. In March five-year-old Billy was baptized at the Episcopal Church of the Epiphany in Vacaville.

On April 1, 1970, deaf, bedridden, and physically spent, Loretta died at home in Rohnert Park, where she and Dad Griffen had moved the year before. Her funeral brought all her surviving children together for the last time. Robert—the oldest son, who had left the family in Hector, Arkansas, to join the navy— was there, as were Pete, Nancy, Gene and all his family, and one of Loretta's brothers, along with friends and some of Loretta's former piano students. However close Loretta's children felt in their mutual grief, Gene was not moved by it for long from the more practical concerns of her will and the insurance.

Loretta had put all her affairs in good order before her death, not that there was much of personal wealth in her estate. The three insurance policies that she carried amounted to little more than three thousand dollars, with Robert, Nancy, and Gene named as joint beneficiaries in her will. Three weeks after the cremation, however, Gene filed a "Statement of Claimant" with the Metropolitan Life Insurance Company asking for the settlement in a single lump sum. He was the sole signatory of the claim.

At about the same time, Gene moved his family off base into a house in the neighboring town of Fairfield, and shortly thereafter he received word that he had been selected for assignment to OSI Headquarters in Washington, D.C., but those orders were canceled within thirty days.

In July Gene's second daughter, Loretta Mae, was born. Loretta would prove the exception in Gene's brood—outgoing, bright, and industrious, never struggling through language as would her brothers and sisters, and never cowed by her father.

But the oppression of Gene's strictures and the general lack of spontaneous expression in the Simmons household were evident in the other children during their first years in school. Little Gene had come out of his slowness by the previous fall, although he was still sloppy and often late with his work. Sheila, on the other hand, was showing many of the characteristics of a child who has not been encouraged to language or independence. "Sheila is rather unsure of herself in reading," her first-grade teacher wrote, "and needs more practice to gain confidence." Sheila was also shy to the point of being noncommunicative and had associative problems attaching sounds to letters, especially with phonetic acronyms such as *TV*, and with all abbreviations.

At work, Gene's fascination with secrecy was taking peculiar turns. Assigned with four OSI special agents to a "Committee to Study Duty Officer/Agent Requirements," Gene began to collect in his personal files the service records of other OSI personnel, as well as the records of airmen under investigation, playing a shadow game of counterespionage. He read with special interest the air force regulations on search and seizure, and he kept a well-thumbed copy of a booklet titled "Use of Wiretapping and Eavesdropping in Conduct of Investigations," as well as a complete set of "Debriefing Certificates" for the men of headquarters.

Concurrently, Gene was also named one of the District 19 "Destroying and Witnessing Officials," whose responsibility was to oversee the destruction of redundant files, superseded orders, and other classified materials. Among the group was an Agent James D.

Wood for whom Gene felt an antipathy that he would later claim as second sight. Wood was smart, articulate, and sophisticated. A flashy dresser, Wood looked ten years younger than his thirty-five and spoke a half dozen Slavic languages, including fluent Russian and Czech. He was the spitting image of the secret agent man, and as such was much that Gene admired and little that he was. Gene's moral pedestal was lofty enough, however, that he could hold Wood in cool disdain.

"I don't like him," Gene told Becky. "He's just too damn know-it-all. There's something fishy about him."

He was vindicated three years later when Wood broke on the witness stand and admitted to spying for the Soviets. Gene kept a clipping of the event for his files as evidence of his prescience.

In January 1971 Gene reenlisted for five years and gained concessions in his choice of career speciality that insured his tenure at OSI. In May he was sent to the Aerospace Defense Command's NCO Academy at Hamilton AFB in California, where he graduated on May 20.

In June and July 1971 Gene took the longest leave period of his military service, actually two consecutive leaves totaling thirty-nine days, most of which he spent traveling alone in Arkansas. With his reenlistment bonus and his mother's legacy in hand, one object of the trip was to investigate the possibility of buying the house in the country near Hector. It had now been twenty years since Gene had left Hector, but the golden period it represented for him was still vivid, those long afternoons with his mother and brothers. Especially his mother. And now she was dead. He had never been closer to her than here at Hector, never felt her loss more than now. The house would recoup something of all that loss. It became a kind of grail for Gene, but it was not for sale.

Disappointed in his effort to buy the house, Gene resumed his life as a rising star in the firmament of OSI, attending two more schools and garnering more high praise from his superiors. The years spent at Travis were the last of something like normalcy for the Simmons family. The physical isolation that Gene would eventually impose was impossible in the Bay Area suburbs, and Gene was more willing in those days for his children, at least, to have interests and activities outside the family, allowing Little Gene to be confirmed that fall in the Episcopal church and serve for the following year and a half as an acolyte.

The shaky equilibrium that the family had gained showed, too, in how well all the children were progressing in school. Little Gene received a reading award and a certificate for participating in the Science and Art Fair. Sheila's grades were only average to good, but she had at last licked her reading problems. Billy, just entering first grade, was also "a good student" who, however, "spends a great deal of his time chatting with his pals" and needed to spend some of it at the base library over Christmas vacation.

Gene, meanwhile, was growing impatient with the changes in (or lack of) orders that had first denied him a posting to Washington and in 1972 denied him an overseas tour accompanied by his family. An accompanied tour offered many financial perks that Gene felt he deserved, and he was beside himself when he was passed over. More immediately, he lay the blame on OSI and initiated a petulant series of memoranda and requests that would signal the end of his career in Special Investigations and the beginning of his emotional disengagement from the air force.

In November 1971 Gene received orders transferring him to the OSI office in Athens. Despite the letter from his sponsor in Greece saying that "local housing [is] scarce . . . cost of living is high [and] . . . roads are extremely dangerous," Gene mobilized the family in eager anticipation of the move. He collected maps and *National Geographic* articles about Greece and the Mediterranean, updated the children's vaccinations, and tried to inject a spirit of adventure into the prospect of leaving a place where Becky and the children were just beginning to feel at home. But on January 17, 1972, the posting to Athens was canceled.

Gene was furious. That very day he filed a request for transfer out of OSI and into the general pool of personnel eligible for accompanied overseas assignment. To this request he attached the following "Memorandum for the Record" in which he details his grievances and, at the end, rises toward that tantrum pitch he used to use when he was a vexed teenager:

In February or March, 1971, I submitted an Airman Assignment Preference Statement, indicating I was a volunteer for an accompanied tour to DO [OSI District Office] 71, Greece. I was subsequently selected for assignment to Greece on 12 November 1971, with a reporting month of June 1972. I understand that there were two vacancies at DO 71, and that the other slot (with a December 1971 shipment) was allocated to SSgt. Alvarez. I have been advised that my assignment to DO 71 has been canceled, due to a manpower slot reduction at that District.

I believe that I should have been programmed for the December shipment to DO 71 [,] since I was more eligible than SSgt. Alvarez for the assignment. I called SSgt. Chase [in Personnel Assignment] this date, and he advised that SSgt. Alvarez and I were selected for our assignments at the same time. I question why, where there was a programmed loss of TSgt. Goodman from DO 71 in November 1971, a replacement should not have been selected more than a month prior to his [date of rotation]. Further, I stated that I should have been given the opportunity of taking the December shipment and waiving the 60-day orders-in-hand requirement. My return date from Vietnam is July 1968. I have more time-on-station than SSgt. Alvarez. I have 14 years of military service and have *never* had an overseas accompanied tour. This should also have given me the edge on SSgt. Alvarez, who had a long accompanied tour to Greece in . . . 1965.

Within a week Headquarters OSI approved the transfer, and Gene moved his kit across base to the 60th Aerial Port Squadron. He regretted it almost at once.

Thirty days after reporting to the 60th Aerial Gene was at the typewriter hammering out a prodigal's lament to OSI. Citing chapter and rule, he writes to his former commander at OSI:

Chapter 3, Table 3-1, Rule 16, AFB 39-11, reflects a minimum controlled special duty assignment with AFOSI as four years. My four years were completed on 8 November 1969. Having more than fulfilled my commitment, I therefore on 17 January 1972 requested release from AFOSI for reassignment by USAFMPC. I was transferred on 31 March 1972 . . . to the 60th Aerial Port Squadron (MAC), Travis AFB, CA. Having now had the opportunity to observe first hand how a non-AFOSI unit functions (particularly from an administrative point of view), I would much prefer to be associated with, and a part of, an organization that is made up of such highly competent people as AFOSI. I now have 37 months on station. I fully understand that reacceptance into AFOSI will result in a new four year controlled tour of duty. . . . I should think it would be in the best interest of AFOSI to select an individual with prior AFOSI experience (6½ years) over someone with no previous AFOSI experience, therefore deleting the necessity for orientation to the varying and unusual facets of an administrative position within AFOSI. In view of the above . . . I respectfully request favorable consideration be given to my request to reenter one of the truly professional organizations in the USAF.

By early May the paperwork had advanced to OSI Headquarters in Washington, where the director of personnel, Major Wilson Kline, received the request favorably, but added that Gene's only possible assignment would be to Washington, not overseas. Gene replied, "An assignment to Hq AFOSI, Washington, D.C., would be acceptable to me."

On May 18 Gene was awarded the Air Force Commendation Medal for meritorious service with OSI. But any hopes he may have had for a return to OSI were dashed just six days later when he received word of his "voluntary selection" for a permanent change of duty station to the 10th Combat Support Group at Alconbury Royal Air Force Base in England, with a reporting month of February 1973.

Gene knew the machinations of air force bureaucracy well enough to resign himself to the byway his career had taken. The furious, fatal day he had spent pounding out his grievances on the typewriter was the casting of the die, but the period that followed was an emotional and behavioral Rubicon as well. The outburst of temper against his superiors was only a hint of what his anger and formless discontent would come to be at home. And yet, publicly at least, he would also turn much of his perfection-haunted energies toward being the perfect papa, and with airmen under his charge he would become increasingly avuncular, if no less judgmental.

Gene began to spend more time with his family, lavishing special attention on the children. He took leave during the summer of 1972 to take the children to Disneyland, where he bought them shirts and souvenir ears, and he was more attentive to Becky. Their house in Fairfield was the happiest she would ever know, filled almost every weekend with family or friends, lots of children, and the smells of cooking. Later Becky would refer to those twenty months as "the good old days." Gene put on his best face for a while, acting the jovial host and tempering his public teasing of Becky. He even let her convince him to have a mail-order "personality analysis." They wrote their names on a cellophane envelope window, and Astrograph of Bellflower, California, sent them a form analysis only a little less silly than your newspaper's daily horoscope.

Christmas was celebrated with a mixture of nostalgia and anticipation that year. Gene asked Dad Griffen and Pete to come for the holiday (in part to ask Pete for the loan of a car), and Becky had her farewell to the good old days in the way she liked best, surrounded by family for whom she was cooking a holiday feast. England would be an adventure, she had convinced herself, but Becky would never be happier than she was during those years at Travis. Increasingly for the next fifteen years, her life and the lives of her children would be ones of abuse, isolation, and lovelessness.

When Gene reported to the 32nd Tactical Recon Squadron at Alconbury in March 1973 he was just approaching thirty-four years old, but could easily have passed for forty-four. He had gained more than thirty pounds since his svelte days as a sailor, his neck was growing wattles, and his thinning hair had started to recede. He sprouted a regulation brush-cut mustache, as appealing as a caterpillar on his lip, and typically wore the faintly irritated scowl of busy rectitude, although he had a quick grin, a sort of bloodless smirk that looked painful when it widened into a smile. Gene's eyes were heavy-lidded, and he walked with the round-shouldered, lumbering gait of a man who doesn't know what to do with his weight. He assumed a better posture when in uniform, however, and his superiors certainly found nothing in him to fault.

Gene was chief clerk at the 32nd Tactical Recon's headquarters, and as Unit Rations NCO was in charge of all rationed goods, including untaxed gasoline and liquor. Prior to his coming, the ration-card system at the 32nd was a disaster of mismanagement. Whole blocks of ration cards, especially for gasoline, were missing, and the entire rationing system had been compromised by ad hoc exceptions for groups and individuals.

Gene's immediate superior, Captain Richard Tessier, was feeling the heat. The hemorrhage of ration cards had to be stanched. In a series of orders and directives that ring with the absolutism characteristic of Gene, Captain Tessier began to tighten the tourniquet on ration privileges. In addition to improving the physical security for the ration booklets and employing new forms to keep track of them, Gene also reviewed each of the special ration allocations, rejecting them by the gross. When things reached the point at which Gene was denying gasoline travel allotments for members of the airmen's Protestant choir, the deputy commander for operations had to step in with a letter telling Gene and Tessier to "ease off." Gene's devotion to efficiency had finally found its limit, although this did nothing to lessen his superiors' appreciation of the job he did.

But any thoughts that Gene may have entertained about extending his air force career beyond twenty years were laid to rest by the time he and his family were settled in England. More and more, as his dreams drew him back toward the forests of Arkansas, he saw the air force solely as a means to that end. He blamed the air force and OSI for his temper tantrum and transfer out of Special Investigations, and he would never again feel the kind of total devotion to the service that he once had. It created a vacuum of purpose in Gene's life that disoriented him. But if he ever doubted himself or his rightness, it was for no longer than it took him to seek sanctuary in perfection. Now, however, as he turned away from the air force, he turned inward, seeking to be a father, not just a provider, to his family. He wanted to be seen as wise, benevolent, strong, and loving, and he had read enough of Ann Landers to believe he knew what those things entailed, but Gene was not eager to compete with reality.

To emphasize his separation from the air force and the fresh importance he attached to his family, Gene scorned any sort of base housing for the remainder of his career and began a steady withdrawal of his family from all society. The house he initially rented in England, in Rushden, Cambridgeshire, was, despite its village air, in too cosmopolitan a town, one with too many other air force families in it. Rushden did not offer the isolation Gene needed for his purpose, and by summer he would be gone from there.

Rural England, however, especially in the Eastern Plain, is nothing like the rural United States. There are no vast tracts of forest, few lone, secluded residences for rent, and one is seldom out of hailing distance of a house. Still, Gene was determined to find something more to his liking, especially now that Becky was due to deliver another child in July.

On July 15, 1973, Edward Davenport Simmons was born at the USAF hospital located on the Royal Air Force base at Lakenheath, Suffolk. On that same day Gene signed a rental agreement for a house called Flat Chestnut Farm in the small village of Honeydon in Bedfordshire.

The Chestnuts, as the house was alternatively called, had many appeals for Gene, the appellation "farm" not the least of them. Honeydon was as remote a hamlet as Gene could hope to find within commuting distance of the base at Alconbury, where he was stationed and the children attended school. By British standards Honeydon was remote indeed: It was surrounded by cultivated fields, and the nearest public house was four miles down the road. It boasted some twenty residences and a Methodist chapel but had no municipal government or law enforcement. It was, however, pin-neat, and the local residents were civil, even friendly, while exhibiting a British reserve and respect for privacy that Gene could not have enjoyed in a community of expatriate servicemen. The slate-roofed, two-story stone house was roomy, with four bedrooms, three baths, a modern kitchen, an inglenook fireplace in the parlor, wood-block floors throughout, and a "tidy and lawned front garden." Out back there was a parking area for the vans and a board-and-batten outbuilding with a galvanized tin roof. There were trees and meadows on either side of the house, although it faced another across the road, and the entire back of the lot was sealed by the blank concrete-block wall of a storage building.

As he had been for so much of his life growing up,

Gene was gripped by a powerful feeling of being the outsider in England. He had insulated himself emotionally and physically from the air force and had no romance about adopting England as his home. He was in each, but not of them. The rootlessness and insecurity that those feelings had once provoked, however, were replaced by a sense of being exempt from society, transcendent. He saw now how to turn that emotional distance to his purposes, how to use it as a shield, a defense against others getting too close to him or his family. It was easier for him to maintain an aloof but civil distance among his neighbors in Honeydon than among his fellow Americans. In the midst of recreating his life Gene could successfully disguise himself from himself as he groped for something that would define him as a father.

While the air force had still been the binding center of Gene's life he traveled in a more or less conventional emotional orbit. Self-centered, narrow-minded, and often mean-spirited, he nevertheless had had few problems existing in the hubbub of life around air force bases—or at least few problems in allowing his family to live there and become absorbed in it while he was consumed with his work. But with his attention shifted toward his family and the creation of a self, Gene slipped from the hold of the military and into a widening, eccentric gyre. Gene's course, like a come's, would take him far into darkness before delivering him into a psychosexual attraction in which he would blaze with ardor. England was the first outbound leg of this ellipse. It would not carry him as far as the ultimate orbit, the one that took him into the deep space of cold-blooded perfection, but it did prefigure those concentric circles of stone, literal and figurative, with which he would wall himself off. The mounting anger and violence that stemmed from Gene's frustration in failing to order affection and happiness in the same way he ordered documents was a sampler of things to come on his wheel of dark karma.

Sometime between Eddy's birth in July 1973 and the winter of 1974–75, Gene began to beat his wife.

His verbal abuse of Becky was no secret. Any of the family who had seen them much together knew the public reprimands and the sarcasm Gene would use with her, the denigrating sneer in his voice, and it caused them concern for what went on in private. But those concerns had no real cause until Gene had his family segregated in a foreign country and more dependent on him than ever before as their liaison with the world. It was, for Gene, like "going native," in that he shed inhibitions, placed himself in a foreign frame of reference where he felt he had greater latitude for action, fewer judging eyes of family or other servicemen. It was not quite the world remade in his image, but it was a beginning. Then the unimaginable happened.

"Gene," Becky said one day, "will you teach me how to drive?"

"Why?" he said. "You don't need to know how. You've never driven in your life."

"I have too drove a car, Gene; you know that. I just need to have a license in case I have to go somewhere and you're not here or if there's an emergency."

"No. It's out of the question."

"Gene, don't, please. I'm a grown woman, and I can learn how to drive if I want to. And I need to, I really do. Mrs. Chessum over at the Methodist Youth Club said she could show me, if you don't want to."

"I said no. You don't need to. Insurance would go up, and we barely have enough gas for what we already do. Besides, if anybody is going to teach you how to drive, it will be me. If you're going to learn, you need to learn right."

But Becky persisted. It was the first time she had ever defied Gene on anything he so vigorously opposed, and he would never forget it. Becky had gained strength through the years, and the love she drew from her children made her stronger. It was the same love and strength that Gene craved so desperately but did not know how to tap. Many years later, as he sat on death row, he had time to ponder this, muttering as he wrote in a long parenthesis in the middle of a paragraph about conspiracies against him, "There was a love locked in me but the right combination never occurred for that love to be unlocked and released. I had Great Plans of Good things to be done but there were some prerequisites."

One of those prerequisites was knowledge that he did, in fact, dominate Becky and the rest of the family entirely. The direct antagonism over her learning to drive and a less specific one of her independence, finally emerging at age thirty-three, gave Gene enough cause to justify hitting her—disciplining her, he said. He had no patience for driving lessons and would slap Becky for mistakes, even when she was at the wheel. He complained about meals, the way his shirts were ironed, the messes made by the kids. And any of those or a hundred other offenses were grounds for an argument that ended in a flurry of fists.

At the same time it was as if Gene were in competition with Becky to see who was the better parent. Even with his lever of manipulation laid on a fulcrum of fear, Gene was matched in unequal contest here— with all except Sheila Marie—for the children loved their mother, and his rages against her, even behind the closed oak door of their bedroom, left the children in curtain-clinging terror.

The children, with the marvelous resilience of their years, were, on the whole, doing fine. There were other children their ages in and around Honeydon, in addition to the friends they made at school. Little Gene enrolled in Molesworth Junior High in the fall of 1973, were he earned As and Bs in everything except dancing, in which he demonstrated his father's lack of affinity for the rosined maple. Sheila Marie, in fifth grade at Alconbury Elementary School, "has trouble completing assignments and maintaining skills previously developed," but she is "always cheerful and ready to help when needed." Billy, a third grader at Alconbury Elementary, alone of the three carried some of the troubles from home with him: Billy shied from other adults. He "came out of his silence with his peers," his teacher wrote, "but not with me. He still prefers not to discuss anything with me and if he's questioned, he quickly withdraws."

The eight-millimeter Christmas record of 1973 shows smiling faces, Becky baking a turkey, evergreens and holly and red berries on a black limb, a tinseled tree, and piles of presents. Eddy was still in arms, and Gene hadn't started hitting Becky regularly.

Before the Christmas ornaments were all down, in January 1974, Gene had added another star to his crown of professional achievements. He was nominated to be the 10th Tactical Recon Wing's NCO of the Year for 1973.

Despite a fulsome endorsement from his commander, Gene was not selected, but he did receive the award for Squadron NCO of the Year, along with a letter from his commanding officer, who obviously did not want his best clerk getting miffed: "Although you were not selected Wing NCO of the Year," the colonel wrote in February 1974, "I am sure that your truly outstanding efforts in helping the squadron maintain its mission capability are being recognized by Wing Headquarters. Keep up the good work, Gene."

As the slow English spring unfolded Gene turned himself a small garden patch in the side lawn of The

Chestnuts, insured the economical Morris panel van he had bought to include Becky as a driver, and found time to wangle a new ventilation system for his office, where his hawking and swallowing provided an ongoing critique of the air quality. In early April he used the extra days of leave he had earned along with his NCO of the Year selection to take Becky and the kids to London, where they visited the zoo and toured the city in a double-decker omnibus, then across the English Channel to Calais for a single night in France. Gene liked visiting London, and he took the family there on four different occasions, making stops at all the sights and taking photos of the children at Tower Bridge, the Houses of Parliament, and beside a roundabout. Gene knew that he was supposed to provide this sort of thing for the children—it was part of the job description—and he did it with a will, making certain that they saw everything from Stonehenge (twice) to Salisbury Cathedral, in addition to two later vacations in continental Europe.

The Simmons family gave every appearance of a happy clan. Becky kept the children clean and tidy; they were polite, and Gene, though seldom seen in the village, was thought an industrious and loving man, albeit rather reticent. But Gene's social backwardness went unnoticed next to Becky's geniality and the sweetness of the children, whom their neighbors saw almost every day. But already the children were having to live a lie, for they knew what really took place in their parents' bedroom, behind The Chestnuts' stout rock walls.

The early 1970s was a tense period for NATO combat units. The Arab oil embargo, the concluding hostilities in Vietnam, Cubans in Angola, and a growing Soviet presence in Afghanistan, among other events, were pushing the Cold War of nerves to more frayed ends. High states of alert, sometimes requiring Gene to remain on base overnight, were frequent at Alconbury, and field maneuvers came up regularly on the schedule, keeping him away from home for days at a time. He dazzled the command of the 32nd Recon with his rampant efficiency, and when he came home he found fault with Becky for not adhering to his domestic discipline.

But if Gene was balked in his efforts to fashion himself and his family into a perfect circle of love, Becky was even more distressed. Her anxiety now when Gene was at the base on alert or out on maneuvers was not over his absence but because she did not know which man would walk through the door when he came home. He was, she knew, often preoccupied with work, and he spent many evenings hunched over papers he had brought home. She knew how terrible his headaches could be, his anger riding them to the top. She was happy when she could do some of the typing for him, and then he would be so loving, and she would feel his hands on her. But there was not always a lot of that—sex, yes, but not the caresses of love. More often Gene was withdrawn, snappish and quick to anger, demanding. One moment he would be swelled with enthusiasm and the next be sulled in brooding silence. Some evenings he was sparkling with plans—for a trip or a garden or some other family project—and Becky would try hard to enter the spirit of his optimism, never dipping her own oar, but urging him on with her agreement.

But Gene had trouble enlisting the interest of the children in his garden or coin collecting, and the trips were never what he expected them to be. No matter how well he organized them and executed his plans, he never found the fulfillment or satisfaction or edification or whatever one was *supposed* to feel. Like the love that Gene felt was locked inside him, waiting for the right combination of external forces and events to be released, he felt his appreciation of all he was experiencing on these holiday jaunts was similarly blunted. Although neither the sweep of history nor the line of architecture thrilled him, he did prefer the megalithic mystery of Stonehenge to the Christian majesty of Salisbury. But among his snapshots there is not one of a castle or a church or bridge that does not contain Becky or his children. They were the reason for all he did now.

Unable to come up with activities that excited the kids, Gene made some effort to find out what they did like. Roller skating was popular among the air force children at Alconbury, and it seemed a wholesome enough thing to Gene for him to take the children to the rink. Gene had never skated in his life, but he had read and copied step-by-step instructions, memorizing the exact sequence: "toe-push, left-push, right-push, swing your arms." Gene had developed such a faith in the immutable truth of the text, the unalterable black and white, that he really believed he could learn to skate from a book, *had* learned to skate from one. At least he acted like it when he rolled onto the hardwood. Toe-push, left-push, and—whiz-bang—Gene was crashing ass over teakettle onto the floor of the rink, giving his right elbow a crack that would ache off and on for the rest of his life. Skating was clearly too dangerous for the children, and they never went again.

Sheila. More and more Gene's thoughts were on his daughter. He blamed Becky for the violence he did to her, and the more he did, the more he blamed her. The threat to his authority symbolized by her learning to drive had pushed her further from him. In his mind, Becky was a cipher now, dutifully filling a joyless role of housekeeper and sexual receptacle. But in Sheila's dependence and unqualified love he saw hope for a condition sufficient to unlock what he thought was love.

"Come here, ladybug," he would say. "Come sit on my lap."

And Sheila would slide onto his knees and rest her head on his chest.

"Mom," Gene said to Becky, "take our picture."

Despite her apprehension over Gene's anger, Becky was yet too trusting and naïve to consider what his hand was doing above Sheila's knee or to think anything of his running a hand inside her shorts when he tucked in Sheila's shirt. Gene took pictures of all his children naked in the bath, but he kept the ones of Sheila separated in an envelope in his dresser drawer.

Gene's fits of anger against Becky were becoming acute, dangerous, and often more cruel than fists. As a fledgling driver, and naturally cautious, Becky was frightened by high speed, which spurred Gene to recklessness.

"Gene," she pleaded as they tore along a gravel lane in a used three-wheel Valiant caravan, "please slow down. You'll wreck us."

"Until you know how to drive, don't be telling me how," he said. "You just shut up and watch and learn something."

The single wheel on the front of the Valiant plowed into deep gravel and sent the car into a right-angle skid. They left the road and struck a reflector post broadside, flipping the Valiant a full loop and landing it on its tires.

"Goddammit," he snapped as he fumbled with the keys and ground the starter. "Goddammit, see what you caused." And he backhanded a sobbing Becky across the face.

Despite Gene's temper, 1975 had the look of a relatively happy time for the family. Gene was in the field a lot, and Becky and the children were beginning to feel that they fit in at Honeydon. The good Mrs. Chessum had the older children involved in her youth dances and walks and other activities centered around the chapel. Pictures of their friends, however, were not taken in the Simmons home, but always outdoors, usually by the chapel, and usually by someone other than Gene. But in April there was another trip to London, and in September a motor vacation on the Continent. Gene had his Dodge van ferried to Zeebrugge in the Netherlands, and from there they toured the Benelux countries, Germany, Switzerland, and France. All that survives of this grand tour are some color slides of mountain scenery and dispirited family groups, a few odd coins, and Loretta's high school list of countries she had seen. In England Becky and the children were all happier, because they were not shut up with Gene twenty-four hours a day, day after day.

In December Gene received both his orders to report to the SAMSO observatory in Cloudcroft, New Mexico, in April 1976, and a belated decoration from the Republic of Vietnam, the Gallantry Cross with Palm, awarded by quota in the failing days of the Saigon government. For Becky and the children there was a happy Christmas, a tall, gaudy tree surrounded by gifts in wrapping foil and bright paper.

Throughout the remaining months of winter and into spring Gene's mind was alive with plans and anticipation. He wasn't familiar with the Alamogordo-Cloudcroft region, but he liked what he read. His nest egg had grown by nearly two thousand dollars in interest, and he had several hundred more in savings bonds. Already he was dreaming of a place in those high, pure mountains of southern New Mexico, a place he could build on, learn on, and eventually sell when he retired to Arkansas. The years in England spent in the bizarre isolation Gene had carved out in the midst of neighbors were the period of incubation for his vision. Cut off from friends and growing more distant from his wife, Gene was intoxicated by his detachment. He saw clearly that to shrink the universe to his size he would have to cast a circle around a piece all his own where his will was uncompromised. His way was not just the right way, it was the only way. It was organized, planned, and operated on established procedures. He took his only joy in the contemplation of this grand, nebulous plan and in the budding sense that Sheila might hold something for him—a key, perhaps—that he had been missing all his life.

PART THREE

THE END

Arkansas,
1981–1987

SHEILA AND THE DEATH OF PAIN

He has fallen into it completely,
like something he has expected forever,
this sudden, surprised dismissal
of the whole world from around him.

—HENRY GRIFFITH
from ''The Lion Trap''

CHAPTER TEN

"He's crazy, Mom. Sick," said Little Gene. His younger brother Billy was outside gathering the last of the tools and building materials, and this was the first chance Little Gene had had to speak to his mother alone. "You can't stay with him. You can't do this."

Becky pretended not to hear. Her son was saying what she knew was true, and her hurt and anger resonated with his words. But she had to think of the children. The only fierceness in her was to protect them, be with them. It made her strong enough to stay. She knelt and folded shut the top of the cardboard box she had been packing.

"Is there any more newspaper, Gene?" she asked, poking at the top of the box. "I need some more for in here."

Little Gene squatted on one heel and took her arm. "Listen to me, Mom," he said. "He needs help, but he's not going to get any better if you keep going along with him. Just think about what he did."

Becky could think of little else, no matter how hard she tried. Not even her terror of being discovered by the police here in Wills Canyon, packing the last of the family belongings into a U-Haul truck in the middle of an August night, could lessen the knowledge of her husband's incest with Sheila Marie. At moments Becky blamed herself. How could she have let it happen? Why had she not seen it coming? And at others she felt a pang of jealousy. Sheila was always the child she had felt least close to—she had always been Gene's girl—but how could Sheila have let it, let him . . . ? Becky felt sobs of guilt balling in her chest, blaming Sheila the way she did, but she had been through so much since that spring, had existed in such a flux of revelations, horror, and chaos, that even her most grotesque imaginings no longer shocked her, only made her sting with guilt.

Becky was torn by ambivalence. Gene had been her everything—father, lover, husband—and now she feared him at least as much as she loved and hated him. And she feared for her children as much as she loved them. All she wanted was to get the truck loaded, get out of New Mexico and back to Arkansas where her children were, where Gene knew she would have to come back, at least for them.

"Little Gene," she said, pushing the box aside and drawing one knee up to her chest. "I can't leave him. What would I do? Where would I go? Who would there be to look after me and the little ones?"

"Me, Mom," said Little Gene. "I would."

Becky smiled and shook her head weakly. Her oldest son was such a good boy—all her children, even Sheila, were dear to her—but he just didn't understand. Becky herself could not put into words the needs and fears and hopes that bound her to her husband, but she was reluctant to see beyond them.

"No," she said. "I can't leave Dad. He's always been a good provider, at least, and that's more than I can do for the kids by myself, Little Gene. He really wants to change. He's been under lots of pressure,

son, but I know he really will change. Really. And
. . . and what else would I do? Sheila is there with
him. And Loretta . . .''

Little Gene didn't know. His outrage and shame
over what his father had done was blinding. He had
been alienated from his father for more than two
years now, maintaining a veneer of civility toward
him only out of his love for his mother and brothers
and sisters. He wanted to protect them all, and at the
same time to hurt the man who was hurting them. But
he felt frustrated and impotent, for Becky was telling
him that to hurt his father was to hurt them all, the
same thing his father might have said, and Little Gene
was sick to death of that. He was sick of himself for
having to agree, for staying in New Mexico to help
the fat bastard sell this scar in the rock he called a
farm, but if it would help his mother, and if it was
what she wanted, he would. Besides, where else would
he go?

"At least just promise me that you won't let him
hurt you or Sheila again," Little Gene said. "You
know you can have him arrested any time you want.
Or get him to come back here, and the sheriff will do
it."

"No," Becky said emphatically. "He's my husband, Gene. You don't understand what it's like for
me. He's all I have, and I want to see him get better.
I could lose everything if I left. I just don't know
what I would do. And I don't want you to say or do
anything either. Please. Not with the sheriff or Social
Services or anybody. Oh, please promise me that."

Unable to deny his mother anything, Little Gene
crumpled a sheet of newsprint and said, "Okay, Mom.
Here's some paper."

Thinking about Gene alone in Arkansas with Sheila
and Loretta and all the younger children made Becky
even more anxious to be packed and gone. With only

Little Gene and Billy to help her, she worked without sleeping until the truck was full for this, its second trip to Arkansas in less than a week.

Gene had been in Arkansas since August 4, 1981, a full week before the arrest warrant on incest charges was issued for him in Otero County, New Mexico. With him he had taken Sheila Marie, the infant Sylvia Gail, Eddy, Marianne, and Little Becky. Never reluctant to call upon the putative obligations of family when it would serve him, Gene imposed his stunned brood on a niece who hardly knew him until he rented a house in the town of Ward, fifty minutes north of Little Rock, on August 6, and sent word for Becky to follow. He would never set foot again in New Mexico.

Towing their old Dodge van behind the U-Haul, Becky moved the first truckload north on August 18, taking Loretta, Billy, and Little Gene. Loretta stayed in Arkansas for the second trip, August 21–24, much against Becky's timorous protests, but sensing his wife's anger and fearing her flight, Gene had insisted. And they were, after all, his children.

For reasons very different from Becky's, Gene also wanted the family brought quickly together. The walls he had built had been breached. He had made an orderly withdrawal—so much so that he would convince himself he had seized an opportunity and not been driven by events—but there was again that old, deep fear of abandonment stirring in him, of being unloved, the nausea that comes with the sense of being utterly alone. And Gene couldn't shake it. He still clung to Sheila, or at the least to the idea of Sheila, as the key to unlock his heart. It was hard, so hard, to be so near and not to touch her. So he would, along with all the rest, even Becky, whom he only endured. He would reach out, make the family one again, his again, Sheila along with all the rest.

Ward was a curious town for Gene to choose as a place of refuge. It is a community of only a few hundred souls set in the verge between the east Arkansas delta and the beginnings of the Ozarks, just off the divided four-lane that runs from Little Rock to nowhere in particular in the flatlands of the northeast. A pedestrian can see most of Ward from the main intersection, the one with the traffic light. There is a modest municipal building and police station to the southwest, and the local grocery diagonally across from it, a garage just down one street, and two churches within sight. Across the street behind the grocery, on a shady corner lot, is the white frame house that Gene Simmons rented.

The biggest news in Ward is tornadoes—which seem to visit the town with unnerving frequency—and everyone who isn't related knows just about everyone else. It's a friendly place where the chief of police will cover for the town clerk at lunch, the woman who owns the grocery will tell you which brand of fried pie is the best, and every other person you meet has the finest vegetable garden in town. The churches and the civic clubs can honestly claim credit for whatever social life Ward has to offer; there are no bars, restaurants, or movie theaters. But Gene never thought of Ward as anything but a way station, a place where he could live anonymously and inexpensively while he consolidated his plans and his money. It is only odd that he should have chosen so conspicuous a house in the center of such a tightly knit yet gregarious community. Publicly, however, Gene had learned how to keep a disarming facade.

He paid Carolyn Jackson, a retired schoolteacher who owned the house and lived nearby, two months rent in advance, then walked the short block to the municipal building and put down a twenty-five-dollar water deposit. On the back of the receipt, while the children mutely tagged along behind him, Gene wrote down the house's shortcomings and damages. Number one on his list was "L.G. [Little Gene]—no help." Little Gene was a slacker and an ingrate, a faithless son. Ever since the day nearly three years before when Gene had beaten his son for stepping between him and Becky during a fight, Little Gene had been a threat and a rebuke to his father. But as long as Gene could use him, manipulate him through Becky, he would.

Outwardly, there was little to remark about Gene's behavior during the two weeks it took Becky, Billy, and Little Gene to complete the move from New Mexico. He was cordial, if fidgety, and quick to display his practiced smile. His inward turmoil, however, was clouding Gene's thinking, compromising his efforts to cover his tracks to Arkansas. He quickly acquired an Arkansas driver's license, then bought another used car, a brown 1970 Chevrolet Nova that would have no records in New Mexico. At the same time, though, he was in touch with a realtor in Cloudcroft, had filed a change of address with the Otero County tax collector, and kept up a bickering correspondence with the Civilian Personnel Office at Holloman AFB concerning the circumstances of his leaving, circumstances involving a piece of facile lying that would haunt him for months.

Gene would also draw the attention of the police in Arkansas with two traffic violations during the coming year, neither of them serious enough to call for more than a routine scan for outstanding Arkansas warrants. New Mexico Social Services did contact its equivalent agency in Arkansas about Gene, but in the absence of any criminal involvement with Arkansas Health and Human Services, which at that time did not have its files on computer, there was little likelihood of his case being noticed by overworked HHS attorneys. The New Mexico warrant was never circulated through the FBI, where it would have been available to any state or local police who requested a check, and in August 1982 the district attorney for Otero County informed the court of his nolle prosequi of Simmons's warrant. The D.A. had a shaky case at best, for Sheila would not testify, and there were other cases on the docket. Gene was just one small, slippery fish who wriggled through the net.

Gene enrolled the three school-age children—Billy, Loretta, and Eddy—in the Cabot school system and applied for free lunches for them. He taught Billy how to shave and took his picture doing it on the morning before his first day of classes. On August 31 Gene drove the brown Nova to the Employment Security Division offices in Jacksonville and began an earnest search for a job.

The satisfaction that Gene felt over getting himself and his family out of New Mexico ahead of the law was tempered by his Damoclean financial situation. He was living on borrowed money, and in less than ten months he had a term payment of more than thirteen thousand dollars due on the mortgage against the Wills Canyon property. Filling out the application with Employment Security, he realized that his leaving the 6585th at Holloman without notice was bound to come to light, and he knew too well how that would play with federal bureaucrats. If he had any hope of getting a civil service job, he had to move fast on preemptive damage control.

The day after completing his job application with Employment Security, Gene sat down to draft a letter to Ken Holland, his civilian boss at Holloman. In it Gene struck a breezy, offhand note and piled up excuse after familiar excuse, all of them stressing that none of it was his fault.

Dear Ken,
Sorry if I slowed down the film scrubbing process.
I didn't know that John was leaving. Ken, I want
to thank you very much for giving me a job. It
had been a year and a half of unemployment.
Don't you go think I am ungrateful by leaving.
But that 90 miles a day trip up and down the
mountain on the cycle with the problem I was
having with the joints of my arm was getting to
me. I couldn't have afforded to get a 4-wheel
drive vehicle which I would have needed anyway
for the winter time. It would have been hard to
get a loan approved for a new vehicle since my
job was temporary and intermittent. I did enjoy
working with you all and would like to have
stayed longer but I needed to get my children
into school. . . Well Ken, again, I say thank you
for everything. Take it easy.

Gene

The same day Gene responded to a letter from
Duane Apprill, the realtor in Cloudcroft who would
handle the sale of the Wills Canyon property. Apprill
had been to inspect the property with Little Gene,
and along with the marketing agreement that he sent
he included a brief note stating that the most Gene
could realistically hope to realize from the sale was
"about $40,000," depending on whether he planned
to make any repairs. Gene responded with a scribble
in the margin to take "$39,500 cash, as is."

Wills Canyon was Gene's ace in the hole. Twice
already he had borrowed against it to see him through
financial crises, such as the one he currently faced,
and he wanted to believe that its sale would smooth
over all his present problems. But as so often was the
case with Gene's financial planning, his execution
foiled his intent. He did not recognize that all the

labor he had forced from the children to build the rock walls did not necessarily constitute an improvement. Time and effort that might have been better spent on completing the cobbled-up sheds and outbuildings was instead spent erecting flimsy chicken coops. Gene never supposed that the remote, unattractive sliver gouged from the side of the mountain might be less than alluring to someone else. He did not see the megalithic austerity of the place, only the shape of his dreams, the emblem of his desire.

Gene's anxiety over the property wouldn't rest. His headaches, he said, had come back to plague him, so he had to dictate his next letter to Little Gene through Becky. Following a chatty paragraph about their new house in Ward and the kids' new school ("no colored kids and . . . free lunches"), it read:

"What's going on back there? It's been over a week since you and Apprill were [at] the house together, and we haven't heard from anyone. We are very concerned. Dad has been going to the PO everyday expecting to receive some word. The place back there is a big worry for us . . . our money is running out fast. . . . You said in your letter that Apprill said there might be some problems working with Security Bank & Trust, what does he mean? What does the Bank have to do with selling the house, how will Apprill be working with the bank? Dad doesn't understand how Apprill would be working with the SB&T. Let us know what he means.

Gene's concern was not just for the sale of the property. One of the pledges he had made when securing the loan to finance his getaway was to remain in Cloudcroft to tend to the sale himself. Gene feared that his reneging on the promise might somehow compromise the loan or, worse, require him to return to New Mexico to close the deal—an unthinkable prospect. In his febrile imagining he even toyed with the notion that the bank was in league with the sheriff and the D.A. to get him back there for prosecution. Perhaps even his son was part of the plot, for Gene would not put it past him.

But Gene's creeping paranoia was no longer confined to fears of prosecution in New Mexico. No sooner had Becky arranged the furniture and unpacked the boxes than Gene began issuing orders to her about domestic economies and security. There was a telephone in the house at Ward that rang through whenever the landlords received a call but on which no one could call out. Gene gave strict orders that it was never to be answered or even picked up. No lights, he said, were to be turned on during the day, and none at night until the children had pulled all the shades and drawn the drapes. The children were not allowed out alone. Even when they went to the corner grocery it was in a line, holding hands. Loretta was the one exception to this, and she would sometimes talk a little with the woman who ran the store. She did not discuss her family, however, preferring instead to profess a Christian faith and tell wishful stories about her imagined church in New Mexico. Not a soul in Ward can recall having had a conversation with Gene or Becky Simmons, save a young Baptist minister who, encouraged by what he had heard of Loretta's Christian witness, came to call one day.

The Reverend Y.—who must remain anonymous— waited a decent interval for the family to get settled before he dropped by to say hello and invite them to his church. Despite the dark windows, he had seen enough of the coming and going around the house to know when he could find Gene and Becky home, judging from which cars were in the drive, and he chose a mild, sunny afternoon in late September to make his pastoral visit.

The Reverend Y. walked from his parsonage to the Simmons house, mounted the steps to the low, covered porch, and assumed his best face, the one that reflected his genuine pleasure in meeting new families in his town and offering them a share of the joy he found in church fellowship. He knocked, thought he saw movement behind one window, then waited for a long minute before he heard footsteps inside.

The front door opened, and indistinctly through the screen the Reverend Y. could see a paunchy, bearded man wearing blue bib overalls over a white T-shirt.

"Yes?" Gene said. "What do you want?"

"Mr. Simmons?" asked the Reverend Y.

Gene nodded.

"I am Brother Y., Mr. Simmons, the pastor over here at the church." The Reverend Y. pointed to his chapel in the middle distance.

"The Baptist church?" Gene asked.

"Yes, the—"

"We're Episcopalians," Gene said.

"Well," the Reverend Y. began, "our fellowship is open to all Christians, and we'd welcome—"

Gene slammed the door in his face.

"Never," he later told the children, "you are never to talk to that man. Don't even answer the door if I'm not at home."

Throughout September, while calling daily at the employment office to check on his application, Gene occupied much of his days writing letters—draft after draft until he got them right. Most of them were part of an unsuccessful campaign he waged against the Civilian Personnel Office at Holloman AFB to repair the damage to his résumé caused when he walked away from his job. Seizing on a technicality, Gene accused the CPO of failing to send him certain documents—documents that had no bearing on the nature of his termination. He cited telephone calls he had made from Arkansas to the CPO informing the office of his leaving. Then he disputed the dates of the calls. Behind this smokescreen he wrote to several different people in his former unit, stressing to each of them that he had made every honest effort to effect his termination according to procedure. He blamed operators and secretaries for not relaying his messages; he accused the entire CPO of ineptitude. The CPO, however, was bureaucratically adamant. The papers terminating him "for cause" had already been filed when he claimed to have called to resign, and that was an end to it. Gene had to back and fill on the dates of employment he listed on his job application. And perhaps no one would bother to check. Still, to be safe, on the Employee Service Statement he filed when he was hired by the Veterans Administration on September 29, Gene cited the umbrella military-civilian liaison unit at Holloman, not the 6585th, as his previous employer.

On September 30 Gene began work as a GS-2 file clerk at the Little Rock Division of the Veterans Administration Medical Center, a job he would hold through the first of the year. Although the salary was disappointing—he had been a GS-4 at Holloman—it did relieve the worst of his immediate financial worries. But by now the specters of persecution were flocking to roost in Gene's mind, and anything he saw might give rise to thoughts of escape, means of removing himself from the world. In 1981, though, his thoughts of death were still figurative. Without any clear idea of how he would use them, Gene cumshawed blank death certificates, enough for his entire family, and collected all the government literature on how to apply for a new Social Security number.

At this time only Becky, Little Gene, Billy, and Loretta knew the truth about Sheila's child, Sylvia Gail, and Gene was making every effort to see that things stayed that way. He was especially concerned that none of Becky's family discover the truth. He knew that there were enough hard feelings toward him and enough influence on Becky from that quarter to threaten his designs. As part of his obsession with controlling all family communication, he alone knew the combination to the post office box—which was in Jacksonville, not Ward—and he alone bought and dispensed stamps. Most of the letters Becky wrote in those first months back in Arkansas were dictated by Gene through many drafts, and he read any others before blessing them with postage. Typical were the scathing letters he had Becky write to Little Gene, upbraiding him for being dilatory and remiss, blaming him for the Wills Canyon property not selling. Gene's intent was, with the letters all written in Becky's hand and made to read as though they were her own, to shame Little Gene into some kind of action. But Little Gene saw through the ruse, and in his replies, although addressed to his mother, he uses language clearly aimed at Gene:

"The end of your letter really pissed me off," he writes on October 12, in a crabbed hand similar to his father's and echoing his father's sense of offended dignity.

> You would have to be here to understand the kind of life I've been leading. Right now it's about 10 minutes to midnight. I'm tired and don't feel good plus I'm in a bad mood. At work, I work anywhere between 9 A.M. and 7 P.M. I work at Pronto Car Wash and Lube across from Safeway. Basically, I wash cars and lube cars and [do] oil changes. In addition to that I do the

manager's job of inventory, opening and closing, and just running the place. The company has been considering making me an asst. manager but they're dragging their feet. Our manager . . . doesn't want me to get the job because I am a threat to her job. She's afraid I'll take it away from her. Even though I seem to be putting in long hours (7 days a week for the past 3 weeks) I'm not making any money. Even though I got my IRS check, it didn't catch me up on my rent. I know you probably think I spend all my money going out, but that's wrong. Nowadays my going out consists of going to [a girlfriend's] house and falling asleep on her couch. I can't tell you anything about the house because I haven't been up there in a while.

After this Gene addressed all his queries about the sale of his property to the realtor.

Gene's single-mindedness soon regained any momentum he'd lost to the move and his anxieties. Within a few weeks he was bringing his files up to date, again clipping self-help and police-beat stories from the local newspapers, and at work he was circulating a memo asking for better ventilation to remove cigarette smoke. Each day he scanned the bulletin board above the water fountain in the hall outside his office, looking for better-paying vacancies within the VA or among the civilian jobs open with the armed forces, especially in the recruiting offices.

By late October, when Sheila Marie's eighteenth birthday arrived, Gene felt on solid enough financial footing that he could turn more of his attention toward reforging his family, with Sheila the meaningful link. Alone among the family, Sheila had never felt the heat of Gene's temper. As her child grew and was accepted by her mother and brothers and sisters as one of their own, and as Sheila regained her figure and sense of being special, the shame and fright she had felt began to dissipate. Closely kept and isolated in a strange place, she felt her attachment to her father begin to reassert itself, and she was no longer shy about showing it. When she went shopping with Gene or sat next to him when he took the family out for hamburgers she sensed her mother's resentment, but he was her sole source of male affection, the strong man who defined her world. More than her mother, Sheila did not know what she would do without him. Only the nagging knowledge that she was at the center of the upheaval in the family, that they were all hiding her secret and sharing its shame, caused Sheila to draw back from Gene. Becky, as gently and uncritically as she could, let Sheila know that what Gene had done was wrong. For his part, he approached her slowly, drawing her to him no faster than the rest, waiting.

The importance that Gene attached to birthdays and Christmas gave him his first clear opportunity to force the pattern of family life he desired. That his wife had withdrawn into emotional shock and his children were mute automatons around the house was not entirely lost on Gene; he at least recognized that something was needed to make the family a reflection of his great plans for good things, to put a happy face on matters, and a party seemed just it. What's more, he could use it to insinuate Sheila into her new, elevated position as mother . . . and as wife.

Becky had no intention of ignoring Sheila's birthday, but she had been reluctant to make much of it. She did not know—as she almost never did—how the family finances really stood, and she did not want to anger and embarrass Gene by suggesting a fete they could not afford. So she was both relieved and apprehensive when Gene brought it up.

"Let's have a real party," he had said. "Sheila deserves that, doesn't she? It'll really be fun."

His enthusiasm was unsettling to Becky, but there was no way she could disagree. She was jealous and resentful of Sheila still, and this made it worse, for Sheila beamed with pleasure at the idea and hugged Gene without being asked. Becky had seen all this before.

Becky baked a chocolate sheet cake, which Gene himself iced and decorated with confectioner's flowers and a looping endearment in blue frosting: "Happy Birthday Sweetheart Sheila Marie." Gene took everyone out for hamburgers at the Burger King in Jacksonville, grinning and making a display of his paternal affection, but Becky was just too sick to eat.

By Thanksgiving Sheila and Sylvia Gail were seated at Gene's right hand, and by Christmas he would hardly pose for the camera without both Sheila and Becky at his side, as though to emphasize their equality. But some are more equal than others. The younger children received dolls and trucks and toys that year. Becky got a waffle iron, and Billy a cheap electronic game. Sheila received her own portable radio, the first one in the family that was not Gene's. He squeezed Sheila's thigh as they knelt for the photo of her with her present.

About a week before Christmas Gene was finally interviewed for a job with the army recruiter in Little Rock, and on January 9, 1982, he resigned from the VA to accept a GS-4 position at the recruiting office, where he was again in his natural element. In many ways, the work Gene would perform in the recruiting office was similar to his old job at OSI. In addition to being in charge of the routine paper shuffling, he also had the responsibility for background checks, judging the medical and moral fitness of potential recruits.

Coincidental with his efforts to redraw the family

ties, especially those with Sheila Marie, Gene was likewise making an attempt to heal some of the rift that had opened between him and Becky, for he knew he would need her compliance to realize his plans. He became flirtatious and affectionate with her. She allowed him to take Polaroids of her in the nude. They began to make love. As it always had, this attention turned Becky's head. Moreover, in a celebratory mood on the day before he shaved his beard—the mustache would remain—and began his job at the recruiting office, Gene had his photo taken with everyone in the family individually. The happiness that shone from Becky's eyes would have been even shorter lived had she known the reason for Gene's. Things had gone as he had connived, and Sheila was again having sex with him.

In his darkened bedroom on afternoons when Becky was at the laundromat with the little ones, in the back of the station wagon when he and Sheila went to the grocery in Jacksonville at night, any time he could, he took Sheila to him and poured out his counterfeits of love. "Honey," he called her, and "my little princess." He fondled her and kissed her on the lips and breasts. He said, "Sheila, honey, I will spend my life making you happy, just don't ever lie to me, don't ever leave me. It's all in your hands, little princess— all my happiness and everyone's. Don't you know that?"

Sheila would dutifully answer, "Yes."

When Sheila did feel the tug of remorse she would try to move behind her mother, telling Gene that she didn't feel right about what they were doing because it hurt Becky so.

"There is so much you don't understand, sweetheart," Gene said to her. "Things can never be right with Mom and me unless they are right with you and me. There is so much I want to do, so much I have to do, but it all depends on you."

This was no dissimulation. Gene believed every word he said. Unfazed by anything else he might have known or felt, Gene was deeply and romantically in love with his own daughter, wholly absorbed in the crippled dependence he had created in her, himself a shuffling Pygmalion.

Torn by humiliation and confusion, but unable to hate or even blame her father, Sheila began to withdraw into the same emotional shell in which Becky took refuge. Billy and Loretta, Eddy and Marianne were terrified by the palpable tension that hung behind the floral curtains of their home, and Little Becky hid behind chairs. Becky did what she could to relieve the atmosphere, hoarding quarters from her laundry money to buy them little treats and, when Gene was at work, allowing them to play on the piano that he had inherited from his mother, something he had always forbidden.

Gene counted February a red-letter month. The truth of his termination from the 6585th at Holloman finally came out, but he successfully tap-danced his way around it, having repeated his fabric of lies often enough that they at last sounded convincing, leaving him secure in his recruiter's job. On the heels of this he received a firm offer of thirty-five thousand dollars for the Wills Canyon property and snapped it up at once. Oblivious to the unhappiness of Becky or any of the children, he made much of taking his wife to a movie on Valentine's Day and treating Billy to hamburgers at Wendy's on his birthday.

Throughout the spring and summer of 1982 Gene did whatever he thought would help put things right. For Mother's Day he took the family to the Little Rock Zoo and gave Becky a new toaster (and Sheila nothing). He pushed himself to spend more time with the younger children, with designs to make allies of them. He bought an inflatable wading pool and splashed with them in it. For weeks there were no photographs of him with Sheila, but he could not disguise his fawning attachment to her. He took her to his office so she could watch him at work and admire his command of the job, and he could not keep from touching her whenever she was near.

In June, much to Becky's delight, Little Gene came up from Alamogordo for a long weekend. He felt his father's eye always on him during the three days he stayed in Ward, but he made the best of things, just to keep his mother happy. The ambiance of the house was only too familiar to Little Gene—if anything, it was more stifling than he remembered—and his mother's insistence that everything was fine did nothing to reassure him. Her family was having a reunion in Colorado in August, and part of Little Gene's coming to Ward was in hope that he could get her to go there with him. But she would not leave the girls alone with Gene, who, always keen to the nuances of power, would not hear of their going.

Certain images in Gene's symbology bore particular significance, and one of these—along with family photos and the trappings of Christmas—was birthday cakes. Gene believed they had a special, almost fetishistic power, especially for Becky. Despite his disregard for her, Gene was apprehensive of what she knew and recognized that her goodwill was important to his holding the children—even Sheila—within his shrinking compass. He ended his physical abuse, and for her birthday in July Gene saw to it that Becky had no less than three cakes—one from Billy, one from Sheila and Loretta, and one from him. The message on the girls' cake read: "Happiness is having you for a mom." Becky was radiant in the glow of the candles. Quid pro quo, she saw to it that Gene and Eddy, who, along with Little Gene, shared July 15 as their birthday, each had a separate cake. Later that month Loretta, too, was lavished with cake and confections and her father's cloying embraces.

Lately Gene had begun to notice Loretta, who was just turning twelve and was prettier than her older sister. He ogled the budding breasts beneath her wet T-shirt when she played in the pool with Little Becky, Eddy, and Marianne. Yet even at age twelve Loretta was too bright, imaginative, and self-confident to be easy prey to Gene's manipulation. He would always know that she was, in some way he could not alter, beyond his reach, and for that he would never be at ease with her, never entirely trust her.

None of Gene's attempts, however, had a happy effect on morale. Becky, try as she might to rationalize her situation, was crushed, beaten. She felt helpless and horrified at what she was witnessing between Gene and Sheila. And her horror only increased her helplessness. Sheila was still being ripped by the emotional crosscurrents of forced sex with her father and his continuing protestations of devotion. Loretta retreated into vivid fantasies of normalcy. The boys, Billy and Eddy, were allowed to drift so long as they did their chores. The younger girls, Marianne and Rebecca, remained cringingly shy.

When Becky's sister Viola and her husband, Roger O'Shields, stopped to visit in August on their way to the family reunion in Walsenburg, they were deeply troubled by the state of the Simmons household. Not able to call and tell Becky that they had arrived, Roger and Vi checked into a motel in Jacksonville and drove up to Ward around suppertime.

"I wrote Becky and told her we were coming," Vi recalls," so they were expecting us. Becky had a little ham fixed"—she holds her cupped hands six inches apart—"and corn and something else. But Gene ate burritos with onions and cheese. She fixed him a separate plate. He didn't say a word, just watched everybody else eat. I hate to say this, but we felt . . . well, I hated to eat very much, because I didn't want to take food out of the kids' mouths.

"Well, there were 'No Smoking' signs, of course, all over the house, and Roger would go outside to smoke, but we sat around inside, talking, and every time I looked at Becky her eyes would fill with tears. Then, I would look around, and Gene would be watching us. I knew there was something wrong.

"We sat and visited, and Gene sat across from us, where he could have eye contact with me and Becky. It got dark, but no lights. I could barely see across the room. When they did turn on the lights, all the kids went around and pulled the shades first. No two words were uttered; they were like robots.

"That's the night when we knew for sure that something was wrong. Sheila was just a shadowy mouse, just completely withdrawn. . . . and Little Becky would hide away.

"But we went back the next day, and I . . . made up Becky's and Sheila's faces and left them some Mary Kay cosmetics. That's when Becky finally started getting some cosmetics, whether he liked it or not. [Gene] came in at noon, . . . and then we all went out to dinner [that night]. We paid, but he told us where to go.

"[Later] the four of us went back to our motel. Becky and I tried to get in a corner and visit. But every time I glanced over, he was, like, tuned in on us, afraid we were going to say something.

"I've always remembered that he always had a kid on his lap, but none of the kids would ever go near him [voluntarily]. Not a one. He tried to get Little Becky to come to him, and Little Becky wouldn't go to his arms."

Aside from her own children, there was no one Becky loved more than Roger and Vi. She had joked with them years before that if anything ever happened to Vi, she would leave Gene for Roger. And she and Vi, despite their long separations, had grown closer through the years. Becky admired—perhaps envied—Viola's religious faith and the strength it gave her. Since their return from England, Gene had proscribed any organized religion, and Vi's visit was like a tonic for Becky. Fortified by this dose of familial love, she rallied her strength to go on, to try to make a family.

Despite Gene's parsimony, he couldn't do too much for Sheila—anything to hold her. Sheila would meekly accept his public displays of affection, but in private she was enough troubled not to say yes to his sexual demands, even when she submitted. She was becoming a young woman, although still a very naïve one, and she had to get out of the house, do something, get a job, she said. Gene was ecstatic. Not a job—no—but education. For Sheila, never a strong student, that meant a vocational business school, and Gene knew just the one. In August, a week following Roger and Vi's visit, Gene enrolled Sheila Marie in the Draughon School of Business in Little Rock, about three blocks from the recruiting office where he worked.

Gene had already gathered and read all the literature and application forms from the school before he had shown them to Sheila. She was happy to go along with the idea. Awkwardly shy from the disjuncture in her life and the almost hermetic isolation of her adolescence, Sheila in fact dreaded the idea of independence, of living in the world and providing for herself and Sylvia Gail. Gene also feared it—for himself. The school, despite the three thousand dollars in fees for its one-year course, seemed a bargain to Gene, if it would keep Sheila near and reliant on him.

Happy and animated, loving and avuncular, Gene sat with Sheila at the Formica table in the kitchen and showed her how to make a double-entry ledger of expenses, reminding her, as the running total grew, of the sacrifices he was making for her. He helped her choose classes and make a schedule that allowed her to commute with him. He gave her money for new clothes, satiny bow-necked blouses and creamy turtlenecks, smart blazers and straight skirts that flattered the slimness of her legs. Her hair fell in a dark wave past her shoulders, or she gathered it in a prim ponytail with bangs. Gene never stopped taking pleasure in looking at her, placing his arm across her shoulders, his hand hovering over her breast, while he explained the columns of figures he had copied in his spiral notebook.

When she had seen the family in Ward, Viola had noticed that Becky insisted on wearing her hair in a bun. Becky still had a trim figure but looked aged with her hair up. Sheila, however, had hers back in a ponytail, her blouse buttoned to the top—and that was Becky, Becky all over when she was a teenager. Everything Sheila said or did reminded Viola of Becky.

In Sheila, Gene sought to recapture the rapture of youth, of his first love with Becky, to erase all the mistakes and hard luck and begin anew on his dream. And the more Sheila turned from him, however slightly, the greater his anxiety and devotion.

In October Gene received a five-hundred-dollar raise and took the entire family to the state fair in Little Rock.

The smells of cotton candy, funnel cakes, dust, broiling hot dogs, and manure from the livestock barns hung thick in the evening air of Indian summer, muffling the shriek of calliopes and diffusing the infernal spinning lights of the midway. Gene held Sylvia in the crook of one arm, the other wrapped around Sheila's shoulders, lost in the synesthesia, a smitten smile pasted across his face. Becky, Billy, and Loretta walked behind with the other three little ones, taking turns carrying Rebecca Lynn when she got tired. The children were excited, but their pleasure was tempered by the rules: no balloon darts or ring toss—no games of chance at all—no overpriced snacks from the travel-trailer kiosks, and no rides except those Dad told them were okay. The younger ones rode ponies and kiddie cars and revolving swings; Billy and Loretta were allowed the Ferris wheel, and everyone rode the carousel. Gene and Sheila shared a car on the body-slamming Mount Everest roller coaster while Becky looked on, holding Sylvia Gail.

Gene led the family on to the livestock barns, then back down the midway where, fifty feet from the exits, he glanced into a cul-de-sac of tents and booths and saw the calendar stand. He had bought some souvenirs and trinkets for the smaller children, stuffed bears for Becky and Loretta, banners for the boys, but nothing for Sheila, or for Sheila and himself.

"Mom," he said to Becky as he reached for his wallet, "don't you think the kids would like one more ride before we go?"

Becky was too surprised to let it show. "Yes, Gene," she said. "I guess so."

He gave her the money and said, "Well, here, the treat's on me. Sheila and I want to look at some things over here. We'll be right here when you're through, so come straight back."

At the stand in the neon cul-de-sac, for seven dollars you could have your picture taken and transferred onto a calendar or metal lapel button. Out of sight of the family, Gene approached the booth holding Sheila tightly to him, running his hand down the curve of her back to her hip.

"And we can have these," he was saying to her,

"and every day I can see you and you can see me, first thing every morning and the last thing at night, just like we were there together."

Sheila squirmed, ducked her head, and smiled. "Okay," she said.

"Gene and Sheila," the legend ran beneath their photos on the two calendars and the buttons, each picture floating in a fuzzy lozenge of light. Later he realized that the calendars could not really be displayed or the buttons worn, so he filed them among his jumble of records, wrapped lovingly in tissue. For the rest of her life—and, really, of his—everything Gene did would grow from or fester in his love of Sheila.

CHAPTER ELEVEN

It was an eerie fall and winter in Arkansas in 1982–83. Freak weather patterns kept off the cold and bent winds in from the south, drawing up epi-tropical warmth from the Gulf and sowing tornadoes like casts of hornets across Little Rock and its suburbs. Japonica began to bloom in December. It was a spring as false as the images that Gene tried to project for the world.

In October, in a letter he censored, Becky wrote to her ailing mother:

> . . . I was real happy to see Viola. The children sure did like her. . . . I hope to make a trip next summer to see you, right now that's my greatest dream. . . . Received a letter from Little Gene [a] while back. In his spare time he is teaching the blind students to play chess. He is a good son, he works and still goes to college. . . . Sheila is going to business school. Got her first report card Friday, all As. . . . Bill is going to college [i.e., vo-tech school] in the morning and high school in the afternoon. . . . He is taking

auto mechanics. . . . Loretta keeps busy with school, reading all the time and sewing. . . . Eddy keeps himself busy with school and just playing on his free time. Marianne is my big help. . . . I have three [children] at home. Sylvia is a very good little girl and minds real well. . . . I've been very lucky.

Becky's sense of good fortune was as real as it was poignantly ironic, for despite Gene's oppression and the jealousy, shame, and guilt that tormented her, there were times when life, for a brief hour or day, was nearly normal for Becky, and she could actually enjoy time spent with Gene as he whirled the family through an odyssey of outings over the coming eight months. From October 1982 until May 1983, much as he had when his temper first began breaking loose in England, Gene took his family to theme parks or playgrounds, toured scenic drives or the Little Rock Zoo almost every weekend. The zoo was his special favorite, for during the unseasonably warm months of winter it charged no admission. Neither the gaiety and spontaneity of the children when they had the zoo essentially to themselves nor Becky's timid relapses of affection clued Gene to the truth, that he and he alone had created the tension in his household. And it was becoming worse.

Gene's desperation to win back Sheila and at the same time have Becky accept the arrangement was becoming acute. He concocted a flattering image of Sheila as a bright young professional—a persona much at odds with her character and her secretarial training—and decorated one of her three birthday cakes with dung-green dollar signs as an emblem of her future prosperity. He showered Sheila with affection and small gifts of clothes and costume jewelry, and once gave her an arrangement of yellow daisies. And she continued meekly to tolerate his affection.

But something had changed in Sheila. Gene could not name it; he knew only that it fanned his jealousy and insecurity, caused him to try harder—or, at least, as best he knew how. There was nothing definite, nothing he could use to justify his anxiety, so he tried to push it from his mind and fill up the time with professions of love, furtive sex, and the manipulations of guilt: "If you love me as much as I love you, you will" was his adolescent refrain, repeated time after time as he drove with her from Ward to Little Rock and back four days each week.

"Remember," he said, "that all this is for you; we're all sacrificing for you. And I need you, sweetheart. You're all that matters to me—you know that, don't you?"

Yes.

"And you'll never do anything to hurt me?"

No.

"And you know that only you can really make things right again, don't you? The whole family is depending on you, little princess. You know that, don't you?"

Yes.

Sheila, however, was on the emotional mend, discovering possibilities in herself that Gene had never allowed her to imagine. Before enrolling in the Draughon School she had spent almost eighteen months virtually cloistered, with little human contact outside the family. Abashed, frightened, and at the same time infatuated with her pride of place in her father's hierarchy, Sheila had been an easy object of Gene's domination. But even Gene could not wholly stunt her maturing. It was this, in part, that he sensed: Sheila was becoming her own person. She did well at her studies and enjoyed the company of the other students at Draughon, especially that of a young man named Dennis McNulty. But emotionally she was held back by her abiding sense of shame, a gloaming knowledge that she was part of something deeply and grotesquely evil.

Gene's arrogance would not admit the possibility that his hold on Sheila had slipped enough to allow for her a real romance, and he forged ahead through Christmas and New Year in ignorance. Loretta and the younger children had made chains of colored paper and plaster-of-paris ornaments at school, and the house and tree were decked in overabundance with tinsel, ornaments, years of Christmas cards, and cardboard cutouts of holiday icons: Frosty, Santa, a one-horse open sleigh.

For his part, Gene made a production of taking the little ones to see Saint Nick at the shopping mall and helping to decorate the house. He was in high and generous spirits, warm within the circle of his family, confident that Sheila was still his. He bought a sackful of toys, dolls, and games, a radio for Bill, jewelry and jewelry boxes for Becky and Sheila Marie, as well as palettes of makeup. And everything he did with Becky, he did with Sheila Marie. Each sits in his lap to show off her new pendant; each kneels with her jewelry box, its drawers open to display the lining. Together they pose with him for pictures of the tree, the other children, the Christmas turkey Sheila baked. Gene seats them on either side of him at table on Christmas Day. They drink California champagne, Sheila only after some coaxing. Morning sickness had made her queasy all day.

Sheila was dazed by the knowledge that she was pregnant again. She had let Gene have her only seldom in the fall and now tried to deny the facts to herself. But when she missed her second period she knew he had to be told.

The news hit Gene like a dash of ice water, sobering his dizzy delusion that things were working out just fine. Suddenly, and briefly, he glimpsed the vulnerability of his deformed moral posture, saw himself as others might. But he would not make the same mistakes he had made before, would not repeat New Mexico. Moreover, now he also knew that not even Becky—especially not Becky—could know. No one could have any hint, most certainly none of Becky's family. Becky was still weepingly distant, and he sensed enough suspicion and resentment from Viola and Becky's half-sister Edith (who also came for a short visit in January 1983) to fear that their knowledge might tear Becky away from him, shatter the bulwarks of family that he had erected around himself. Protecting that cobbled edifice was paramount, more important to him than his espoused convictions. Gene stood on highly vocal principle against abortion, but this was a special case—his.

On January 30, 1983, a Sunday, Gene took the family to the zoo, despite its being one of the rare chilly days that winter, puckering their smiles with the cold. The next day he took off from work, pulled Sheila out of classes, and drove her to the doctor.

Dr. Chu Iy Tan was a cultural castaway in Dermott, a small farming community in southeast Arkansas lying between the Bayou Bartholomew and the Mississippi River. The town had recruited Dr. Chu from Canada, and in exchange for all sorts of incentives he had agreed to practice in the rural area for five years, which soon would be up. He had many patients whom he saw only once, country people who harbored an aversion to doctors and those who canceled follow-up visits. He was counting weeks until he was free and not trying to ingratiate himself in the community, not making an effort to remember everyone he saw. He thought nothing of not recognizing a Mr. Allen, who brought his daughter, Sheila, in for a routine pregnancy test.

How Gene found Dr. Chu or chose Dermott is a complete mystery, as are the details of the subsequent abortion. Gene destroyed everything relating to the incident except for people's memories and the form Dr. Chu filled out certifying Sheila's pregnancy. It somehow slipped down the back of a folder containing old automobile records.

The abortion was a turning point for Sheila Marie. The small voice, an echo of her mother's, that had been telling her what she was doing with her father was horribly wrong finally began to ring clear. She could sense, if not articulate, the wonderful difference between how she felt when she talked with Dennis at school and her self-loathing when she was with Gene. With Dennis she felt clean, vicariously cleansed by the Catholic faith that he so cheerfully discussed with her. He was a friend, but she knew he thought she was pretty. She told Dennis she had a daughter, and his reaction was to ask to meet her. When she was self-deprecating he would protest it. Sheila was still some way from breaking completely with her father, but she never again had sex with him.

Wholly incapable of walking a mile in another's shoes, Gene nevertheless put on a countenance of concern for Sheila's feelings, making his mawkish attempts to soothe her while at the same time coercing her with veiled threats of what it would do to the family if anyone found out. He was willing to accept her further withdrawal and physical distance from him for a while.

As the weird winter slid imperceptibly into spring Gene had two goals: to complete his reconciliation with Sheila and at last to buy that place in the hills where all his dreams could come true, his love for Sheila be eternally requited.

Toward his first end, Gene knew that he must complete his reordering of the family. Especially so long

as Becky held back from him, refused to enter into
the happiness of his designs, he could not enjoy the
blessing of inner peace that Sheila would bring him.
While Becky was as visibly battered by events as she
had become, Gene knew that Sheila would never
come all the way back. He had to instill in both wife
and daughter a sense of the *three* of them as one, the
core of the family, and he had to do this without
revealing to Becky his true motives. Out of this need
the weekends of enforced togetherness intensified,
with trip after trip to the zoo, to Greers Ferry Lake,
to Hot Springs, to the Toad Suck Recreation Area on
the Arkansas River near Conway. But the apogee of
this flurry came in May, on Mother's Day, when
Gene took both Becky and Sheila to a concert by the
country-rock group Alabama.

Gene was not much drawn to music, although he
did have a few country-and-western records, and
Becky's taste ran increasingly to gospel, so it was
largely for Sheila that he undertook the detailed planning of the occasion. Barton Coliseum, where the
concert was to be held, is on the state fairgrounds,
and Gene knew the parking areas nearby, but he had
never been in the coliseum itself, a vast barn of a
building with entrances on every side. He gathered
multiple copies of the floor plan, with their seats and
entrances marked, so he, Becky, and Sheila could
each have one in case they got lost or separated.
Then he carefully instructed them on what to do and
where to meet him if that happened. Gene fretted for
days that he might lose face by failing to navigate
them to their seats, but he did not. He sat between
Becky and Sheila and bought them souvenir T-shirts
afterward, satisfied that he had shown himself to be a
really with-it guy. Later, forced to pose with Rebecca
Lynn on her lap, seated next to Sheila and Sylvia
Gail, Becky is a picture of misery.

With his attention so tightly focused on frequencies of the triangle he formed with Becky and Sheila, Gene neglected the rest of the family more than ever. After Little Gene's rebellion Gene had never taken a particular interest in his sons or felt especially threatened by them. Eddy was too young, and Billy was too malleable. But without the anchor of a happy home easygoing Billy drifted into bored delinquency. His schoolwork was "below capacity, nearly failing . . . and always late." But that did not directly affect Gene, and he could ignore it. Not so when Billy was caught with three other boys trying to break into the school and start a fire. There was no property damage, however, and the incident was soon forgotten. But to Gene it demonstrated more than ever the importance of getting his family away from the immorality that seemed to turn up on every hand. It was the only way he could protect them.

To the west of Ward the land begins to roll and rise, and the vegetation marks a shift from delta to Ozark: hackberry and cypress give way to oak and red cedar. The rock is closer to the skin of the earth here, and water is the blood of the land: Springs flow from the ridges like the redeeming wounds of martyrs. Here the streams run clear in rock-bottomed beds through a million acres of forest dotted by small farms and abandoned homesteads. This was the country of Gene's longing, of the town of Hector and the happy days of childhood. Now, with the sale of the property in New Mexico and a personal loan wheedled from his incipiently senile stepfather, Gene could at last go home again.

He made an inquiry about the house in Hector where he had spent his early childhood, even clipped a photo of it that appeared by chance in a local paper, but it was not for sale. He likewise scanned the realtors' multiple listing book and called the "for sale by owner" ads in the paper. What he did most, however, was drive. And he was driven all the harder by his discovery of Sheila's affection for Dennis McNulty.

How much Gene knew and when is not clear. What is clear is that once he had the least hint of Dennis, who had started dating Sheila that spring, Gene accelerated his efforts to find a farm, covering every mile of two-lane blacktop in four different counties along the southern escarpment of the Ozark Plateau.

The turning point for Sheila naturally marked one for Gene as well, and not one for the better. His relations with Becky, in conflict with his attempts to win her over, were curdled by anger, resentment, and fear. As a self-serving concession to her, Gene permitted his wife and her youngest child, Rebecca Lynn, to travel by bus to Colorado in July, shortly after Gene had signed an agreement to purchase a house and thirteen-odd acres near the town of Dover, north of Russellville and only a dozen miles from Hector. For her part, Becky needed the break so badly that she was willing to see Sheila and Loretta stay behind. Gene's now-undeniable depression actually helped Becky find the heart to go. She had recently ceased to sleep with Gene, indulging any one of the children who asked her to sleep with them, and he spent more and more time in his room alone. Usually meticulous and orderly, Gene was growing sloppy in everything from his biographical files to his personal appearance. Most unlikely of all, because it was so odd and, therefore, hung a nervous pall over the household, he would sometimes simply sit in silence, drinking Schlitz and watching anything that was on the television. His enervation was a comfort to her.

But Gene's moods were also more unpredictable nowadays, veering wildly from doting to violent. Loretta, in particular, was the object of Gene's frequent scorn. Gene called her "conceited," a "know-it-all," and an "ingrate." She could hardly speak to him without encountering some deprecation, but all the children used Gene's isolation in his room as an excuse not to talk to him. Instead they slipped notes under the door. And even gentle Billy, now eighteen and finishing high school, was discovering a will to bait his father, although he never mustered the sarcasm that Loretta commanded. In one note that she passed under Gene's door, Loretta wrote: "Dad, Loretta needs $2 for class dues. If you don't know what class dues are, ask Mom. She should know. Loretta, you're [sic] smartest chick."

At other times Gene would plead for affection, putting a comic face on it. When Sheila wrote a note to Becky saying, "I love you Mom, I like the dinner you made tonite," Gene scrawled at the bottom, "How about me, Dad, Dad!"

In fact, the children hardly knew where to turn for kind, undivided attention. Gene's obsession with Sheila was patent even to the youngest, as one drawing of Marianne's reveals. In it, a bloated stick-figure labeled "Fat Dad" is covered with Valentine hearts, each bearing Sheila's name. Even Becky was preoccupied, often neurasthenic to the point of taking to her own bed, where the children passed her notes as well. Loretta asks in one of them, "Mom, are you my friend? Yes or no. If you are lend me the following items: $1, a good book, a brand new stuffed animal, an hour of junk food eating, loud playing rock and roll, a good, good book, and ten minutes to tell you something with out Bill or any of the kids."

What Loretta had to relate may have been the onset of puberty. She had her first period in July, which she recorded on a three-by-five card that she kept in a shoe box, along with sentimental poems she cut from newspapers, booklets on contraception, and a growing collection of inspirational and devotional literature. Bright and curious and self-possessed, Loretta would suffer her family life least easily of anyone. Her rite of passage was lost in the flurry of regimented activity that typified Gene's moves.

Within thirty days of signing the contract to purchase the property near Dover, Gene had given notice at the recruiting office, overseen the packing of the household goods, gathered all the school and medical records for the children, and told his landlords he was leaving. Still fearful of being traced from New Mexico, he threw one additional red herring across his paper trail: He rented a post office box in Ward, in addition to those he had just rented in both Dover and Russellville, after canceling the one he had kept for nearly two years in Jacksonville.

That fear of New Mexico authorities, however, like his purpose in renting the post office boxes, was less real than it was a symptom of the panic Gene was experiencing as a result of Sheila's attachment to Dennis McNulty. It was clear even to him that the closer she drew to Dennis, the better able Sheila was to reject Gene's blandishments and advances. He could not put enough distance between Sheila and Dennis soon enough, not with his fear of discovery and Becky's encouraging the young couple.

With Gene leading in a U-Haul truck and Becky, Sheila, and Billy driving the old cars in caravan behind, Gene at last moved his family to the land of dreams. His fear and jealousy over Sheila's friendship with Dennis McNulty was simmering inside him, spiced with morbid self-pity. Filed neatly at the front of Gene's folder on the new property was a single sheet of paper with the notation "He Stopped Loving Her Today—George Jones" printed neatly in the center, the song in which the day he stopped loving her was the day he died.

CHAPTER TWELVE

He called the place Mockingbird Hill. Gene's thirteen-plus acres lay on a low ridge that runs east-west, parallel to a paved county highway called Broomfield Road, about four miles from the town of Dover. The rutted red-clay driveway rises steeply from the road to where the half-mobile home, half-clapboard house sat at the top, just beyond where the ridge crests and flattens. Most of the ridge facing Broomfield Road is covered in small pine and young, scrubby oak, and the woods sweep back around the house and pond, defining Gene's dominion before melding into the larger forest and ridges to the north.

The house itself was dispiriting—rude, plain, and jerry-built—sitting in a weed-choked clearing too rocky for a lawn, without shade or relief for the eye. From the roofless, unscreened front porch Becky walked into an oversize family room more than twenty-five feet long, carpeted in cheap brown shag. To her right were a small kitchen and a dining room. A shotgun hallway ran the rest of the length of the house, giving onto three small bedrooms, a bath, and two larger bedrooms under the added roof. The walls were thin, and there was no plumbing. The only heat was from a fireplace in the family room, its concrete-block chimney too short to provide a proper draw.

None of this bleakness seemed to dampen Gene's enthusiasm as he threw himself and his family into a series of half-baked home improvements. He pressed Billy, Loretta, Eddy, even little Marianne into duty digging ditches for drainage pipes and a hole for the privy—"our waste disposal system," Gene called it— which was no more than a crude seat over the hole, screened for privacy by sheets of galvanized tin roofing that he wired to metal fence posts and braced with an old headboard from a double bed. Gene set Billy the job of building a greenhouse and a shed from plans found in *Mother Earth News* while he began combing local lumberyards and building supply stores for concrete blocks.

Never since his return from England had Gene been in a tighter financial corner than the one he put himself in with the purchase of Mockingbird Hill. Neither his blissful disregard for reality nor his forgetfulness of botched projects at Wills Canyon, however, could deny that his dream home needed a lot of work, and most of it not cheap—plumbing, heating, wiring, and new outbuildings. So Gene looked for bargains, sometimes driving thirty miles to save five cents apiece on twenty blocks. And that was how he bought them, a few at a time, usually used ones or seconds, crumbly things cast from soured concrete and soft as chalk. Continuing until the spring of 1984, he would regularly buy small lots of blocks, barbed wire, galvanized roofing, corrugated fiberglass panels, plastic pipe, and electrical fixtures, seldom making two purchases in a row from the same store, and often visiting several in a single day for small lots of the same thing.

But if Gene was enthusiastic about the work on

Mockingbird Hill, he was also fretful and apprehensive on several other counts. His family endured in name only, an outward show of normalcy devoid of reciprocal affection. Becky was ever more withdrawn, taking the younger children with her. Billy and Loretta were standoffish and restive. And Sheila—God, how he ached for her. He had sworn to Becky that there was nothing more between him and Sheila, but he knew he was watched by his wife, by Billy, and by Loretta, who all knew the truth. He was miserable with jealousy over Dennis but had to pretend to a grudging acceptance. At low moments he would take from his wallet a typed copy of a poem and read it:

Heavenly Father up above,
Please protect the girl I love.
Keep her ever safe and sound,
No matter when or where she's found.
Help her to know, help her to see,
That I love her, let her love me,
And then, oh Lord, help me to be
The kind of man she expects me to be.
Keep us now, keep us forever,
Always in love, always together.
Grant, oh Lord, to my content,
And thank you for the girl you sent.

Gene was not only being squeezed out of the family and denied Sheila, he was overwhelmed with debts and the need for home improvements that he had no resources—manual or material—to address. Faced with the silent condemnation of his family and haunted by the fear that others would discover the truth, Gene found himself scuttling for justification, any moral crack to wriggle through. He even took comfort in a religious pamphlet entitled "The Unpardonable Sin," in which he was assured that only blasphemy could not be forgiven. Within Gene's moral cast, that which he called love for Sheila legitimized all his acts, and it was part of his misery that no one else could comprehend the fact.

Throughout the first three weeks of August Gene kept up a steady cadence of labor from dawn until dark. The children too young to wield the pinchbar or a shovel hauled dirt and rocks in buckets and toy wagons to fill the gullies in the drive. Billy, who was always good with his hands, found some refuge in building sheds and, on the sly, some satisfaction making a playhouse in the woods for the little ones. Sheila, like Becky, was consigned to child care and housekeeping. Their only break came on the twentieth, the weekend before school started, when Gene took the family up Highway 7 to the Dogpatch USA theme park near Harrison, Arkansas. But Billy was out of school now, and the Daylight Savings afternoons were still long enough that the kids could get plenty done after they came home, by flashlight, if need be. Gene's vision was relentless. Save school and trips to the laundromat or grocery, none of the Simmons family left Mockingbird Hill for weeks. There was just too much to be done.

Gene's success at losing himself in activity and ignoring his gradual loss of Sheila foundered in September, when Dennis McNulty again started coming regularly to call.

Gene could never deny Sheila, not even when she got the first letters from Dennis. Fearing Sheila's anger as much as her loss, he delivered them unopened. He remained impassive when Sheila told him that Dennis was coming over from Little Rock one Saturday. When Dennis arrived Gene was sullen and quietly contemptuous, threatened to his marrow by the intelligent, good-looking young man who lit a smile on Sheila's face, played with the children, and made Becky blush with his modest flattery. Gene stopped short of being rude—the following year he would use Dennis as a reference on an employment application—and Dennis, not knowing him, might easily have taken his frostiness as habitual. The rest of the family, however, could sense Gene's resentment. Becky, in particular, could see the coming crisis, but she liked Dennis immediately and let Gene know that she would stand by Sheila if Dennis was the man her daughter loved.

Gene tightened his grip. He kept up the dogged attempts at improvements, bought chickens and a propane tank, had the children scrounge deadfalls for firewood (he never bought a chain saw), and made sure Billy stayed busy with the carpentry. He was almost constantly short-tempered these days, hurling verbal abuse and threats of worse at everyone. There was too much work, not enough money, and the damned old cars kept breaking down. By November Gene could no longer afford the cost of constant vigilance over his family, and he began looking for a job.

The prospects were not heartening. The office skills that had served him so well in the military and with the military recruiter were not in high demand among the retail stores and food processors who did most of the hiring in the small towns down in the Arkansas River valley, and his military experience in general didn't cut much ice with people looking for minimum-wage employees. He applied at a frozen-food factory, an office-supply store, and a service station before finally landing a job as an "industrial cleaner" at the Atkins Pickle Company, where he also filled in netting pickles from the vats and processing the brine at four dollars and sixty-seven cents an hour. No one clearly recalls Gene from his months at the pickle plant, but he took note of them, quite literally: "Daniel Cavander, beard, relish," he wrote in his notebook; "Lucby, phillipino, brine man; Roger C., big tall engineer . . ."—identifying each man on his shift by his job and some physical trait. It was as deeply as Gene understood others or cared to.

The job, the weather, and the seventy-five-mile daily round-trip commute put many of Gene's projects at home on hold. He had to content himself with posting "No Trespassing" signs "to keep out the dope fiends and perverts," he said, and with the odd weekend of hectic, ill-planned puttering—laying a few blocks for the wall he was building between his house and the road, slapping down fiberglass panels to roof the porch, posting a hand-painted sign that read "Little Princess Lane" along the path in the woods where the children went to play. And the farther he fell behind in his projects, the more of them he planned and the more scrap materials he hoarded. But water was his chief concern. His well was erratic, easily pumped dry and slow to refill, so he plumbed it only into the shower in the house. He would supervise the filling of bottles and trash barrels from it for drinking water. Water for washing and the garden he caught in a row of plastic milk jugs sitting under the drip line of the roof. He kept dozens and dozens of these cached all over his property. He said they were to fight fires.

Frustrated, forced to take a job beneath his abilities, and terrorized by his jealousy of Dennis, Gene never retreated from his bullying, especially of Becky. Confined and brutalized, without friends or family near, Becky kept from breaking only through her devotion to her children, and even then she was sometimes immobilized by her grief, her sense of lost love. Gene's stinginess caused her to have to scrimp on meals—"They get a good lunch at school," he said. Sometimes she just could not face it, and she took to her room.

"Dear Mom," Eddy wrote in a note to her shortly after the move to Dover, "Hurry up and come out of the bedroom. Are we going to have lunch before you come out of the bedroom. I'm very hungry (so is Loretta, Becky, & Sylvia). It is very boring and everyone is starved and in a bad mood and cranky!" To which Loretta added, "Mom hurry! LS" and "Hurry Grandma, I'm starved From Sylvia." Sheila was off shopping with Gene.

Gene did not, until the last months of her life, give up on having Sheila Marie. He appealed to her in every way he knew, to their "special bond" and "all we have done together." He told her Dennis would make her miserable, that he would never accept Sylvia Gail. Gene's hope was that she would not tell Dennis the truth about Sylvia's parentage, but in this he profoundly misjudged both Sheila and Dennis. Dennis had come by a few times in Ward to take Sheila to the movies, and Gene knew that they had been corresponding; but, forgetting his own courtship of Becky, he willed himself to believe that the distance he had put between them was eroding their devotion, when it in fact was making it stronger.

In March 1984, as winter began to lift and Gene's grim optimism tried to renew itself, critical cogs in his life began to spin out of control. The pickle plant reduced its shifts and put Gene out of a job. Both Billy and Sheila had determined to get work in town. No one in the house would speak to him unbidden or without a particular reason. Worst of all, Sheila was unquestionably in love with Dennis. Gene's vanity seldom allowed him to sense a loss of self-esteem, but Sheila's love for Dennis shook Gene to the bone. Here was proof positive that he could not command his family or even provide for them, that he could not have the only one who mattered to him. He applied for unemployment compensation and set to work on his wall.

Billy and Sheila both found jobs at Hardee's in Russellville a month before Gene was hired at a Del Monte frozen-food plant, where he was assigned as a "processor" on the second shift, from three to eleven P.M., beginning April 16. He listed Dennis as one of his references.

On Easter weekend, shortly after Gene went back to work, Becky's half-sister Edith Nesby came by on her way from a visit in Walsenburg to her home in Texas. Edith and Becky had had their differences in the past and were never as close as Becky and Vi, but Edith and Gene frankly despised each other.

"My husband disliked Gene, just really disliked the man," says Edith. "Couldn't stand him, as a matter of fact, and he refused to ever go back. He said, 'Honey, you can go and see Becky, if you want to. She's your sister, and I won't keep you from her, but I won't go back. I can't stand him. I'll hit him.' "

Gene, who once impressed all the Novaks with his new van and camper trailer, couldn't have been unaffected by Edith's arriving in an RV worth more than his house, and Becky later said that she was embarrassed by the bareness of their pantry.

"I brought food and everything," says Edith, "and Becky cried, because they didn't have food in the house—very little. Gene still had those "No Smoking" signs all over the house [his cough was chronic now, noted on his physical at Del Monte], so Becky and I would sit on the front porch. I'd smoke, and we'd talk. I think he was trying to keep me away. All the time that I was there, Gene would not talk to me. If I was in the living room, he would go through the kitchen to go out. If I was in the kitchen, he would go through the living room. He would not speak to me at all. . . . He worked nights, [but] he'd leave, like, two hours early for his job and not come back until, like, two hours after his job. [Usually] when he was there and I was there, he stayed in his bedroom with the door shut, the room with the air conditioner in it. He'd just stay locked up in there. He had a lot of reel-to-reel tapes, and Becky would say, 'Well, he's probably working on his tapes,' or 'He's working on his important papers.' Becky never knew what he did, because that was his room. She would sleep in the far back bedroom, the little girls' room.

"When we got there, he had the kids digging a latrine. He had a second latrine he wanted dug, and he had the kids digging it. Little Eddy was real tiny; they're all fragile kids. He had them out there in that hard ground trying to dig that latrine. He used to make the kids bring him the turkeys and chickens every night and put them in a box and put it on the porch and put a piece of plywood over them. Then, in the morning, he would take them out back and put them in his little pen beside the house.

"When I left, he said, 'Well, I hear you're leaving. Goodbye.' That is the only words he spoke to me. He was just real strange, you know. He's always been strange."

Not long after Easter, Sheila announced her engagement to Dennis. On May 5 Gene bought a snubnose Harrington & Richardson .22 revolver at the Wal-Mart store in Russellville, adding it to his arsenal, which included the Buntline-barreled Ruger .22 and the high-velocity Winchester he kept under his bed. He also quit his job at Del Monte in May, no reason given, and drew unemployment compensation until late June, when he took a part-time position as cashier at the Russellville Mini Mart, a job he would hold until December 1987.

The summer of 1984 was an eventful, pivotal season in Gene's life. He completed his concrete-block wall and finished much of the fencing around the property, built a proper privy and chicken coop, and began to feel the full weight of his tyranny rebounding on him. Billy bought his own truck and was making plans to move out of the house now that he was working full-time at Hardee's. Little Gene had married earlier that year, and he and his wife were expecting their first child. But the event that loomed largest in Gene's mind was Sheila's impending marriage, planned for August.

Becky's determination to protect her children, including Sheila, from Gene, Sheila's ecstatic love for Dennis, and Gene's own fears of being exposed all conspired to quell his hopes of ever having Sheila again. As her wedding date approached he told her over and over again that she was making a mistake, that she would make her mother miserable, that she would destroy him. Sheila knew better.

"And what about Sylvia Gail, our Sylvia Gail—what will he think when you tell him?" Gene demanded.

When Sheila said that Dennis knew the truth about Sylvia, Gene's gorge rose in fear and anger. He washed his hands of the marriage, refused his blessing, and would not buy Sheila clothes or even a wedding gift. Dennis sent her an outfit to wear to her bridal shower, given by his twin sister and family friends, but Gene would not let her wear it. And it was Dennis who bought her white wedding gown. Gene drove the family to the ceremony in Camden, however, and sat in seething silence throughout it. Everything he had tied his hopes to was coming unraveled. Everyone he had done so much for was turning against him.

A month after Sheila's wedding, in September 1984, Roger and Viola brought Ma Novak to Arkansas for a visit. Unlike Edith, who stayed at Mockingbird Hill and made Gene surly by her very presence, Roger and Vi preferred to stay in motels when they came, in part not to feel that they were imposing themselves, and in part so they would not have to endure the oppressive atmosphere of the house. By sending them a list of rates for triple occupancy at three different Russellville motels, Gene made it additionally clear to them that he expected Ma Novak to do the same. But once she arrived, the children made such a clamor about having their grandmother—the only grandparent that the little ones had known—spend the night that Gene grunted his consent. He was glad to have the excuse of a weekend job to remove himself from the happiness the rest of them enjoyed. When Sheila and Dennis arrived the following day—Ma Novak had never seen Sylvia—Gene changed clothes and left early for work. In a spirit of meanness he pled car trouble and borrowed Billy's truck, causing Billy to mutter about the way his father drove and say he wished he had waited until his father was at work before he came out from town to see Ma Novak. Becky put on a brave face for her mother.

"Those kids," Vi recalls, "didn't pass by Becky without getting a hug and giving her one when we were there. And they made a wide sweep around Gene when he was home."

The clichés of quiet desperation and silent suffering cannot begin to hint what life was like in the Simmons home the following year, although Becky certainly was desperate, suffering, and silent. Gene still quarreled with her violently, sending the children scattering to their playhouses and hideouts in the woods, but he had not hit her since the move from New Mexico. Becky had learned to defend herself with threats of exposure, strengthened by the support she got from Billy and Little Gene. Billy was dating a girl he had met at Hardee's and had plans to start his own family, and he and his brother were beginning to urge their mother to leave. She was too tied by her own commitment as a wife and mother to seriously consider divorcing Gene—she still did his washing and ironing and prepared his meals separate from the rest—but her sons' urgings did make it seem possible to her. Yet she held out, imagining that Gene would get over Sheila. The time he spent alone in his room helped, too.

School made life tolerable for the children. Eddy was proving himself a B-plus student, and Loretta even better. Her dark good looks and outgoing nature had made her a hit at Dover High School. Even Marianne and Little Becky needed no prompting to be ready for the bus. For them, school was like Never-Never Land compared to the grueling chores that Gene piled on them. And when he was not upbraiding them or barking commands he would launch rambling, scolding lectures. The subject might be drugs, the Equal Rights Amendment, or the Democratic party, but always something that Gene condemned and none of the children could comprehend. And when Loretta, always the bold one, asked permission to go on a date, he replied, "Hell, no. You see what happened to your sister, don't you? That's what comes of dating."

Gene quit taking photos almost entirely after Sheila's marriage. He did not sort his records or edit his tapes while alone in his room. He ate and he masturbated. On metal shelves beside the locked door to his room—the only door in the house that could be locked from the inside—he kept a supply of peanuts, chips, and candy. In the bottom drawer of the dresser beside his bed he had a tube of surgical jelly and women's slips and panties made stiff with jism. He called Sheila's name when he came on his bloated belly. All his pain and pleasure had her name.

Despite Gene's work schedule and the hours he spent behind his door, his presence hung like a malignancy on the spirits of his family. Collectively they ignored Gene, developed a tacit conspiracy of silence, but they could not completely deny their fear of him, their dread of his moods and capricious discipline. Gene was still in control—of the mail, the money, the car—and he used that leverage to keep them all in their places. Only Loretta had the courage to face him and struggle for the normal life of a pretty, popular teenager, though to little effect. There were no outings, no nights spent with friends, no after-school activities, no movies, and only the occasional carry-out pizzas when the children won them in reading contests at school. There were, however, lots of chores, proliferating projects that were never quite finished or done right. Becky's neat housekeeping did not extend past the front door, and Gene's hoards of used car parts and building materials were littered everywhere.

In January 1985 Gene at last found a clerical position at Woodline Motor Freight in Russellville, which he held in addition to his weekend shifts at the Mini Mart. He was the only man among a half dozen women in his office at Woodline, and the clerk with the least seniority. Being at the bottom of the pecking order was not a condition Gene could accept with any grace, and having a woman for a boss would ultimately prove explosive. For the moment, however, Gene was grateful for the added income, and his family was equally relieved to have him away from the house.

With the coming of summer's long afternoons and the end of the children's school term Gene once again began to push his repairs and improvements forward, anything to kill the pain of Sheila's loss. The pressure he put on Becky and the children to complete the chores was unrelenting. He bawled orders and berated them, and none of them left the hill for the first two months of summer except for the necessary trips to the grocery or laundromat. Without a mowing machine or even a Weed Eater, however, there was nothing they could do to keep down the brambles, broom sage, and johnson grass. Seed ticks multiplied in the undergrowth, and copperheads invaded the foundations of the house, seeking the mice that bred there. Killing the scorpions in the piles of scrap lumber was a weekly event.

Becky had reached her limit. As if the condition of her life was not bad enough, she also had to listen to Gene's tirades against Sheila and Dennis, for whom he no longer tried to conceal his hatred. Sheila would come back, Gene said, growing angry when Becky disputed him. She would see what a mistake she had made, how she could never be happy with Dennis. The worst of all this for Becky was not having anyone to lean on or with whom she could share her troubles. She had to find release.

In August her family was having another reunion in Colorado, and Roger and Vi again came by on their way to ask Becky to go with them. Becky's desire to go and her fear of leaving the children alone with Gene were patent behind her feeble excuses, and the suspicions and rumors about Gene and Sheila that floated among the relatives at the reunion caused the O'Shieldses' concern to turn to worry. On their way back to their home in Alabama, where they had settled after Roger's retirement from the navy, they dropped in unannounced at Mockingbird Hill, on a Saturday afternoon, when they knew Gene would be at work.

Eight years before, Roger and Vi had gone through a bad patch in their own marriage, and Becky had been the only one of Viola's family who wrote regularly to offer support and understanding. Vi was reluctant to intrude on Becky's obvious problems without being asked, but the sight of her sister's misery and the memory of her kindness would not let her remain silent. She and Roger sat with Becky at the small table in the kitchen and told her they knew things were terribly wrong between her and Gene. They did not mention the rumors of incest and beatings that had circulated at the reunion, but they let Becky know they loved her and were concerned and would do anything to help her. Loretta, sensing something, took the children outside to play, and Roger and Vi looked at Becky in silence.

Becky leaned over into Viola's arms and began to cry. In a stammering torrent of words that grew stronger as she spoke, Becky told them everything. With frozen, shock-pried faces, Roger and Vi heard the narrative of Gene's deterioration, the anger, isolation, violence, incest, and paranoia. Becky detailed for them his smoldering, enduring love/hate for Sheila and his ongoing delusions about having her back. She revealed her fears for them all, especially Loretta, whom she had seen Gene beginning to treat in the same ways he had Sheila Marie.

"I can never leave home," Becky said, "and leave any of my children with him anymore, especially the girls." Choking back the emotion in her voice, she added, "That's why I couldn't go with you [to Colorado]. I wanted to see Mom, but I couldn't unless I could take all the kids."

"I wish you had told me," Viola said, "at least written and told me."

Becky explained to them the way Gene controlled the mail and her access to telephones, so the three of them devised a plan. By enlisting Billy, who still lived in Russellville and came to see his mother regularly, they would be able to communicate by mail. Any of Becky's letters that arrived without a return address were secret from Gene and should be answered through Billy. Others would be the letters censored by Gene and should be answered through the regular post, to keep him from getting suspicious. Roger and Vi left without Gene's ever knowing of their visit.

Those few hours spent at the kitchen table infused Becky with a courage that she had previously only imagined was within her. Between the strength she drew from Billy and Little Gene and the love of her favorite sister and brother-in-law, Becky determined to rid herself, one way or another, of Gene's tyranny.

Becky felt lighter, buoyed and confident, but she also felt bad that she had brought Vi and Roger into her problems. Between her isolation from her family and the isolation that her marriage to Gene had imposed, she had come to believe that she should not—indeed, could not—rely on anyone besides Gene. Now that was beginning to change.

". . . Dad can no longer push me around," she wrote to Vi two weeks after their visit. "I've gotten to be strong. . . . In fact, he is more afraid of me than me of him. He already knows any false move with my girls & I'll turn him in. . . . I won't kill him because . . . I could lose my children & even end up in prison. I'll get more joy by watching him suffer. He is suffering now, he can't have Sheila."

By this time Becky was convinced that Gene was mentally ill. Little Gene had written her what he had been reading in his psychology text, outlining for his mother the traits of an obsessive-compulsive personality disorder, those of the sociopath, and the typical profile of an incestuous father. Even without this Becky knew that Gene's admission to her that he had done wrong was not sincere, that it was only to keep her quiet.

Her shameful feelings toward Sheila—the jealousy and blame that had once tortured Becky—had turned to pity and love. Becky had never felt so close to all her children before, united by their contempt for Gene.

The runaway course of events—Sheila's and Billy's happy marriages, Becky's stiffening resolve, and Loretta's sometimes open defiance of him—left Gene furious, wounded and bewildered. He did not relax his hold on the purse or car keys, but neither did he fly into rages over the challenges to his authority. He saved his anger for people, and his family were becoming a collection of objects. The thing he had created had turned on him, become his enemy, an object of indifference, so he began to look outside the family for fulfillment, especially toward a young woman named Kathy Kendrick, with whom he worked at Woodline.

Kathy was in her early twenties, dark and slim, with high cheekbones and a brilliant smile. At certain angles she bore a striking resemblance to Sheila. Rumor had it that her marriage was not happy, and Gene sensed her vulnerability. He chatted her up at work, hung around her desk, and put on the face of a fatherly confidant. Kathy fell for it at first. She told Gene of her troubles, and he pretended to understand, making consoling noises and touching her on the shoulder. Sometimes he would get her to sit alone with him during breaks. Otherwise, he rarely spoke to anyone in his office about anything other than work. Usually he took his breaks alone and went out to his car, sometimes returning with booze on his breath. Kathy —or her looks—became an icon for Gene, a surrogate for Sheila, and his fantasies about her ran wild.

Unknown to Gene, his fear of Becky's family discovering the truth about his relations with Sheila had in fact been realized. Viola had kept her promise to Becky not to tell their mother, but Little Gene had not felt so bound.

Little Gene and his wife, Wilma, had gone to Walsenburg in September, and under the questioning of Edith and others he had told all he knew. Later he called Billy, who informed Becky that the story was now out.

"Of course fat Gene knows nothing," Becky wrote to Vi in late September. "We keep an awful lot from him."

What Becky was no longer keeping to herself, however, were her threats and fears.

"Touch any of my daughters or anyone I keep in my house," she told Gene, "and I will put you in prison."

She also began to caution the younger girls, who were ignorant of their father's relations with Sheila, not to undress with their doors open or allow their father in the bathroom alone with them. She felt her children were safe now, that she could protect them, and that Billy and Little Gene would stand by her.

Gene, meanwhile, was becoming a ragged shadow of his old self. Still driven by the emptiness inside him to strive for some sort of perfection, his goal now was reduced to denying reality, attempting to ignore his fear that others knew the truth, especially Dennis; Billy's girlfriend Renata; Becky's family; and Little Gene, all of whom he suspected. Appearances were all he had left, but his relaxing the strict confinement of Loretta and the other children would not last.

Becky, on the other hand, was more and more taking on the hard definition of independence. Ironically, the concern and love of her sons and her sister and their assurances that they would help her if she left Gene gave her the will to stay on, for the unknown angel of freedom was at least as daunting to her as the familiar demons of Gene's degenerating psyche. Too, the newfound outlet for her in the secret postal system at last gave Becky an opportunity to vent all her anxieties and lighten her emotional load. Two weeks before Billy's marriage in October 1985 she wrote Vi a long back-channel letter that makes plain her hopes, fears, and ambivalence about continuing a life with Gene: "Bill brought your letter yesterday," she wrote, followed by some details of Bill's impending wedding and his plans to move to San Antonio, Texas, where Little Gene was now employed as a food-service manager at an air force base.

This is the first time that I have seen Gene upset about any of his kids leaving. [Billy had continued to help Gene with his improvements at Mockingbird Hill.] He didn't act this way with Little Gene or Sheila. He has been different with all of us. . . . Ever since I told him Sheila is pregnant, he treats everyone better. I know he thought he would have her home forever as long as he gave her everything she wanted. Now he realizes he can't hold on to them.

The reason I'm not going to tell anybody about Gene is at least a dozen reasons. I have too much to lose if I get careless. If it got out Gene could lose his jobs, the school could interfere, I would have to move again. The children like this school. I don't want people to know about us. I like this place. I have 14 acres [sic] & in the future I can give [a] couple of my kids 5 acres to put a mobil home on. We have about 12 more years to pay this place off. Gene has two jobs to fix this place up. I've got medical care, life insurance, a home, a good school for the kids & if I decided to divorce Gene I would lose [all that] and would have to work and maybe have problems with my health. As it is I have all this, I don't know how to work & I'm here when my children get home from school & maybe someday all this will be mine. Am I wrong? I could never trust another man as long as I got girls, so I would never

remarry, so I would have many years alone. . . .
At least Gene is working, taking care of all of us.

Viola was not the only outlet for her feelings that
Becky was finding. With Gene now a topic of open
conversation within the family, she began to confide
in Billy's wife, Renata, as well.

One night she told Renata all about what had happened in New Mexico, and Renata could hardly contain it.

"I'd have gone crazy if I'd been in your shoes,"
Renata said.

"No," Becky said, "you wouldn't have let yourself. If I had gone crazy, I would have lost all my
kids. People would have said I was unfit. Fatso was
already the crazy one in the family, so I had to be
strong."

Becky was showing ever greater strength, but it
was not without real concerns. Despite her assertions
that she could protect her children, Becky knew that
Gene was dangerous and that her defenses were not
absolute. In another of the several letters she wrote
to Vi that fall Becky's fears and confidence are both
clear:

> I got Gene where I want. He is scared to death
> the family is going to find out. . . . I don't want
> Gene to know L. Gene told. . . . I want my family
> to all come visit me & not feel uneasy because of
> all this. If Gene thinks no one knows, the better.
> This way I can threaten to tell, ha! Since he
> reads my letters, just keep reminding me that you
> care. If Gene knows that you all care, he too will
> be more careful. . . . I don't want [any of the
> family] to mention to me [in a letter] that they
> know. I don't want Little Gene to be afraid to
> come here.

Another thing I try always to remember, "A man who hates suffers more than the man hated." I used to feel . . . so much hatred for Gene. I also know he is a sick man. No matter what, I will always be one step ahead of him & always on my guard. He will never push me around again. He knows I can leave him anytime, and I can fix it to where he will never see his kids again. He messed up his own life. *He knows he has already lost the battle.* I get a thrill when I tell him to get out [of my sight], ha! . . . He didn't feel sorry for me or help me when I needed him. Whatever, he will pay. That's why I want so much to go to heaven & I don't want to meet him in hell. . . . Gene . . . has promised me many times that he would not touch his daughters, to give him a chance [but] he became mentally disturbed. He knows I watch every move he makes.

CHAPTER THIRTEEN

Gene was lost on familiar ground, living a sustained and terrifying déjà vu. He could remember how it had been nearly four decades before in Hector, when he spent the happiest time of his life competing for his mother's love against his handsome older brother, against the babies, Pete and Nancy, and on weekends against his stepfather, whom he never seemed to please. No matter how good he tried to be, how careful and precise, he never knew the confidence of his mother's undivided love. He could remember the aching solitude he came to feel, the pain he tried to roar away. He felt it now as an emptiness, a sense of infinite loss. Why had they done this to him—Sheila and Becky, Billy and Loretta and all the rest?

Gene could not comprehend his distress over Billy's marriage and planned move to San Antonio, but it did not lessen when Renata's father found Billy a job in Fordyce, Arkansas, about thirty miles from Sheila and Dennis's home in Camden. No one had told Gene that Renata was pregnant when she and Billy married in October, and he betrayed no feelings when Becky told him that Sheila and Renata were due to deliver within a month of each other in the spring. He still ordered the children around and would quarrel with Becky over a pin, but in the main he showed no affect beyond his stiff and practiced grin.

To Gene, the source of his unhappiness was all Sheila, and he had to find some way to make contact with her, to leave the door open for her return to him someday. Now that their secret was common knowledge, and Becky and Dennis and Little Gene had poisoned her mind against him, he felt cornered, stripped of all options or of any power to control events, the helplessness of a child. If Sheila did hate him, he had to have her forgiveness. He couldn't live like this.

Neither could Becky, as she was beginning to realize. Despite her newfound strength, there was little unalloyed joy in her life. The love of her children and the happy times she spent with them baking cakes or working in the garden were darkened by Gene's shadow. She found herself resentful that Gene lay on the sofa that Billy gave her for Christmas that year, eating candy and drinking beer in silence, watching hour after hour of holiday television specials. The tree and the chockablock decorations went up, but neither Sheila nor Billy was at home on Christmas Day, and Little Gene had stayed in San Antonio. It was a hollow season on the hill.

Gene was little more than a bitter observer of his family through the spring of 1986. He said nothing about Becky's cooking or her listening to the new gospel radio station all day. He did not protest Loretta's makeup or the expense of her formal for the Valentine's Day Sweetheart Ball at school. In fact, he kept a picture of her in that dress on his desk at work and frequently even allowed Loretta to spend the night with a friend. He had no comment on Sheila's activities in the Catholic church or on Billy's turn toward religion through his father-in-law, who was a preacher. He felt disconnected from his family. He despised their judging him but could see no alternative to playing off that judgment, if he were ever to make them a part of him again.

In the eighteen months since Sheila's marriage he had not once been alone with her. That was torment, but worse was his anxiety over whom else she had told about them. His contempt for Dennis was set, for he could sense the same contempt for him in Dennis, and he hated the younger man's easy familiarity with women, how he could make them laugh and glow. Dennis had defied him, and the women had taken Dennis's side. He had brainwashed Sheila and now was doing the same with Becky and Loretta, who had passed from spiteful jealousy toward her older sister to a longing envy for her freedom. He could not understand why Loretta resisted his love, where he had gone wrong with her.

Had he seen her diary, he could have had a clue. Less than a year before Loretta wrote, "I'm writing to li' Gene. Dad'll probably grip[e]. Oh I hate him sometimes. He says it[']s because of Mom. To hell with that! I have a memory. I remember how it was. Him yelling at everyone except little Sheila. Sometimes I hate her too. She let him take her every where & never said a word. Life is the pits sometimes. Only sometimes. I sometimes think 'I can't wait for Dad to die.' Then we can get a phone & start being normal people & going places & having some fun. Going to church too."

In late April, about six weeks after the birth of Sheila and Dennis's son, Michael, Gene invited them all to come to visit Becky, who was eager to see her new grandson. Becky was delighted by the idea—and curious. Gene had been no more or less withdrawn and testy lately, but she could sense that he had something planned. When she speculated what it might be there was always one grain of fear in her thoughts.

Becky and Loretta and the little girls made a tremendous fuss over Michael and his baby-blue eyes, but Sheila did not offer to let her father hold him. Gene sat and watched in smiling silence, bouncing Sylvia Gail on his knee. When it was time for Michael and Sylvia to take a nap he shooed Eddy, Marianne, and Little Becky outdoors to play and told the others that he had something to say.

Becky, Loretta, Sheila, and Dennis sat in the living room, but Gene could not be still. His chest felt ready to explode, and he had to stand and pace to keep it from bursting. He had rehearsed this over and over in his mind, but the words seemed to flee from him now.

"I'm sorry. I'm sorry," was all he could manage at first. "I'm sorry," he said, "for what I've done, for what I've put everyone through."

Sheila squirmed closer to Dennis on the sofa. Gene felt a weight sink in his stomach.

"I'm sorry," he said, "for everything." He looked at Sheila, who would not meet his eyes. "I do love you, Sheila, and I want you to forgive me. What I did was wrong, but I can never be happy again unless you forgive me. I should never have done what I did."

He turned to Becky, who was staring at the floor, and said, "I have changed, Becky. You must believe me, that I have changed. I will make it all up to you and the kids, but you have to love me, help me bring this family back together. I'm miserably sorry. Let's just all love each other again. There's so much we have to do, so much work. You just don't know what it's been like for me."

He appealed to each of them, pouring out his confession in the vain hope of canceling the past and giving himself some spark of a chance to be alone, just one more time, with Sheila. And as the pressure in his chest subsided to a throb he opened his arms to her.

Becky and Loretta looked away, and Sheila clung to her husband in silence. Dennis disengaged his arm from hers, stared Gene in the face, and let his hands fall together in flat, mechanical applause. "You deserve an Oscar, Gene," he said, and with each clap the mockery rained down on Gene like lead through a shot-tower sieve.

He walked stiffly to his room and locked the door behind him.

All that Gene had left was loss, anger, and a ravenous infatuation for Kathy Kendrick.

Kathy had already grown uncomfortable with Gene's attentions when he began to act more like a suitor than an older friend. He started bringing flowers for her desk and once dropped by her house before work and invited himself in for coffee. Kathy did nothing to encourage him, but she didn't know how to tell him to stop, until it had gone on too long.

Gene's relations with the other women in his office were poles apart from his doting on Kathy. Women were the root of all his suffering—his mother, his wife, his daughter. It was their weakness that had caused it. That made his having to take orders from Joyce Butts, his supervisor, that much harder, for Gene was equally assured that he was superior to her as a clerk. At the Mini Mart other employees had begun to notice an edge of irritability in Gene that they hadn't seen before. But at Woodline he exploded.

On July 8 Joyce Butts took Gene to task for failing to code a stack of bills. He protested, saying that the coding was unnecessary and that the bills were better tracked in other ways. Joyce said she didn't care. She wanted the bills coded, and he *would* code them. The argument flared into a shouting match in which Gene's vehemence shocked everyone. Joyce called Gene to her office, reprimanded him, and put a memo on the incident in his personnel file. No one in his office had before had any inkling of Gene's volatility—indeed, they hardly knew him. As Vicki Jackson, who worked in Gene's office, said, "He was always the outsider."

He was also desperate to find ways, however small, to lash out at the world. When Mae Novak suffered a serious heart attack that July, Vi and Roger showed up at Dover on their way to Walsenburg, having written to tell Becky they were coming, but no one at Mockingbird Hill was expecting them.

"Didn't you get my letter?" Vi asked.

Gene looked up from his cheese-and-onion sandwich in innocent surprise. "Oh," he said to Becky, "I forgot to give it to you," and then he continued to eat.

Despite Becky's assurances that she was growing stronger and had command of her life, they could see that Gene still dominated the family. Again Roger and Vi urged her to leave. Viola told her, after Gene had left for work, "Becky, you've been married to him for over twenty years. If you divorce him, you can get half his retirement pay, and probably the other half in child support. You won't be hurting for money."

But Becky wasn't yet sure, and she feared that a separation might upset her mother and aggravate her heart condition. What's more, Little Gene and Wilma, his wife, were going through a divorce and custody battle themselves, and Becky, knowing that Little Gene would do all he could for her, did not want to saddle him with an additional responsibility. Becky believed she was finding the strength of inner peace. As she said in a letter to Viola shortly after seeing her, "I just want to keep learning about the Bible & life itself. When I was growing up I wouldn't even read a book, now

I'm so grateful . . . to be able to read and keep learning.''

Never having the overt friction with his father that his older brother had, Billy continued to see Becky regularly, although it was a three-and-one-half-hour drive from Fordyce to Dover. Becky was thrilled by the visits and the chance to see Billy and Renata's son, Trae, and they also gave her the opportunity to keep up her secret correspondence with Vi, to whom she wrote in late August:

> I don't see Sheila often but seems like Dennis & Dad don't get along. It's Dad's jealousy. . . . It's Dad who hurts the most.
>
> Dennis was supposed to adopt Sylvia [this month] before she started school. Dad (Gene) knows nothing of it, and I don't intend to tell him. . . . I want you to know that everything is well here, don't worry over me any. God is with me and my children are my happiness. . . . Gene is not as mean as he used to be, but maybe its because I don't care, or he knows I can be just as mean. . . .

In November Gene's frustrations and infatuations at work came to a head. Unable to read anything he did not want to believe into Kathy Kendrick's discomfort over his affection, Gene had pressed his suit to the point of serious embarrassment for her. Unable to bring herself to tell Gene directly how she felt, Kathy went to Joyce Butts with her problem. Joyce still carried a grudge against Gene, and she did not hesitate to tell him how Kathy felt and reprimand him for being a disruption in the office.

The following Monday and Tuesday, November 17 and 18, Gene called in sick at Woodline for the first time. On Wednesday morning he came in late and went directly to Kathy Kendrick's desk, where she was speaking on the phone. He pushed the hold button and said to her, "I hope you're happy now," and he turned and left before she could say a word. Taking one of the other women in the office as a witness, he walked into Joyce's office and said, "You can take this job and shove it."

"What's wrong?" Joyce asked.

"Nothing," Gene said, turning to leave. Then, over his shoulder, he added, "Why don't you ask Kathy?" But in his mind it was Sheila who had caused it all.

Gene turned back to the land, to the piece of the earth he called his, shrinking his cosmos to thirteen-point-seven acres of flint-shot Ozark ridge. With time and piles of secondhand materials on his hands, he flew into a fury of fence building, setting cedar posts and stretching stiff ranks of barbed wire around his defensive perimeter, enlisting Becky, Loretta, and even Eddy, the frailest of his sons. Any relaxation that Becky and the children had previously enjoyed was canceled by Gene's renewed activity. But his equilibrium was not restored by it. Unknown to Becky, he lashed out even at Sheila, calling her to say she was no longer welcome in his home, and never to bring Dennis there again. For the first time in her life Sheila openly defied him, as Becky recounts in a letter to Vi, written at the end of January 1987:

> ... we were out building fences with old crazy. ... I am doing fine considering Gene is home *all* week. HE JUST QUIT HIS JOB ALL OF A SUDDEN. He is a jerk. We get along pretty well considering how I feel about him. He doesn't argue with me. I'm ready to fight back. ... Besides if I give him a hard time he will be back to work, or looking for work sooner, ha!

Sheila came for several days right after Christmas & Bill & family for New Years. Sheila has really grown up and I now know she loves me. She is a mother & wife and she now has herself in my place. She has nothing but hatred for her father. . . . Anyway, she wrote right before Christmas saying they might come. After we received the card Dad (Gene) called her up and told her not to come, which I didn't know.

On the Friday morning when Sheila and Dennis were due to arrive Gene was visibly agitated and made an excuse to go into town earlier than usual to pick up his paycheck. And when Sheila arrived she told her mother about his call. Becky continued in her letter:

Sheila said he wasn't going to stop her from seeing me. We all had such a wonderful time. Too bad Gene can't be part of it. Sheila stayed for several days . . . Dennis pitching in and helps me cook, even helps me some with housework. He even serves me food. . . . Thank God, Gene at least works weekends at the store. That's when I do my writing. . . . I was makeing blankets [and] I'll start back up once I can get Fatso to get a job. He eats alot now, as the kids say, let him, maybe he will die. . . . don't worry about me, I'm fine, strong & mean [but] now that Gene is home we do alot of work, & we don't go to town as often to mail letters.

Gene still had the power to command the obedience of his family when it came to work on the house and property, but the respect and intimidation with which he once held sway were gone. Now petty acts of manipulation and the power of the purse were his

224

sole authority. Gene bought candies and nuts for himself and kept them locked in his room, but he would dole out cinnamon red hots to Eddy, Marianne, and Little Becky in exchange for hugs and declarations of love.

Along with the recurrent angst of adolescence, Gene was also experiencing an unfamiliar disruption in his concentration and memory, as though losing his grip on his family had loosened his psychological hold on everything. He found it necessary—not just habitual—to make lists and notes concerning practically everything he did, and even in these his grasp of what he was doing would slip. In one rambling script that he prepared before trying to call Sheila he apologizes for this: "Try to understand if it sounds like I keep changing subjects, but I can't rely on memory." At the Mini Mart, where his behavior and performance, with minor exceptions, had always been exemplary, he began to make errors in simple math and forget to do routine tasks. To compensate, he would latch onto niggling details as handholds to one-upmanship. One Saturday that spring David Davis, a county deputy who was a regular customer at the Mini Mart, dropped in to pick up some snacks and, finding he was short of cash, gave Gene his credit card to charge them. Gene refused to accept it, claiming that the embossed numbers were too worn to make a carbon impression. There were words exchanged, but Gene refused to take the card. He turned away and waited on another customer.

This public surliness was wholly new in Gene. He'd often written arrogant, insulting letters to clerks and officials whose competence didn't measure up, but directly confronting anyone outside his family was unheard of. It was only a thin vent, however, for the horrific pressures building inside him. Especially now, since Kathy Kendrick had shown herself unworthy and deceitful, he longed for Sheila more than ever. But they were all women, weren't they? Silly, devious, and weak. Despite Sheila's telling him she did not want to talk to him, he continued to try to call her, preparing disjointed notes for himself to follow during the conversations, scripts that swung wildly from invective to adoration but always with the underlying theme of Sheila's cruelty to him:

"Is anyone else there?" he planned to say on one occasion.

Are you recording this?
Please don't lie to me. You have lied to me too much already. . . .

I want to start by saying, Honey, I love you. . . . I love you and I will go to my grave loving you. You have destroyed me and you have destroyed my trust in you. . . .

You and D[ennis] have seen to it that things can never be right with you and me. . . .

You have caused me a great deal of pain, suffering, sorrow, and loneliness. You claim D. won't let you talk to me alone, well he is going to regret that and so will you. . . .

I miss you so very much. . . .

I will see you in Hell.

He ends the note with another protestation of his love.

Loretta, the strongest of Gene's daughters, the one he could not manipulate, and the one he went to greatest lengths to denigrate, was now the oldest of the children still at home, and she felt bereft by her father's rejection and capricious temper, utterly alone and unloved. Her adolescent crises, whether infatuations with boys or conflicts with her mother, were magnified by her sense of isolation and her hatred of her father. During the 1986–87 school year even the limited freedom she had enjoyed began to evaporate as Gene became more clutching, demanding, and censorious. Unable to ask him for anything without hazarding a lecture or a scolding, Loretta was reduced to pleading her case through the notes she slipped under his door. To justify a request to stay after school and work on a class project, Loretta pointed out her load of chores: "I've been working hard in the chicken yard for the last 3 nights. I deserve a break!" And in other notes she had to beg for everything from her daily lunch money to permission to go to a high school ballgame. Outside school, her most frequent contact with any of her friends was at the end of Little Princess Lane, where a girl who briefly lived down the ridge would sometimes meet her in the woods. Her diaries and poems all reflect her loneliness and hatred of her father, whom she described to a classmate as "a drunken bum." Twice, unknown to her parents, she cried for help through halfhearted suicide attempts, each time eating handfuls of aspirins and patent medicines, making herself violently ill, jackknifed with cramps, begging her friends who knew not to tell her mother.

By summer Gene was murderous in his mind, if not yet in his intent. The isolation that as a child had caused him such pain, and that he would later turn into an emotional buffer between him and the world, had now come full circle, cutting him off from his family. Wild schemes to win them back, especially Sheila, multiplied like mushrooms in his mind. But the spawn was deadly, each notion carrying the spores of its defeat. In effect, Gene had no idea what to do. He would sit alone in his room recording songs of lost love off the country-and-western radio station to send to Sheila. In the background and between the cuts he could be heard sobbing and grinding his teeth, blubbering a paranoid glossolalia of love and hate: "Darling, sweetheart, Sheila Marie. How could you, how could you do this to me? You've ruined us, ruined us all. Oh, God, God. I'll be with you in hell someday."

Unable to relax or even sit still except when numbed by television and beer, Gene always kept busy—and kept the children busy—on his jackleg improvements to Mockingbird Hill. Without Billy's clever hands to aid him, however, Gene's work had the improbable conformation of a Rube Goldberg contraption or a wheelbarrow by Picasso, cobbled together from scrap iron, a laundry cart, and a tricycle tire. He was more successful at fencing or digging holes, which the children could do alone. He liked to have several shallow holes always open for the stray dogs and marauding armadillos that he shot, always covering the carcasses with roofing tin and barbed wire to prevent other dogs and coyotes from digging them up. He doted on his poultry to the extent of making any of Loretta's privileges contingent upon her taking care of the birds. And there was always one or more of his decrepit cars that needed work. His biggest and most practical project, however, was moving the privy. The outhouse that he had originally built sat directly behind the house and below the crest of the ridge. In heavy rains the runoff would flood the cess pit and flow into his pond, so he chose a new site at the top of the ridge in the edge of the woods, where all the digging was through roots and the coarse strata of sandstone and flint that are the bones of that land. He did not mind that the children found it hard going; it was enough that he kept them working, gouging through the rock with pinchbar and pick, working out slabs fully half their size and scooping up loose earth with their hands.

Throughout June and July no one except Gene left the hill alone. Friday through Sunday his job at the Mini Mart took up his afternoons and evenings, but he was gone more often than that. Some of those lost hours he spent parked near Kathy Kendrick's house in Russellville or across the street from the law office where she had gone to work after leaving Woodline. But during all of them his resentments simmered. His mind was alive with all the wrongs done to him, all the derision he had to endure from Becky and Dennis, all the reasons he had for getting even. That summer he kept Becky and the children in an isolation as complete as any they had known, clinging to the last straws of his authority, repeating the only patterns he knew to hammer out a loyal and loving home.

In late July and again in early August Roger and Vi dropped by at Dover on their way to and from visiting Ma Novak in Walsenburg, and each time Viola experienced an unnerving sense of dread. They had timed their arrivals for when Gene was at work, but Vi could not shake the feeling that his eyes were on her, burning into the back of her neck. And Becky's behavior only made her discomfort worse.

Loretta and Becky had been going through the sorts of mother-daughter frictions that are commonplace when girls reach their teens, and Becky had translated this into a need to talk with Loretta about boys, dating, and sex—topics about which Becky was either ill-informed or ill at ease. When Loretta brought her scrapbook in to show to Vi, Becky joined them on the couch. It was clear to Vi that both of them were starved for conversation, desperate for someone to talk to, competing for her attention.

"I felt like I was being pulled," Vi says, "and then

Becky was talking to Loretta through me . . . about keeping herself a virgin, about boyfriends, about how we handled the sex questions [when we were young].

"She kept saying, 'Tell her about the boy you dated so long and then broke up with, because you wouldn't . . . you know,' and things like that. I just sat there between both of them, with both of them talking through me."

Vi was touched by their loneliness, and one part of her wanted to stay, but "I had a fear of something," she says. Becky was openly hurt when Vi and Roger would not stay for dinner, but they did not want to be there when Gene came home.

"We had our nine-year-old grandson with us," Vi explains, "and I just felt something bad in the air."

Vi wanted her sister out of that house, and she was not alone. Billy had been putting increasing pressure on his mother to move out also, just as Little Gene had been doing for years. And now Sheila and Dennis were putting their weight behind the idea as well. None of this was supposed to get back to Gene, but he already sensed something was afoot when Sheila and Dennis came up on the weekend of August 15.

Saturday passed easily enough, with Gene leaving early for work and not coming home until after midnight, but Sunday morning was anything but a period of peace.

"I told you," Gene said to Dennis, "that you are not welcome here. Sheila can come anytime she wants, but I don't want you ever to set foot on my property again."

"I'm not coming here by myself," Sheila said, "and you're not going to stop me from seeing Mom."

"That's right," said Becky. "It's my house, too, Gene, and my daughter can come here and bring her husband, and you're not going to stop her."

"Then all of you can get out," Gene bellowed. "Out of my house."

No one moved except Dennis, who stepped between Gene and the women.

After a moment of deafening silence Gene stomped into his room, then came back with the snub-nosed revolver in his hand and went outside. In a minute they heard the repeated crack of the .22—nine shots, a pause, another nine. Dennis started for the door.

"Please, Dennis, don't," Sheila said. Sylvia was clinging to her leg.

"It's okay," Dennis told her, and he went outside.

Gene had walked toward the pond north of the house, where Eddy was fishing with the rod and reel that Dennis had brought him. Gene was lumbering through the high weeds taking potshots at bottles and clods of dirt. When Dennis called to him he stopped to reload and turned back toward the house, grinning. His eyes were bright and narrow. He shot into the ground to the left and right, then splattered a sandstone rock into powder ten feet from where Dennis stood. Gene looked at him, swung out the revolver's cylinder, ejected the empty cartridges on the ground, and went into the house and back into his room without a word.

All Dennis said to Sheila was, "I think it's time for us to go."

Three weeks later, on Labor Day Weekend, Little Gene came up from Texas with his daughter Barbara. He had won custody of her in his divorce, but now he and Wilma were trying to patch up their marriage, and he thought Barbara would be better off with Becky while they did, instead of living in the bachelor digs that he was sharing with another young man in San Antonio. On Sunday, September 6, Billy and Renata drove up from Fordyce, and while Gene was at work they all held a family conference about him.

The youngsters were sent out to play, and Renata took Loretta aside to talk clothes and hair while Becky sat at the small kitchen table with her two oldest sons, each of them holding one of her hands. They tried to convince their mother that it was time. Gene was only getting worse, perhaps dangerous, they said, and it was not safe for her and the kids. There was no telling what he might do. Becky agreed to all except the leaving. Both boys were gone before Gene got home to an angry, troubled wife, whom he hardly noticed.

It was nearly a month before Becky could get any mail off the hill, and she had been doing a lot of thinking in that time. She wrote to Billy and Renata:

> I've been thinking of all you said Bill & I know you are right. I don't want to live the rest of my life with Dad, but I'm still trying to figure out how to start. What if I couldn't find a job for some time . . . ? It all would be so much easier if it were just me, but I have 3 kids also. . . . So if you want to do any checking by telephone [about divorce and child support], go ahead & check & we can talk about it when you come. . . . I'm still very confused but like I said I do know I don't want to stay with Dad, but I don't want him getting more than he deserves. . . . I am a prisoner here & the kids too. I know when I get out, I might need help, [because] Dad has had me [so] like a prisoner, that the freedom might be hard for me to take, yet I know it would be great, having my children visit me anytime, having a telephone, going shop[p]ing if I want, going to church. Every time I think of freedom I want out as soon as possible.

In a similar vein and at about the same time she wrote to Sheila and Dennis:

> I want to wish you both a happy birthday. [Theirs were eight days apart.] I planned on buying you both a card, but Fatso will not let me. . . . Fatso hasn't asked one question about you all. He did ask Little Gene if he had heard from you. . . . I think he was curious to see if you told anybody about him [and the shooting incident]. We found the shells for his gun on the ground outside a couple of days [after the incident]. I gave them to him and told him if he ever tried pointing a gun at us I would get him for assault with a deadly weapon. . . . Just be careful whenever you do come. Bill, I know, worries over me so I have been doing a lot of thinking of leaving Dad. I've been a prisoner long enough and Bill and I are trying to find a way. Just don't want to give Dad anything. He has mistreated us all long enough, so I feel no pity for him and being alone is what he deserves. . . . I don't want to continue life with Fatso.

Becky had reasons aplenty for wanting to leave, but she might have stayed with the known demon— her statements to the contrary notwithstanding—had it not been for the children. However much she had learned to shield herself emotionally from Gene, she still could find no way to wholly protect the children from him. He would drive them like fieldhands, working them well into the night, until one day eight-year-old Becky had to be sent to the school nurse to treat a festered blister on her hand. When asked how she got it, Rebecca Lynn said, "Hoeing." And later in October another eruption of Gene's anger at them all helped to seal Becky's decision to leave.

Billy, Renata, and Trae had come to Dover to lobby Becky again and to bring some small presents for the kids. Renata, who was a practiced hairstylist and had done wonders with Sheila's hair and makeup, offered to give Becky and the girls a cut. She bobbed and trimmed and poufed, taking years off Becky and turning Loretta absolutely glamorous. When Gene came home from work and saw the results he was incensed.

"You look stupid, dumb," he growled at Loretta. "What do you think you are, some sort of beauty queen, Little Miss Stuck-up?"

Then to them all, "Who told you you could do this, anyway? Did Renata talk you into it? You look like a bunch of whores."

It riled even laconic Billy, but Loretta got in ahead of him.

"Shut up," she said. "Shut up and stop it. We're not your slaves, no matter what you think we are. It's not your hair; you don't even have any hair. So just shut up and let us do what we want."

Becky *shh*-ed her and said to Gene. "She's right. You can't order us around like that. We have rights, too, Gene. *I* said it was all right, and I asked Renata to do it."

"To hell with you then," Gene said. "To hell with all of you; that's where you'll all end up some day, and don't you ever forget it."

That was the final nail. Although neither knew it at the time, the next sixty days would be a race between Gene's intent and Becky's determination. Gene knew now what he had to do. All that remained was to establish the procedures. And Becky was likewise determined to leave. The only question was when. She still had not only her children but Little Gene's daughter, Barbara, to consider, and she wasn't going to do anything until she heard more from Billy.

November passed like an armed truce on Mockingbird Hill. Sheila, Dennis, Billy, and Renata did not come there that month. Loretta was given permission to have a friend over and to spend the night at the friend's house once. Gene did not object when she went one evening to a Christian youth group, and on another occasion he gave her money to go to a football game. But neither she nor Becky mistook any of this for a lapse of Gene's volcanic temper. On those few occasions when he emerged from his room he was no less irritable, only more distracted, preoccupied with something, something that filled Becky with apprehension.

The more Gene thought about things, the wider the net he cast for enemies. His list already included Little Gene, Sheila, Dennis, Becky, Renata, Joyce Butts, and Kathy Kendrick, but others soon came to mind. On November 28 Gene told Paul Epperson, a deliveryman for Wonder Bread, that he didn't like Rusty Taylor, who had owned the Mini Mart when Gene first went to work there. He also told Epperson that he had been insulted and maligned by "several other people" and that he would "get even with them."

Everything Gene ever hoped or dreamed was reduced to nothing, and he in turn distilled all resolutions to a single act: He would kill the pain. It was all he had left to do, a final correction in his life, deliverance. He had been grievously wronged in word and deed by every member of his family and every employer he had had. They owed him for his pain, and it was time to settle the books.

A satisfying job, he once told Loretta, is one that "adheres to established procedures," adding that adhering to those procedures is "the meaning of integ-

rity." All action now was a function of satisfying
Gene's integrity, establishing procedures that would
annihilate all sources—and himself, the sole object—
of pain. Deep in his mind a dark design had already
formed, moving like a dance. Gene's heart went cold,
and then he relaxed.

He would welcome hell—at times because he believed he had earned it, and at others because he
knew that Sheila was damned for hurting him, and
he would meet her there. Fearful and maddened as he
was by the thought of being alone, he would not die
alone or leave anyone alive who might gloat over it if
he did. First there would be the little deaths, the ones
who deserved to die in preparation for the final death,
his own, which would put an end to the world.

Gene's sense of urgency had a parallel among his
children. Sheila, now twenty-four, and Billy, twenty-
two, had grown close since their marriages. She and
Dennis spent many weekends and evenings with Billy
and Renata, and they all often talked about the situation on Mockingbird Hill. Gradually the four of them
came to be of a single mind about getting Becky away
from Gene. Little Gene had reconciled with Wilma—
they planned to be remarried in February—and he
would be coming up at Christmas to get Barbara.
Perhaps with all of them there to lend their mother
support and present a force of wills and numbers to
Gene they could make the final break then, celebrat-
ing the birth of Christ and the rebirth of man with
their mother's salvation.

On December 1 Sheila called Little Gene in San
Antonio and talked to him for more than a half hour.
Some uncertainty about whether Wilma would be com-
ing and the vagaries of traveling with young children
made a detailed plan difficult, but in the end Little
Gene agreed that sometime over the Christmas holi-

days, while all of them were there, they had to get their mother out.

Dennis and Sheila knew that their going to Dover would challenge Gene and might make what they had to do more difficult. They didn't take lightly the caution in Becky's letters "to be careful." In order both to see Becky and to make a placating gesture to Gene, they called him at work and asked if he and Becky would mind keeping Sylvia Gail one day while Sheila and Dennis went to a going-away party for one of Dennis's friends.

They dropped seven-year-old Sylvia off at Dover on December 5 (Dennis's parents in Camden kept twenty-one-month-old Michael), and Gene invited them to come back and spend the night to avoid a long drive home in the dark. He seemed so genuinely happy to see Sylvia, and so willing to ignore the recent past, that they accepted. The weekend went without incident, but on Sunday morning Gene did not come out of his room before Dennis and Sheila were to leave. Only when they were headed for the car did he lean from his doorway, look down the hall and through the length of the family room, and say in a loud, strained voice, "Oh, you're leaving. Good-bye."

Two days later, on December 8, Gene rented a 1987 Ford and drove to Camden and Fordyce. If things did not work out, he needed contingency plans. He had to see where Sheila worked and find her new mobile home in a wooded development outside town. He needed to learn the approaches to town and the ways out.

Gene was not inconspicuous in the new Ford, for his appearance had deteriorated badly in the past two years. Long overweight, he had also acquired the puffiness of a chronic drinker, and his thinning hair had gone lusterless, hanging in limp, damp strands from beneath his baseball cap. Sometimes he went from Monday until Friday without shaving. Dennis's mother saw him that way when he went into Harold's Pharmacy in Fairview, just outside Camden, and bought two greeting cards. She wasn't certain that it had been Gene until he was gone. He hadn't seen her, and she didn't mention it until a month later, when reporters and the police began to ask questions.

On December 11 Gene renewed his safe-deposit box at the People's Bank and Trust Company in Russellville.

Christmas—it backlit the design, completed the circle, drew everything together. He saw the little ones tenting last year's cards over cheap cotton string above the doors, himself smiling and putting up the tree, Becky cooking in the kitchen, and Sheila dead on the floor.

Gene never knew greater joy than he had known on Christmas, and neither had his family. He had given them so much joy, and they had given him . . . nothing. He had given them his entire life; his work and worry was all for them. They had taken everything, and he was going to take it back.

Sheila at Christmas, that had been his greatest joy. Her eyes, her smile, on him—him and him alone. How could she forget that joy? Flinch when he touched her now?

Christmas: death and rebirth, the end of change and the beginning of renewal. Even Christ was born to die, end his pain in suffering. Having never known the trauma of birth, Gene sought rebirth only in surcease of pain. There was a way to do it, to have them all around him again, to erase a mistake. Christmas would bring them together, and he would bind them to him forever.

The vision burned in his head, cauterizing all feeling and reason. It had a cadence, the roll and gathering of thunder, that drowned out all else. It was stillness and motion, the beginning and the end, rushing toward him the way the prostrate earth rushes to meet a ballistic warhead. How simple, coherent, and understandable it made everything. Shrinking his world to ever smaller diameters, Gene had achieved critical mass.

On Friday, December 18, Gene collected his paycheck from the Mini Mart before noon, saying he would be back for his one o'clock shift. But shortly before one he called David Salyer, owner of the convenience store, and told him he was quitting.

"I want to submit my resignation immediately," Gene said. "As of now, I quit."

Salyer was incredulous. "What's the matter?" he asked.

"I've just burned out," Gene replied, "just tired of it."

"Is there something I can do, or can we talk?" Salyer asked.

"That is what I'm doing now," Gene said. "I'm telling you I'm tired of it. I've got the worst hours and the worst pay of anybody here." Changing abruptly to familiar apologies, he added, "And my old car is not running all that good, and I won't be able to make it down the mountains in the cold weather. I'm just tired of it." And then he hung up.

The trees and trimmings went up that weekend, and Gene seemed almost in the spirit of the season, almost the way he used to be at Christmas time.

When he read Sheila's letter that said they might not be able to make it because Michael had a cold, Becky was briefly touched by Gene's concern over not getting to see them. Now forty-six, she had decided she would not spend her forty-seventh Christmas with Gene, and the gentler, forgiving part of her was glad her last could be a happy one, although, in a way, that would be a punishment to him as well. Becky was so filled with the anticipation and apprehension of leaving that she was surprised Gene could not sense it. She was glad Little Gene was on his way.

Seventeen-year-old Loretta was especially helpful to her mother that weekend and sweet with the children, particularly in her affection for little Barbara. Loretta was trying harder to be accepting and forgiving and to do more for others. The week before, Fatso had allowed her to spend the night with her friend Angie, and Angie, after weeks of talking and a gospel-rock concert, had at last brought Loretta to Jesus. Loretta was still warm with the glow she felt when she opened her adolescent heart to God. She only felt a little selfish for helping out by taking care of Barbara, because she liked doing it so much. She hoped God thought it was okay; she hoped He would forgive her for wishing her father dead.

Eddy was small and thin for fourteen, but he loved being outdoors, playing or fishing. He hoped it would warm up over Christmas, and he and Dennis or Billy or Little Gene could catch a mess of bream and catfish in the pond. As the only boy left at home, he longed for visits by his big brothers and his brother-in-law. For now he had to put up with all his sisters, but Loretta was not acting so know-it-all, at least.

Marianne and Rebecca Lynn, eleven and eight, were the good spirits of the season whose delight it was to find one more ornament to put on the tree, one last place to hang a strand of tinsel. They were eager to see who had the biggest present.

Little Gene arrived alone on Monday, December 21, planning to stay through Christmas, then take Barbara back to Texas for New Year's with Wilma. His aloofness toward Gene made Becky uneasy, fearful that Gene could read their thoughts and would do something bad. Instead he was mute, civil, distant. He spent most of Monday away from the house, buying presents and making another visit to his safe-deposit box.

Gene hardly slept on Monday night; his senses were too alive to every sound and feeling. He was a maelstrom of fears and elation, hallucinating in the dark of his soul, his room, watching patterns on the wall. After dawn he heard Becky dressing in the bathroom across the hall. He heard Loretta and Eddy and the little girls having breakfast and leaving for the bus. He heard Becky go back down the hall to the room where she slept with Barbara and Rebecca Lynn. He rose, dressed, put the snub-nosed pistol in his waistband, and stepped out in the hall.

CHAPTER FOURTEEN

On Friday morning, December 26, 1987, a shaft of early sunlight penetrated the overcast, the small pines, the winter branches of gnarled scrub oak, and fell on a figure stooping at the edge of the clearing behind the house on Mockingbird Hill. Gene's face was dirty and ashen beneath a four-day growth of beard. He squatted unsteadily on his haunches and with exaggerated care placed a newly opened bottle of Château LaSalle on the bare ground beside him, near the empty Schlitz cans he had left here during the past three days. He paused before raising the sheet of corrugated roofing lying before him, blinking the weak sun from his eyes. Shifting to one knee, he lifted the metal and looked blankly at the fresh earth underneath.

A car door slammed somewhere across the hollow, momentarily startling Gene from his concentration on the patch of red, rocky dirt with its half-dozen protruding loops of barbed wire. Satisfied that the site was unmolested, Gene lowered the sheet of roofing, rocked back on his heels, and reached for the bottle. He took a long swallow, then rose on stiffened knees and lurched across the clearing toward the house, once more satisfied that the bodies of Becky, Little Gene, and the five children were safe.

He had put them all there on Tuesday evening, finishing up by flashlight, Becky and Little Gene with their gunshot-shattered heads, and the strangled children on top. Even with the kerosene that he kept adding and the buried barbed wire as precautions, he kept coming back to make sure no dog or coyote had been scratching around.

Over the past three days the grave had become a regular station on Gene's ritual circuit of the hill, and he was especially relieved on this trip to find nothing disturbed around it. As he walked away from the smell of coal oil that hung above it he knew that this would have to be his last visit here. The others were coming today, and he had to be at home for them.

As he rounded the southeast corner of the house a restless cackling reminded him that there were still chores to do. He set the bottle of wine on the concrete steps at the front of the house and walked down the grade to the north to let the chickens out. He spread some feed for them, returned to the house, picked up the bottle as he stepped into the front porch, and walked through the sliding glass door to the living room. Voices from the television and the flicker of the Christmas tree lights in the darkened room greeted him again. Without a glance he turned right into the small dining area and sat down at the table with its clutter of wrappers from microwave burritos, empty Schlitz cans, and two small-caliber revolvers.

Gene settled into the chair next to the north wall so he could see the television in the other room and, through the kitchen window, the front yard. The rest of his family would be coming soon to join their mother and brothers and sisters.

*   *   *

Gene sat down on Mockingbird Hill, and one hundred sixty miles southeast of him, near Fordyce, Billy and Renata were picking up the wrapping paper that twenty-month-old Trae had scattered across their trailer's small living room when he ripped open the last of his presents the night before.

"I think he liked the paper more than his presents," Billy said as Renata struggled to put a coat on their wriggling son.

She finally gave up, telling Billy she would take Trae on to the truck and get him dressed there. "Hurry up, I don't want him to get cold," she said over her shoulder as she hurried Trae through the door.

Billy hesitated before closing the door of the trailer. "Are you sure we aren't forgetting something?" he called to his wife, but he got no answer. Renata, bent half in and half out of the pickup, had reached a giggling standoff with Trae in the struggle to fasten his seat belt. She could not think of anything else they needed, and she ignored Billy's question.

Billy closed the trailer door and tugged on his jacket as he walked to the pickup. Despite his nervous preoccupation with the plans for getting his mother away from Gene, Billy couldn't help smiling as he neared the Toyota truck and saw Trae shove his mother's head down and fill his tiny fists with her mussed brown hair. Renata retreated from his grasp, straightened the Christmas bell pinned to her pink sweater, and ran a hand through her hair, trying vainly to smooth away Trae's handiwork.

Billy opened the door and started to slide under the steering wheel but stopped before he was in the seat. Renata got in and looked at him.

"Be right back," Billy said. He started the engine that he and Dennis McNulty had spent their fall weekends overhauling and, leaving it to warm, ran quickly back to the trailer, went in, and returned almost at once. Soon Trae was nodding in his car seat, and Renata was watching the familiar scenery glide past along their way to U.S. Highway 167, north out of Fordyce toward Little Rock.

Renata was used to her husband's long silences, but after a few miles she was hoping he would turn to meet her eye and talk to her. She knew what was on his mind—they had talked about little else these past few days when they were alone—and she wished they could find something pleasant to say, something else to talk about today.

Billy hardly noticed the familiar road or Renata's uneasiness. What troubled him most was why his older brother Gene hadn't called.

When the phone rang at 6:25 that morning Billy had hoped it might be Little Gene. But it was Sheila, and practically the first words out of her mouth were, "Has Little Gene called yet?"

"No, Sis," Billy told her, "he hasn't." Renata stopped what she was doing to listen.

"Well, Dennis wanted me to call. He thinks it might be good if we follow each other," his sister had said, "in case there's any car trouble."

They talked only another minute, Sheila saying Dennis wanted to leave about 7:15 and Billy agreeing to leave Fordyce about 7:45, giving his brother-in-law time to cover the thirty miles from Camden and overtake him somewhere north of Fordyce around eight o'clock. They expected to arrive at their mother's shortly before noon.

"I called Grandma Novak a while ago," Billy said as they ended the conversation. "She asked me to get Mother to a phone so she could talk to her. She was worried about Mom. I didn't tell her anything but that I would try to get Mom to call."

245

As he hung up Billy took little comfort from knowing that his sister and Dennis had been thinking about the same things that had troubled him the past few days, and he decided to try one more time to convince Renata not to make this trip. There really could be trouble. Little Gene should have called by now, no matter what had delayed him. In his last phone conversation with Sheila and Dennis on December 1 Little Gene had said he planned to arrive at Mockingbird Hill on the Monday before Christmas, and he pledged that he would convince his mother that it was time "to leave the fat bastard. I'll drive up early and call to let you know what's going on," he had said.

Sheila and Dennis visited Becky the weekend following the call, and after returning home that Sunday Dennis reported to Billy that although Becky was still vacillating, as she had throughout the fall, she seemed ready to do *something*.

"She said your dad is acting even weirder," Dennis told him. "She's really afraid for the kids, but Loretta told us she is afraid for her mother. I think she'll listen to Little Gene this time. She also said, whatever happens, she didn't think it would be a good idea for me and Sheila to go back Christmas, but I think he ought to see the whole family is behind her."

Billy agreed—Sheila and Dennis's presence might stir up an ugly scene—but he also agreed that there was safety in numbers.

Twice that morning, once before leaving their bed and again after Sheila's phone call, Billy had told Renata, "Everything is probably going to be all right, but I would feel better if you and Trae stayed home. I can come right back, and we can go on to your mother's in the morning. You know you can't stand being around him anyway, and he sure may not be nice this time."

Renata wouldn't hear of it. Everyone else will be

there, she argued, and Becky would probably not make up her mind anyway. Besides, it's silly to do all that extra driving. It was a much shorter trip from Dover than it was from Fordyce to her mother's home in Waldron.

Billy gave in and retreated to his thoughts.

Now, as they reached the outskirts of Fordyce and her husband had yet to break his silence, Renata remembered her father-in-law's eyes. Since October he had hardly spoken to her, but his look was enough for her to feel the condescension and hatred. She shuddered, and Billy glanced at her.

"That heater's taking its time warming up," Renata said. "It's a little cool in here. Are you cold, honey?" she asked Trae, who was already asleep.

As they turned onto Highway 167 north of Fordyce Billy looked at his watch—about 8:10—and told Renata to start watching for Sheila and Dennis. "Sheila said they would leave the house around seven-fifteen and should hit Fordyce about eight, because they had to make a stop for gas," Billy said. "We're right on time. If we drive slow, they should catch up soon. We should see them before we get to Sheridan."

By the time he reached Sheridan, thirty-five miles north of Fordyce, Billy was doing less than fifty miles an hour, and Dennis was nowhere in sight. He whipped the truck into a convenience-store parking lot at the main intersection with Highway 270 and told Renata, "We'll wait here a few minutes. If they don't catch us before we get on the interstate, we might as well quit slow-poking and drive on to Mom's. Keep an eye out for them, and I'll go in and get us some Coke and munchies. Honk the horn if you see them go by."

Billy was back in minutes and gave Renata the small sack of sodas and snacks. Out of his jacket pocket he drew the half pint of bourbon that he had fetched from the trailer just before they left.

"What's *that?*" Renata asked archly. "And for breakfast. I really don't understand how you can do that, Bill, with Trae in the truck."

Billy didn't try to answer. He reached across and pulled a Coke and a Styrofoam cup from the sack sitting on her lap. As he mixed his bourbon and Coke a large drop of rain fell on the windshield. In the few minutes before they left the sky darkened further, and a pouring rain forced him to turn on his headlights. This should really end any hopes of hooking up with Sheila and Dennis, he thought. It was good bourbon weather, though, and he hoped a couple of drinks between Sheridan and Dover would calm his anxiety about the trip.

Billy nursed his drink until they reached the rest stop on Interstate 40 just south of Morrilton—about forty-five miles from Mockingbird Hill—where he pulled in and, despite a glare from Renata, mixed himself another bourbon. Trae awoke, sucked his bottle for a while, and was asleep again before they had gone another five miles.

Renata finally shrugged off her irritation at Billy, and they began discussing plans for their trip the next day to visit her mother in Waldron. It was just past ten A.M. As they talked Billy's eyes returned again and again to the rearview mirror.

Sheila's and Dennis's imaginations had also been working overtime as they waited for the call from Little Gene. At one point on Tuesday, the twenty-second, Sheila had become so withdrawn that Dennis was worried the children's Christmas would be ruined. As it was, Sylvia, sensing her mother's tension, had trailed Sheila constantly the past few days. "It will be okay," Sylvia would say to her, patting her arm when she thought no one was watching.

Dennis, though worried himself, had worked hard

to reassure Sheila and distract Sylvia. By tacit consent Fatso had not been mentioned when Billy, Renata, and Trae visited them on Christmas Eve. The two couples had concentrated on enjoying the children, with Sheila following them everywhere and snapping shots with her camera as they opened presents and played with their new toys. Conversation at dinner centered on Sheila's plans to enroll part-time in the local branch of Ouachita Baptist University. Billy, ever confounded by Dennis's insistence on sharing the housework with Sheila, teased his brother-in-law. "With Sheila working and going to school you'll have to get a whole new set of aprons or hire yourself a good-looking maid."

Renata, reminding Billy of his days frying burgers at Hardee's, said, "For the right price I'll rent *you* out to cook for them."

Dennis was pleased to see his wife lose herself in the banter and to see her good mood continue through the next day's Christmas gathering with his parents.

Neither Sheila nor Dennis said anything on Christmas Day about the trip to see her parents until Sheila started gathering presents and bundling up the children about six that evening, saying she had to wash clothes tonight, since they were leaving before eight the next morning.

Dennis, who was a notorious sleepyhead, grinned pitifully and said, "Love, you know I can't get up at any six in the morning."

Sheila picked up an umbrella and hit him playfully on the head. "Sylvia," she said, "make your daddy carry you to the car so you won't get wet."

Sheila hugged her mother-in-law and father-in-law. "We'll see you in a couple of days, if I can keep your lazy son moving," she said as she left.

Dennis returned to the house laughing, scooped up Michael, who was standing by the door, and shouted

"Merry Christmas" as he ran back to the car. The McNultys stood just inside the door, out of the rain, as their son and his family drove away. By the light from the porch they could see Sylvia's face pressed to the window as she waved at them from the car.

It was just a few miles to their home, and soon Sheila was putting a load of laundry into the machine and telling Sylvia to start getting ready for bed. When she finished, Dennis was waiting in the living room with a bottle of champagne. "If you're going to make me get up at that ungodly hour, let's at least enjoy ourselves a little first," he said, cocking an eyebrow.

"I would love to," Sheila said coyly, "if you think you can handle it and still get up at six. And I'll bet you won't be this romantic then."

The champagne bottle was emptied that evening; the washing machine was not.

At 7:15 the next morning Dennis had just finished gassing up the car and was inside the station putting a small pile of chips, doughnuts, and sodas on the counter when Sheila, who had stayed in the car with the children, came in laughing.

The attendant had worked with Sheila at the Valentine Sinclair Oil Company, and he smiled as she said to Dennis, "The early wakeup, the champagne, or something has kicked our brains out of gear. We've got to go back to the house. We forgot Michael's tennis shoes."

Dennis shook his head then pointed across the counter, and with a big grin he said, "I think you better give me some of that." The man at the counter was chuckling with Sheila as he handed Dennis a pack of BC headache powders.

"We'd better hurry," Dennis said as they started back to their trailer. "Maybe we can catch Bill before they leave. Anyway, the later we are, the less time we'll have to spend with Gene before he goes to work."

When they arrived at the trailer Dennis ran from the car to unlock the door and hurry to the phone. Thirty miles away the phone rang in Billy and Renata's trailer. Billy had just closed the pickup door after having fetched his bourbon and was backing out of the driveway, windows rolled up to keep out the cold. After ten rings Dennis hung up and walked into Michael's room to get the shoes. They weren't there. Dennis made a short search, walked back to the kitchen, and, as he was mixing a BC powder, he glanced around the living room and at once saw Michael's shoes sitting by the front door—exactly where he had left them that morning so they wouldn't be forgotten.

"We still may catch them. Bill may wait on us," Dennis said as he got back in the car.

Sheila, leaning into the back seat and teasing Michael with a candy cane, turned and looked at her husband. "Let's really try. I would feel a whole lot better if we all got there at the same time."

"I wish we had some of that champagne now," Dennis said playfully, trying to ease the tension creased on Sheila's face. They both knew there was little chance that they could overtake Billy and Renata now. Behind his smile Dennis silently cursed their luck as, for the second time that morning, they started the trip to Dover.

On the hill, Gene flickered in and out of contact with his surroundings. Sitting at the dining room table, he would slide slowly into torpor, fatigued by four days of drinking, fitful sleep, and all the details he had to attend to. But then a passing car on the road below or the bark of a neighbor's dog would jolt him to attention, and he would pace through the house, peeking out windows, sometimes slipping outside to view his driveway and Broomfield Road from the cover of his concrete-block wall. He had to force himself away from the path to the makeshift grave, however. It could be disastrous for him to be caught far from the house today.

Gene ended his circuit back in the dining room, checking his pistols and the cartridges in his pockets, then rewinding the nylon fish stringer in loose loops around his hand and stuffing it back into his field jacket. He took a long drink of wine from a plastic cup. He was tossing it back like medicine now that its sweetness had begun to cloy, and he wasn't really feeling the effects anymore. He had been drinking since Tuesday night and had long since lost track of the bottles of Château LaSalle and the brown cans of Schlitz.

However, on Wednesday morning, the twenty-third, he did put the bottle aside for one trip to town. Gene would not hazard his procedures on a chance arrest for drunk driving. He did not bother to shave that morning, but he brushed his teeth and gargled and changed into fresh clothes that Becky had ironed the previous Saturday. Sober and rid of the wine's sweet reek, Gene drove his son's Toyota to People's Bank and Trust in Russellville and signed for his safe-deposit box at 10:10 A.M. Along with the mad, threatening note that he had written to read to Sheila in March and had left in the box on Monday he placed an envelope containing two hundred sixty dollars that he had taken from Little Gene's wallet. He turned to the last page of the note and added a line in pencil: *Kathy Kendrick was a contributing factor.* He didn't need to read the rest; it scrolled like a Möbius through his mind. And now the police couldn't steal his money.

Gene drove from the bank to the Sears catalog store to pick up a stereo system he had ordered for Becky. The delivery notice had arrived on Monday, the day before he killed her. Instead of driving back north toward home Gene turned east out of Russellville on Interstate 40, toward the crossroads at Blackwell, about twenty miles away, and the nearest liquor store. Gene bought more wine and beer and drank straight from a bottle of Château LaSalle as he drove. He left the interstate at the Highway 105 exit and tacked northwest toward Hector, winding through the hills out of the river valley, choking on nostalgia, self-pity, and rage. What he had wanted had been so little, so simple, and so good, but everything he loved had betrayed him—his wife, his daughter/lover, and his life. It was not what he wanted to do, to be a destroyer, but they had left him no choice. All of the pain that he faced and had to annihilate fed on itself, consuming him. Everything was lost except his integrity, and he would see the job done right.

When he arrived at Mockingbird Hill he once again checked the grave before carrying the stereo and the wine and beer into the house. He put the shipping package under the Christmas tree and returned to his drinking, letting ballgames and holiday specials on the television mute the chatter in his mind. He would nap; some sound would wake him. He would pace and peer from windows and heat burritos in the microwave oven. He went outside to relieve himself and checked the grave each time he did.

By Christmas Day the drinking and the television could not contain the buzzing mantra in Gene's head, the endless loop of thoughts he had locked in his safe-deposit box: *Sheila, you have lied to me, hurt me, destroyed me, and it will hurt you more than it will hurt me. I will see you in hell.* The memory of the lies and pain sanctified him and steeled his resolve as much as he was saddened by the images he quarried from the past—baby Sheila squealing with delight as he tossed her in the air; Sheila in her early teens sitting at his feet, with long, dark hair flowing over his thighs as she leaned into his strength; and Sheila the lover, opening her arms and, he had thought, her soul to him. *You forgot about all the little things I have done for you and with you. You were my best friend, my confidant, and my love. You gave me the best years of my life, and the worst. You have destroyed me. But I will see you in hell.*

Gene had reached a state of grace where moral sense and physical sensation were reduced to broad and insignificant abstractions. He felt the enormity of what he was doing only as a rising note that resonated through him, filling him with more than he could contain. Memories, visions, details of what he had to do crowded for attention. Goaded to do something, Gene went through the house gathering emblems of his past—Becky's wedding gown, his mother's family Bible, the letters he never mailed to Sheila—and piled them in the fireplace. He doused the pile with kerosene and lit the last fire built on Mockingbird Hill until vandals burned the house in March 1989. Gene watched until the flames had licked away the past, and the fire lay dying ghostly blue on the ashes. He let the house go cold as a morgue or the purpose in his eyes. *You have destroyed me. I will see you in hell.* He thought of phoning Billy and telling him not to come but decided that would not be fair to the others in the grave, that it would leave the work unfinished. And he could not spare Billy when Renata had to die. Worse, they might tell Sheila, and then she might not come, and he had not gone this far to be denied her.

At noon on Saturday, December 26, Gene had stepped outside to urinate when he heard a car door slam by his driveway at the foot of the hill. He froze for an instant, his bladder seizing in spurts with the sudden swell of adrenaline. He wet his hand and pants as he stuffed his penis back into his underwear and ran for the front door. Was it Sheila? Billy and his bitch? Please, oh please, don't let it be the police—not yet, Lord, not just yet.

Gene's body was a hot pulse. He ran inside to the dining room table where he had left the six-shot Ruger .22. Wheezing and clammy and fighting for calm, he patted the nine-shot snub-nose and the ammunition in his pockets and tucked the Ruger in his waistband at the small of his back, the long barrel hard and cold and disconcerting between his buttocks. He hurried back out on the porch, cracked the door, and listened.

Gene caught his breath and held it, and his body tingled as he heard Billy's voice telling Renata to drive through the lower gate so that he could close it behind them. Calmer now, Gene could not stop the grin spreading across his face. He retreated into the kitchen and waited by the curtain-covered windows.

He heard Billy's truck stop at the second gate near the top of the hill, and in a moment the pickup pulled in to park behind the big cedar out front. The tree blocked them from his sight, and he strained to hear their voices.

"Come on, Trae, stop crying. We're at Grandma's house," Billy said as he rounded the cedar tree, carrying his son.

Renata, walking behind them with her arms full of diaper bags and toys, said, "He's not even awake yet, honey. He'll brighten up when he sees the girls."

Gene watched as they crossed the trampled path between the cedar and the house. He looked into the living room, and how he would do what he had to do became clear to him.

After a last glance outside Gene took the H&R revolver from his pocket, slipped it into the front of his waistband under the field jacket, and walked to the sliding glass front door. Billy was opening the door to the porch, balancing Trae over his shoulder with one hand and pulling on the knob with the other.

"Is anybody at home?" Billy shouted as he stepped into the cold clutter of the porch.

"Yeah, come on in."

Gene's instant reply startled Billy, who could hardly make out his father's figure against the weak glow from the television and the lights on the Christmas tree. He had seen Little Gene's car outside and might have expected his brother or his mother or Loretta to meet them. But at the sight of his father standing alone by the door he felt his stomach tighten. Gene never met anyone at the door. Usually the girls rushed to the car to greet them before they could get out, and his mother would wait at the door with hugs and kisses. Having grown up in his father's house, Billy thought nothing of the lights being off.

"Come on in," Gene repeated. He slid the glass door open and stepped back into the living room. "Do you need any help with anything?"

"No, We'll get the other stuff later," Billy said. Renata came in behind him and put her bags and boxes on the floor just inside the door. She stepped next to Billy and took Trae from him. Both of them knew that something was very wrong in that house.

"Where is everybody?" Billy asked. The cold was beginning to seep through his jacket. His father was indistinct against the pale backlight, a voice disembodied.

"Oh, Loretta and Little Gene talked everybody into going on a walk for me," Gene replied evenly. "I wanted everyone to get here before I gave your mother her present, but I had to get her out of the house so I could wrap it and put it under the tree."

Knowing how his father enjoyed the holidays, especially his role as Father Christmas, Billy relaxed a little. Clutching Trae closer to her, Renata did not move from his side.

"Come on back here and I'll show you, Bill. I haven't finished wrapping it yet. See if you think she'll like it," Gene said as he turned and walked toward the hall. Trae was cold and whimpering again. "Honey, why don't you give Trae his bottle?" Billy said. Sensing her apprehension, he patted her shoulder and lowered his voice. "It's going to be okay, honey. I'll be right back." He walked her over to the couch and went on to his dad's bedroom, turning as he entered the hall to give her a smile and a shrug.

Renata sat Trae on the couch and gave him his bottle. She turned, shivered, and took three steps toward the hall.

"Dad, no!" she heard her husband shout. Then she heard the gunshots—she never knew how many—and Renata turned and tried to run back to Trae. It was all like a dream, a horrible dream, one of those slow-motion nightmares in which she could only stare toward Trae, unable to hear his screams or move fast enough down the tunnel between them.

Gene had entered the bedroom and walked directly to the curtained closet in the southwest corner. He stood with his back to the door and pulled the pistol from the front of his pants, softly thumbing back the hammer. He could feel Billy drawing closer. Gene was bathed in a warm glow. He felt the floor shift beneath him as Billy stepped into the room. Gene whirled to his right and, in one motion, straightened his arm and fired, cutting off Billy's scream. Fired from less than a foot away, the hollow-point round hit Billy in the right cheek and penetrated the soft palate, going into his brain.

Billy's hands came to his face as he collapsed toward his father. His head struck the bedpost, and he rolled to the right, coming to rest on his back. Gene didn't want Billy to suffer. He stepped to his right, measuring the angle of fire, took careful aim, and shot his son two inches above the right ear.

Renata had taken two running steps toward the couch, wailing in her dream, "Trae. Run, Trae. Run!" when Gene burst into the living room.

Renata's screams excited Gene. He lurched to a halt in the mouth of the hall and snapped off a single shot that hit Renata in the back of the neck. She flinched and stiffened as his next shot shattered her left jaw, and she turned a clumsy pirouette to the floor. Gene fired two more shots—one to the right side of her neck and another to her right jaw—as he closed the distance to her body. He wanted her to see his face when he put a full stop to her insolence. He wanted to see the understanding there, he wanted to see the fear he had heard in her voice. Quaking with anticipation, he was oblivious to Trae's wailing on the couch.

Gene was fulfilled. Renata was still moaning and jerking when he stepped astride her and pointed the gun at her head. He squinted, thought he saw recognition in her dying eyes, and grinned as he shot her above her right eyebrow. Her head snapped to the right. Gene stood back and fired the two last rounds in his chambers, one shot striking her above the left ear and the other in the left cheek.

Gene was taking his breath in gulps as he straightened and stepped away from her body. At once he became aware of Trae. The child was balled on the couch, heaving muted sobs of terror.

"Hush, hush, son," Gene said. He approached Trae slowly, easing the pistol into his pocket. "Grandpa won't hurt you. Come here to Grandpa."

Trae continued crying as Gene lifted him to his shoulder, patted him on the back, and walked to the front door. "Hush now," Gene said, gripping Trae hard. He listened at the open door for a minute, then turned and walked back into the dining room. Gene sat at the table and put Trae on his knee. He took the length of nylon cord from his jacket and looped it swiftly around Trae's neck. "Hush, son," he said. He tightened the garrote with a violent parting of his arms, as though ripping the fabric of the air, and he held the cord trembling-taut for fully five minutes, until the child's face darkened and his body hung limp in the noose.

Gene carried Trae's body to the water barrel in the kitchen, submerged his head and saw no bubbles, then took him back to the dining room and laid him beneath the table. Working fast now but with deliberation, he dragged Billy's and Renata's bodies into the dining room and laid them next to Trae's.

Gene sat at the table with his feet resting near Renata's head. He replaced the spent rounds in the pistol and took another hard slash of the wine. He felt more alive than he had in three days. An image of Dennis smirking and clapping his hands was burning in his brain, and he prayed for him and Sheila to arrive. *He turned you against me. Little princess, you have lied to me, defied me, betrayed me. You have destroyed me and us all. And I will see you in hell.*

Gene was startled when he heard the McNultys' car coming up the drive; it seemed he had just sat down. But he was not anxious the way he had been when Billy arrived. In fact, he was quite calm now that everything was going according to plan.

He walked into the living room and stood by the glass door, where he could see that the overcast had turned to rain. He saw Sheila come from behind the cedar with Michael in her arms, herding Sylvia ahead of her and saying, "Hurry, hurry, or you'll melt." Gene began to feel again that feverish swelling of his entire being, an almost sexual excitement. Sheila paused on the porch to shake the rain from her hair and slide back the door with her foot, letting Sylvia in ahead of her.

Sylvia ran into the room without seeing Gene. "Loretta, Barbara," she called, "we're here." Sheila came in right behind her, wiping water from Michael's hair. She, too, almost passed Gene, who was standing to the left of the sliding glass door, before she registered the silence and the chill in the room. She saw something from the corner of her eye and turned to face her father, taking a step backward into the room and gasping at what she saw.

Gene was grinning and red-eyed, and his face seemed to float out of the darkness. Clutching Michael to her, Sheila began to tremble and make high, pleading sounds in her throat. Her eyes raced to find Sylvia, who had reached the end of the couch and stood looking solemnly back at Gene and her mother. Sheila wanted to run to her, to cover her, but she stood transfixed by Gene's grin.

Gene enjoyed what he saw on Sheila's face. "I'm glad you could come, little princess," he said, taking a step toward her. "Is there something wrong? You're not frightened, are you? I told you over and over what you were doing to this family, so I know you're not surprised."

As Gene spoke Sheila backed toward Sylvia, who was standing near the west end of the living room, her back to the Christmas tree. Sheila's face had gone rigid, drained of all color.

"What are you doing? What is wrong with you?" she said, forcing the words through her fear.

"It's time, precious," Gene said. "I love you more than anything in life. I've told you that. But you and Dennis have destroyed us, destroyed me. You've destroyed everybody, so don't look at me that way. You could have stopped all this. You know that. I really do feel sorry for you. You had someone who really cared for you. But you turned your back on me and the family, and now we all have to pay.''

Sylvia was gripping Sheila's leg now, and both of them were whimpering. "Please don't hurt my children,'' Sheila said as she lowered Michael to the floor and touched Sylvia on the head. "For God's sake, Sylvia is yours, and Michael has never hurt you.''

"I'm not going to hurt them,'' Gene said, pulling the snub-nosed pistol from his waistband. "I didn't want to hurt anybody, but you betrayed me. I told you. I told you. If only you had been honest . . .'' His voice trailed off, then he motioned toward the dining room with the pistol and said, "Anyway, we've all been waiting for you.''

Sheila's eyes followed the pistol, and at the end of its arc she saw what at first were only three indistinct bundles lying parallel to each other on the floor by the dining table. Then cold recognition cut through her to the heart. *Billy,* her mind screamed. *Renata.* "Oh, God, no,'' she said, her voice rising. "No.''

Gene's grin furrowed his face as he swung the gun back on her. "I still love you, princess. I'll always love you. And I'll meet you again in hell.'' Gene started across the few feet separating them, firing three times and feeling a release like ejaculation as each round left the gun. The first shot hit Sheila in the right upper lip, the second in the right cheek, and the third, from about a foot away, below her right eye as she fell between her children.

Sylvia screamed, "Mommy, Mommy,'' and she held tight to Sheila's body. Michael threw himself on the couch and covered his head with his hands, keening in elemental terror. Gene wheeled away from Sheila toward the door.

When Dennis heard Sheila's scream and the flat crack of the .22 it was as if he had known it was coming. He broke into a run, shedding the bags in his hands as he went. The door to the porch was still open, and he leapt through it, almost losing his footing on the muddy pine floor. Through the glass door he could see Sylvia kneeling by a figure on the floor at the far end of the room, and he forgot all fear as he rushed inside.

Gene was ready to punish Dennis, to beat and humiliate him, but Dennis was not caught completely by surprise. Gene stepped from the shadows inside the door, the pistol raised in his right hand to strike Dennis in the head. Dennis saw the movement and turned to meet it, raising his arms instinctively. Gene brought the pistol down like a hatchet, scraping Dennis's right wrist, his forehead, the side of his nose, and his chin. Dennis snatched at the gun with his left hand, but Gene jerked away, pushed him back, thrust the gun toward Dennis's head, and pulled the trigger, hitting him behind the left ear. Dennis was dead as he fell. Gene felt cheated, frustrated. That was not the way it was supposed to be. He had died too quickly and too easily.

Sheila, however, was still alive, breathing in great shuddering gasps through a froth of blood and saliva. Gene genuflected beside her, swung out the cylinder of his revolver, and checked the number of live rounds left in it.

"It's almost over, princess. Soon there will be no more pain, no more lies, and we'll be together again."

Sheila's eyes rolled back into her skull. Gene stroked her hair, lifted her head, and brought the pistol to within six inches of her left temple. He said, "I love you very, very deeply, little princess. Good-bye, my precious. Good-bye, my love. Good-bye, good-bye . . ." The shot sprayed a fine mist of blood over the cuff of Gene's field jacket.

Gene dropped her head and fired two more shots as he stood up, aiming at her eyes.

Sylvia, terrified into silence, was staring at him from the shadows behind the Christmas tree. Gene saw Sheila again in Sylvia's eyes, and he threw the pistol to the floor. He took the yellow-and-white nylon stringer from his jacket pocket and started toward her. He had a swifter, quieter way to deal with children. Sylvia did not even cry out when he grabbed her roughly by the shoulder, spun her around, and twisted the cord around her neck. The force he used to seat the cord in her flesh threw him against the wall. Sylvia's head rolled loose in the loop. Blood was streaming out of her mouth, from the tongue she bit through. Gene worked frantically to reset the noose around her throat. He jerked it tight again and again, many times after her body had gone slack.

Gene calmed himself and slowed his breathing. Michael lay just a few feet away at the end of the couch, shrunk into a fetal ball. His rib cage heaved in terror.

Gene picked Sylvia up as though she were asleep and he didn't want to wake her. He carried her back to Loretta's bed, lay her facedown, pulled a blanket over her body, and tucked her in.

He returned to Michael and gently picked him up, crooning reassurances as he carried the boy into his bedroom and strangled him there. Gene forced Michael's head into the water barrel in the bathroom off the hall, then carried him to the dining room and laid him on the table.

Seeing the neat array of bodies filled Gene with relief, a sense of accomplishment, and the stiff grin slowly returned to his face as he raised his wine in a toast—to the perfection of his life's work on the coming Monday.

Gene wrapped Trae and Michael in plastic garbage

bags and left their bodies in the trunks of two abandoned cars at the end of Little Princess Lane. He
covered the adults with coats and blankets where
they lay, except for Sheila. He moved her closer to
the tree, where the twinkling lights could play across
her shattered face, and there he arranged her in state,
hands folded virginally across her breast, covered
with Becky's best tablecloth.

CHAPTER FIFTEEN

Late Saturday night Gene awoke from his first real sleep since Tuesday feeling refreshed, groggy, slightly euphoric, despite the sting of cordite in his nose and the sour aftertaste of Château LaSalle in the back of his throat. His breath hung ghostly in the dark of the house as he plodded from his bedroom to the kitchen, picked up a saucepan from the counter, and dipped it full from the water barrel. He dashed his face and shivered and rinsed his mouth with the water in which he had held Trae.

Gene shook his head hard, turned on the kitchen light, and went into the living room. He walked the circle from the living room to the dining room and back to the kitchen, pausing at each body to satisfy himself that he was nearly there, almost free. He took a beer, an onion, and a block of cheese from the refrigerator and sat in front of the television eating the onion like an apple, chasing it with plugs of cheese and long draughts of beer.

As he ate, his eyes moved from Sheila to Dennis. By the time he finished the beer and the onion his head had cleared, and the stiff grin returned to his face. He lowered his head and shook it slowly.

He looked at his watch and saw that it was 11:45 P.M.; he had slept almost eight hours. Fully awake now and content that his work had been good, Gene's mild euphoria swelled, filling him with a feeling of accomplishment, something worthy of celebration. He changed his shirt, put on his field jacket and cowboy hat, and left Mockingbird Hill at midnight, driving Little Gene's brown Toyota.

The North 40 is a private club just across the interstate from Russellville, and the waitress there noticed Gene because at first glance he reminded her of a regular customer, Robert E. "Doc" Irwin. The resemblance was spurious but prophetic: Two days later Gene's life would become the charge of Doc Irwin, who, with fellow Russellville attorney John Harris, would be appointed to defend him.

Gene ignored the noisy crowd and walked directly to the end of the bar where the waitresses filled their drink orders. In his cowboy hat and boots he fit with the Saturday-night crowd of local professionals gone slumming and flannel-shirted lumbermen from the hills who had come to town. Nobody noticed as he sat down at the table by the wall with his two mixed drinks and, grinning broadly, raised one glass to the empty chair across from him.

"Sheila, honey," he said softly, "I'm coming." He slid the second drink across the table and drank his own off in long swallows. "We will be together forever in hell."

He left Sheila's drink untouched, returned to the bar, and ordered two more. Again he sat one of the fresh drinks opposite him, and he leaned back in his chair, sipping his second drink slowly and staring across the table. Fifteen minutes later he left without leaving a tip.

Gene's confidence and sense of satisfaction endured throughout the next day. He spent Sunday watching football and drinking beer, indifferent to the bodies strewn through the cold house. From time to time he rose to stretch or urinate or inspect the mass grave outside, and constantly his mind cast forward to tomorrow, for which he made a list:

1) Kathy (You're partly the cause) at Peel, Eddy: S. Glenwood—leave west on Main
2) Taylor at Oil company: Main—leave east on Main
3) Salyer at mini mart: leave east
4) Joyce (Know nothing bitch) at Woodline: Airport Rd.—leave to Sheila?

The way was paved now, his own death its destination. Already the pain was gone, and everything left was but a matter of integrity. The endless loop of details, preparations, and invectives had grown shorter, until at last he could see all the world at once, the universe in a .22 round and eternity in a moment, just a moment.

Near midnight Gene wrapped himself in a blanket and stretched out on the couch with his face toward the front door and both pistols in easy reach on the floor beside him. Within minutes he was asleep, as near to Sheila as he had been in years.

Gene awoke early, stiff with cold, and immediately went out to check the grave. He walked the length of the cinder-block wall along the military crest of the ridge, crossed the barren garden past the sign that read "Mom's Playground," and circled the house once more before going back inside. He opened his last bottle of the sweet yellow wine, drank from it, and made ready for his last trip down from Mockingbird Hill. He counted the money in his wallet, more than two hundred fifty dollars, and put it in an envelope with a letter to Ma Novak:

Dear Ma,
Sometimes you reap many more times what you sow. You have given so much to this family, this is just a little token of our appreciation. Keep it in remembrance of us.

Love,
Gene and family

He then wrote brief notes of thanks to his two nieces in Little Rock, whom he almost never saw. Mary Mason and Sharon Quandah would receive the greeting cards while watching reports of the killings on television.

Shortly after nine o'clock Gene walked through the house and pulled the curtains and drapes, still fearful a curious neighbor or friend of the children could turn up and undo his best-laid plan, for there was a possibility that he might need the refuge of Mockingbird Hill again. If either Kathy Kendrick or Joyce Butts had decided to take an extra holiday, he would have to wait until tomorrow to complete his will.

Gene put the snub-nosed revolver in the pocket of his coat and the six-shot Ruger in a paper bag, along with a box of saltines, the letters, an empty envelope, and the bottle of wine. He wedged a length of broomstick in the metal runner of the sliding glass door to lock it and unlatched a window on the south side of the house. Before wriggling through it he paused to look again at Sheila's body. "Soon, precious, soon," he said, and then he was out the window into the cold December morning.

He started Little Gene's Toyota and left it to warm

while he turned out the chickens and spread some feed for them. Then he removed the Toyota's Texas license tag and replaced it with one off his Chevrolet, turning the screws only finger-tight, pleased that he had thought of the birds, so no one could accuse him of being heartless enough to let them starve.

Leaving the hill for the last time, he drove south on Highway 7, eating crackers and washing them down with sips of wine. With the energy that possessed him now he did not need the confidence of alcohol, only its companionship, and he did not want to be so muddled that his endgame failed.

Ten minutes later he rounded the gentle left-hand curve into Dover and pulled slowly into the post office parking lot. He left the engine idling and dropped the letters to his nieces and mother-in-law into the box outside. He passed through Dover and down the valley toward Russellville eight miles away, never going more than fifty miles an hour.

At about 9:40 Gene crossed the interstate and wound through the deserted campus of Arkansas Tech University into Russellville proper. He drove first to Kathy Kendrick's house to see whether her car was there before he traveled on to the Peel & Eddy law firm, where she now worked. Gene's heart raced with anticipation when he saw that her car was not at home.

He forced himself to drive slowly down Glenwood, where he saw her car parked at the law office, but he did not stop. He continued along the route he had plotted on his map of Russellville, wanting one final rehearsal to insure the integrity of his plan. Shortly after ten o'clock he finished the circuit, stopped at the side of the road a few blocks from Woodline Motor Freight, where his design was to conclude, and removed the loose license plate from the car's bumper. He didn't want to make it easy for the police, not until he was through.

It was 10:15 when he pulled into the law firm parking lot. Leaving the motor running, Gene patted his jacket, felt the pistol in one pocket, and put the empty envelope in the other. He tugged the cowboy hat low over his eyes, got out, and walked directly into the office, keeping his eyes on the ground until he was inside.

As he came through the door Gene was relieved to see only two people, a young woman client in the reception area and Kathy Kendrick sitting behind her desk. Kathy did not look up from her paperwork when Gene approached and slid the diversionary envelope across to her. "May I help you?" she asked. Gene started to pull the revolver from his right pocket and hung its hammer on the seam. Kathy looked up, and her eyes met Gene's as he jerked the pistol free.

"Oh, no," Kathy said, her voice small and desperate. She pushed her chair away from the desk and started to rise.

Gene shot her in the head, and Kathy fell in a bundle back into her chair. He fired three more rounds into her skull before wheeling around and bolting through the door. Kathy Kendrick, twenty-four years old, died later that day at St. Mary's Regional Medical Center in Russellville.

At 10:17 A.M. Cathy Casey answered the telephone at the Russellville Police Department, and hearing the terrified voice of Linda Breashears, a legal secretary at the Peel & Eddy firm, at once transferred the call to the department communications operator and dispatcher, Donna Jones.

"Communications."

"Yes, I need the police at Judge Peel's office immediately. Someone's here with a gun shooting."

"Your name, please."

"Linda Breashears. I'm in his office now."

"PD one-oh-seven. Seven, I need you to go to

Judge Peel's office. I have a report of a subject inside the office shooting at this time."

"Someone is hurt. Call an ambulance, too, please. Oh, my God. Who did it? Oh, my God. Is she hurt bad?"

As Linda Breashears was dialing the police Gene was driving west on Main toward Taylor Oil Company, whose owner, Rusty Taylor, Gene had long held in contempt for failing to recognize his value as an employee. He drove slowly and tuned the car radio to the Russellville station to wait for the news bulletin. Gene was exhilarated. Pain was escaping from him like gas from a punctured balloon, driving him, and his hand shook with adrenaline as he reloaded the gun between his knees.

Gene had not dared to glance at the patrol car as it sped past him in the opposite direction, its lights flashing, for the possibility of not being able to make it back across town to Jim Salyer and Joyce Butts after finishing with Rusty Taylor was too cruel to consider. Still, he could not shake the notion, and that anxiety made him hasty when he entered the oil company office.

Gene spotted Rusty Taylor through his open office door and didn't wait for a close shot. He stopped just outside the door and fired two rounds. Taylor fell behind his desk, hit twice in the left chest, and Gene quickly turned to leave without making sure that he was dead. The door by the dock opened and a man with a pager on his belt started through. Imagining a threat from the pager, Gene fired without breaking stride, and J.D. "Jim" Chaffin, thirty-four, a Russellville firefighter and part-time worker at Taylor Oil, fell. Gene's shot hit Chaffin in the right eye, and he died where he lay. Gene immediately sensed more movement behind him and spun to meet it, firing one round.

Juli Money, on her first day of work at Taylor Oil, was coming out of the restroom when the bullet cracked past her head. She as lucky. Gene was in a hurry, firing on instinct, and only to cover his dash to the car.

At 10:27 A.M. Cathy Casey answered the telephone again:

"Russellville Police Department."

"Please send an ambulance immediately to Taylor Oil. There has been a shooting here. There's one man dead and one man shot."

Cathy transferred the call at once to the dispatcher.

"Your name, please," Donna Jones said.

"My name is Juli Money."

"Did you need an ambulance?"

"Yes, yes."

"Stay on the line with me."

As she relayed the report of the second shooting to the squad cars Donna could hear the panic running among Juli and the others who had rushed into the office:

"Yes. Rusty's shot. Do you have something you can wrap around to stop the blood? Okay, hold still, Rusty. I've got the ambulance on the way."

"I thought it was a joke."

"Oh, my God, that man pointed that thing right at me."

"Who was he?"

"I don't know. I don't think I've been hit. It went right over my head. Oh, my God, Jim's shot. Where's he shot?"

"He needs something laid over him. Jim's dead."

"Yes, shot in the eye."

"No. Jim's still alive."

"Oh, my God, there's nothing we can do. There's the police; there's the police. Wave them down. Oh, my God, that man left."

"In a brown Toyota."

"Toyota Corolla. He just took off. I don't know which way."

Donna came back on the line: "Okay, the police are there. Calm down. Can you tell me anything about the person?"

Juli said, "It was a older man, I'd say. He looked like he had gray hair. He had . . ."

"A white cowboy hat?"

"Yes, yes."

Gene punched the accelerator and almost lost control of the car as he careened out of the parking lot and turned back east on Main, in the direction of the Sinclair Mini Mart, four miles across town, through a gauntlet of patrol cars. He forced himself to take several deep breaths as the first bulletin about the shootings came over the radio. The report described the assailant as wearing a cowboy hat, and Gene grinned as he took his off and replaced it with a baseball cap just seconds before meeting another police car speeding toward Taylor Oil. He maneuvered warily within the flow of heavy traffic, but as he passed the intersection with Glenwood his anticipation began to build, and he eased the accelerator down, trusting that most of the police were on the other side of the city by now. His plan was going well, and the urgent voice of the radio announcer combined with the screaming of police cars down Main Street to make him nearly giddy as he turned sharply into the parking lot of the Mini Mart that he had swept so many times at midnight.

The wail of sirens was dying behind him as Gene stepped from the car, and he ducked as another patrol car sped by with its lights flashing. He walked toward the door, his pistol held close to his leg, and he could see Roberta Woolery, a woman he had worked with at the store, turn to watch the police car through the convenience store's plate-glass windows. He had no quarrel with Roberta. She had always treated him right, but she would not stand between Gene and what he had to do.

Gene was afraid of David Salyer, his ex-boss, and hated both himself and Salyer for it. He didn't want Salyer even to know what hit him. Salyer and a friend, Tony Serta, were sitting at a table in a far corner of the store, talking and drinking coffee, when Gene came through the door and fired from thirty feet away. Salyer ducked as the bullet missed him and whined off the wall.

"I really didn't know if it was a real situation," Salyer recalls. "I thought somebody was playing a joke. I asked Tony, 'Is this for real?'"

Serta and Roberta Woolery recognized Gene even with the bill of the baseball cap pulled low over his eyes and realized immediately that it was not a joke. As Roberta screamed, "What are you doing?" and grabbed for the telephone Serta dived for cover and yelled at Salyer, "It ain't no joke. The guy's got a gun, and he's shooting for your head."

Gene, standing just six feet from Roberta, saw her grab for the phone. He fired two quick shots, one striking her in the mouth and the other grazing her shoulder as she went down behind the counter still holding the receiver. Gene turned back on Salyer and started to close in for a better shot.

Salyer made a split-second decision that probably saved his life and Roberta's. With no place to hide and no stomach for cowering in a corner while Gene killed Roberta Woolery, he picked up a chair and charged across the store, screaming, "Get out, you son of a bitch."

Gene jerked to a halt and slung a rattled shot that ricocheted off the wooden chair Salyer was swinging at him, wounding Salyer in the head. Salyer went down, throwing the chair at Gene as he dropped.

Serta, a robust, white-bearded seventy-one-year-old, had dodged behind the cover of a shopping aisle after the first shot, but he could still see Woolery and Salyer fall and decided he did not want to be next. He had spent many hours in the store talking to the two, considered them friends, and he wasn't going to do nothing while Gene shot the prostrate pair. Serta grabbed the first thing that came to hand, a six-pack of soft drinks, and hurled it across the top of the aisle at Gene, narrowly missing his head. Then he was grabbing can after can, throwing them and screaming, "You son of a bitch."

Gene was overwhelmed. He fired wildly at the flying cans, then turned and ran out the door.

Roberta Woolery, though bleeding heavily from the wound in her cheek, completed her call to the Russellville Police Department at 10:39, even before Gene was out the door, and spoke with a calm born of either shock or courage.

"Communications, Donna," the dispatcher said.

"This is Salyer Mini Mart on Sixty-four East, Sinclair, across from T-Berry's. You got it?"

"Yes, ma'am."

"A man just come in here and started shooting, and he's got me in the chin, and another guy is down on the floor."

"Okay, which way did he head when he left there?"

"Headed east."

"Okay. Stay on the line with me, okay?"

"Okay, but please hurry. Our blood is dripping everywhere."

Donna radioed to the squad cars, "The suspect is headed east at this time. We have just had another shooting at Sinclair, across from T-Berry's mobile home, PD one-two-one." Then, panic beginning to take an edge in her own voice, she said to Roberta Woolery, "Okay. Calm down for me, okay."

"I'm trying, hon," Roberta said, her own voice steady, "but I've got blood dripping everywhere." She saw Serta and asked, "Are you shot? Would you get me more towels? We do need an ambulance, don't we?"

"Oh, you need an ambulance?" Donna said.

"There's a man on the floor."

"Okay," Donna said, now clearly agitated. "I want you to calm down with me, okay?" She interrupted herself to respond to a patrol car: "She advised that he was headed east," then returned to Roberta. "Okay, your name, please, again."

"Roberta Woolery."

"Okay. Do you need an ambulance there?"

"Yes, ma'am."

"Okay. You calm down."

"Okay. I'm trying, hon," Roberta said reassuringly, turning calmly to Serta to add, "Would you get that guy's gas money when he gets done? I'm shutting the pumps off. Is David still conscious?"

"Roberta, we've got to get help right away," Serta said.

"I'm trying. It was Gene Simmons, wasn't it?"

"I think so," Serta replied, bending over the wounded Salyer.

"I do, too. This guy owes me seven dollars, sixty cents. He's coming in. Oh, God, he just missed my head. Tell him not to move."

"Just lay still, David," Serta told his friend.

"Oh, lady, where are you?" Roberta said into the phone. "I'm about to pass out."

Donna came back on the line. "I've got an ambulance on the way, and I've got an officer on the way."

"I'm pretty sure I know who it is," said Roberta.

"Who do you think it is?"

"Gene Simmons. He used to be an employee here. He just quit about two weeks ago."

"Okay, Mister Simmons . . . uh, thank you."

Gene was shaking violently as he pushed the accelerator to the floor and peeled away from the Mini Mart, not caring now if he attracted attention. He had to get to Woodline Motor Freight. He knew that by this time he was positively identified and that every police officer in the county had his description. His only fear, however, was of failure and the uncertainty that his .22 would deliver him to Sheila. He had had to shoot them all so many times, so many times.

It had been only twenty minutes since he had walked into the Peel & Eddy law firm when he pulled into the Woodline Motor Freight lot and drew a mental line through the last name on his list, Joyce Butts. Here he had planned to join Sheila, with all accounts settled. But the seed of doubt planted in his mind six days earlier when he pumped round after round into Little Gene, trying to end his frenzied flopping on the bedroom floor, and nourished by repeated demonstrations of his .22 pistol's ineffectiveness, now blossomed full-blown.

Gene reckoned the possible outcomes of putting his gun to his head, and two of the three terrified him. He recoiled from the idea of ending his life a paralytic vegetable or awakening helpless in a hospital mental ward. And he didn't think the odds much better in forcing the police to do the job. He had dealt with them regularly as a clerk at the Mini Mart and had nothing but disdain for their professional competence.

As his doubt grew that suicide or a forced gunfight would insure his own end, Gene took refuge in believing no jury would let him live after what he had done. He could convince them of that.

As Gene got out of his car at Woodline he knew he

did not have long before the dragnet closed in on him, but he wouldn't need long to finish what he had come for. With the snub-nose in his pocket and the Ruger in the paper sack under his left arm he entered the building through the shop door in the back. No one saw him come into the office and stand by the Christmas tree, pausing to locate Joyce Butts at her desk before walking briskly toward her, pulling the short-barreled revolver from his coat.

Gene fired twice, striking Joyce in the head and chest, as the other seven people in the office disappeared under their desks. Months later, after surviving open-heart surgery, Joyce Butts still would not be able to remember what happened that day. As she fell behind her desk Gene turned and walked to the computer room at the back of the office area.

Charles Sawrie, the company's data processing manager, and Vicki Jackson had witnessed the shooting from inside the computer room and dropped to the floor at once. When they heard Gene fumbling at their door Sawrie bolted for the rear door that led to the loading dock, shouting at Vicki to follow him. But Vicki was frozen with fear.

Vicki had known Gene as well as anyone during his two years at Woodline, and he had even talked to her occasionally about her friend Kathy Kendrick. As he came into the office Vicki looked up from the floor, numb with dread. He stopped above her, motioned toward her with the gun, and said, "Vicki, get up. I'm not going to hurt you."

Vicki looked up at his face and saw it serene and malevolent. "Gene," she said, "please don't shoot me."

He backed away to reassure her. "I'm not going to hurt you," he said chidingly. Then, as though it were a casual conversation, he added: "But why haven't you come to Sinclair to see me?"

"Gene, I've been down there before, and you weren't there," she said as she stood up, almost as shocked by his tone as by what he had done. "You know I just work on weekends," he said. He walked to the glass partition between the computer room and the office and saw that no one had moved from beneath the desks. "I just want you to call the police," he said, turning again to face Vicki. "I'm going to turn myself in. I want to turn myself in to you, because you've never done anything to me."

Vicki sidled cautiously toward the phone on her desk. "But Gene," she said, struggling to keep her voice calm, "what's going on?"

Gene shrugged. "Nothing. It's all over now. I just want to turn myself in. Call the police."

As Vicki lifted the receiver Gene walked over, took the Ruger from the sack, and tried to hand it to her.

"Just lay it on the desk," she said. "I don't want it."

"Would you like a cigarette?" Gene asked. "I'll get them for you."

"They're in the other room," Vicki said, motioning toward Sawrie's private office. As she dialed the phone and watched Gene lumber away Vicki kept telling herself to be calm, not to scream or run. Something in Gene's tone and sagging carriage made her believe that he would let her live.

Vicki was talking to the police dispatcher when Gene returned and handed her the cigarettes. Hearing what she was saying, he interrupted her. "Everything is all over with," he told Vicki. "I just wanted to kill Joyce, just Joyce. I didn't want to hurt anybody else. Just call an officer."

At 10:48 a rattled Donna Jones took Vicki Jackson's call:

"Communications."

"Yes. I need someone here at Woodline Motor Freight."

"Yes, ma'am. I have an officer on the way. Is the suspect still there?"

"Yes, he is still in my office."

"Okay. Does he have the gun now?"

"Yes."

"Do you know his name? Does he know you're talking to the police?"

"Yes."

"Did he ask you to call us?"

"Yes. He didn't want anybody barging in here. He's giving himself up."

"You advise the subject—advised he is going to give hisself up, stand by. Okay, your name please."

"Vicki Jackson."

"Okay, Vicki, where are you at, at Woodline?"

"I'm in the back, in the computer room."

"Unit one or one-oh-one, he does not want anybody to barge in. He advised that he is going to release hisself. He is with Vicki Jackson. She is at Woodline Motor Freight back in the computer room. What is his name, please?"

"What?"

"Ask him if his name is Gene Simmons."

"Yes."

"His name is Gene Simmons?"

"Yes."

"Has he turned the gun over to you?"

"No."

"Is he holding it?"

"I've got one, and he's holding one. But he is not pointing it at me. He said he has give up to me."

"Okay. All right, Vicki, are you calm?"

"No."

"Calm down as much as you possibly can. We're

going to get you through this, believe it or not. Is there anybody else in the office with you?''

''No.''

''Just you and him?''

''Yes, but one's shot. I don't know where she's at. I don't know if they took her out or not.''

''One is shot, and you don't know if they've took her . . . uh, he does want to turn hisself in?''

''Yes, he does want to turn himself in.''

''Ask him if he will give you the gun.''

''He says he is not going to have them barging in. He says when he sees the police officer he will give me the gun.''

''Okay.''

''And I've got one of the guns already. He gave me one, and he's holding one, and he says when he sees a police officer he will give me the gun. But he will not have them barging in.''

''Okay. PD one-oh-one, somebody, have radio contact with me. Come on, I need to talk to somebody who's going into Woodline.''

Within minutes the building was surrounded by city police and county deputies, rifles, shotguns, and pistols trained on the windows and back door of the computer office. Russellville Police Chief Herb Johnston, who had been en route to the Sinclair shootings when Vicki's call came through, arrived at the scene and ordered all the officers away from the building. Police Major Ron Stobaugh, however, had already positioned himself inside the office, within easy gunshot range. He saw Gene standing with Vicki behind the glass partition and ordered him to throw out his gun.

As Stobaugh ordered Gene to drop the gun Chief Johnston came in the office area unarmed, and Gene ignored the command.

''Find out who that is,'' he said to Vicki, and on

the other end of the line Donna confirmed that the silver-haired man in the blue sweater was Chief Johnston. Still ignoring Stobaugh, Gene walked to the door and opened it.

"Give me the damned gun," Johnston ordered, and Gene handed over the pistol without a word. In seven days he had killed sixteen people and left four others wounded.

Gene dropped his head and retreated inside himself, refusing at first to speak at all to the police who handcuffed him and hustled him away. He entered his cell wearily at the Pope County Detention Center, less than a mile away, walked to the bunk, and lay down, his hands cushioning his head as he stared at the ceiling and let a pleasant fatigue blot him out, disconnect him from events, the rough beast's hour come round at last.

EPILOGUE

MUTATIS MUTANDIS

Lockup,
1988–1990

THE DYING OF THE LIGHT

Exhausted fireflies stalk the window screen
spreading dim luminescence on the wire.
Then one by one, like dogged ideas, they pause,
pulse, and gasp their terminal bursts of fire.

—PAUL WILLIAMS
from "A Nocturne"

James Hardy had a bad feeling in his stomach. During his fifteen years as a deputy and investigator for the Pope County Sheriff's Department he had had to look through a lot of keyholes and half-drawn drapes, but there was something eerily unsettling about the stillness inside the Simmons house on Mockingbird Hill, something made more disturbing by all the signs of recent occupation outside, the chickens running loose, the children's tricycles and toys scattered across the cold hard-pack, the four automobiles parked beneath the big cedar in front.

Hardy did not know what he was looking for, only that it had something to do with the spree of murders that morning in Russellville, but all his instincts told him that there was more here than he could see without a search warrant. He made a final circuit of the place, squinting in each of the darkened windows, then returned to his patrol car and radioed the license numbers of the vehicles to his headquarters. He ended his transmission at about 12:40 P.M. with the words "There's nobody here, no sign of life."

A half hour later Hardy was back in Russellville,

concluding his report to Sheriff James Bolin and Lt. Jay Winters. Winters looked questioningly at Bolin, jerking his head in the direction of the cell block where Gene Simmons was being held. The sheriff nodded and said, "Try talking to him one more time, Jay. This situation may be getting a whole lot worse."

Gene had nearly collapsed during the booking process that morning and had to be held up by two deputies to be fingerprinted. Since then he had lain in silence on his bunk, staring at the ceiling and refusing to answer any questions. But from talking to witnesses and Gene's intended victims Bolin knew that the prisoner had a large family in Dover. The sheriff was hoping against hope, just as James Hardy had, that his gut feeling about this was wrong.

The judge who would normally issue a search warrant was out of town at a trial, but Bolin was increasingly certain that they needed to have a look inside that house.

"Okay," Bolin said when Winters came back and reported that Gene still was not talking, "we don't have to get a search warrant. There's something really wrong here. We can go in under emergency search."

Coincidentally, Robert E. "Doc" Irwin, a Russellville attorney who had been in municipal court when the first reports began coming in of Gene's rampage through the town, he had returned later to follow events with the sheriff, and he turned to him now and said, "Sheriff, this is big. You better get a search warrant and cover all your bases. If I were representing this guy, I would sure as hell question the legitimacy of the search."

Irwin lost that argument with the sheriff just as he would against Prosecutor John Bynum a year later, after Irwin and John Harris, another Russellville attorney, were appointed to conduct Gene's defense.

At three o'clock that afternoon Bolin squirmed through the window that Gene had used when he last left the house. The sheriff found the floor with his hands and lowered himself inside, nearly falling across Sheila's body beside the Christmas tree. He threw back the curtains and started for the sliding glass front door, where he saw Dennis McNulty lying, his face covered with his jacket, and children's clothes over his legs and arms. Bolin removed the length of broomstick that held the door shut and told his deputies to come inside with the videotape camera they had borrowed from the state highway patrol.

Just after five o'clock vans from the state medical examiner's office in Little Rock pulled onto Broomfield Road, carrying the bodies of Sheila, Dennis, Sylvia, Billy, and Renata, followed by a line of police cars returning to Russellville. Throughout the evening radio and television bulletins flashed across Arkansas and the nation, and by morning dozens of reporters and photographers had converged on Pope County.

Investigators from the Arkansas Highway Patrol, the Pope County Sheriff's Office, and the Russellville Police Department worked throughout the night to piece together the facts, and by Tuesday morning, December 29, they were convinced that the scope of Gene's slaughter was greater than even Bolin had feared. According to what they had learned from relatives, there might be as many as nine more bodies awaiting discovery on Mockingbird Hill.

Gene was arraigned before Judge John Patterson the next morning at 8:30 for a probable-cause hearing. He still wore the same slump of exhaustion, the haggard eyes, and the thick stubble of beard. He stood with his head bowed, refusing to respond to the judge's questions until Patterson asked in exasperation, "You want to give me a nod or any kind of response?"

Gene remained motionless.

Patterson ordered Gene held without bond and appointed Irwin and Harris to represent him. It would be a frustrating alliance for them all.

As the door fell shut on Gene's cell at the Pope County Detention Center law officers combing the ridge east of Dover discovered the grave site, the scent of kerosene still lingering beneath the corrugated tin. Wearing gloves, they dug gingerly through the rocks and loose dirt, pulling the loops and strands of barbed wire free until one of them hung on something. A deputy felt along the wire and brushed the area clean to find the body of Rebecca Lynn. In quick order the searchers unearthed the bodies of Marianne, Loretta, Eddy, Barbara, Becky, and Little Gene. A grim, funereal silence hung over the men as they worked. Some of them turned away when the bodies of the children were lifted out—Loretta in a "Jesus Loves You" T-shirt, little Barbara in her yellow pajamas. Some muttered, and some cried.

Two hours earlier and one hundred yards away from the makeshift grave, Lt. Winters and Deputy Tim Wittenberg had pried open the trunks of the two abandoned automobiles at the end of Little Princess Lane and found the bodies of Trae Simmons and Michael McNulty in them, wrapped in plastic garbage bags.

The following day, Wednesday, December 30, as accounts from relatives began to sketch Gene's family past, Judge Patterson ordered him to the state hospital at Benton for immediate psychiatric evaluation. Before Gene left, however, he broke his silence and asked to see his attorneys.

Horrified and rapt, Irwin and Harris sat in silence as Gene recited the events of the past week, enumerating the facts in a telegraphic monotone, devoid of emotion. At moments Gene would look up at them and speak of Sheila. "If only she would have talked to me," he would say. "If only she hadn't lied to me, none of this would have had to happen." And then he would fall back into the cadences of a staff NCO delivering a training evaluation.

It had taken Gene fully two days to compose himself this far. He knew his thoughts were disordered, that he was emotionally spent, and he feared appearing foolish or insane. He had reflected enough, however, to realize the importance of telling his lawyers exactly what he had done. There could be no doubt in their minds about his guilt. He was going to do all he could to insure his conviction, and he did not want his lawyers believing that they represented an innocent man.

The day after Gene's removal to the state hospital a new prisoner sent to his cell found a handful of .22-caliber cartridges stashed behind the commode.

Greater than Gene's fear of failing to secure his own conviction, greater than his anxiety over a life sentence was his terror of being judged insane and confined indefinitely to a mental ward. He was glad to have had the days in the detention center to gather himself before going to the hospital at Benton. He assumed that everyone, including his attorneys, was somehow in collusion to have him committed. He knew he had to watch his every move, for everyone else was certain to be watching, especially while he was confined for evaluation.

Gene knew they wouldn't make it easy for him, so he was not surprised at the gas being pumped through the ventilators at Rogers Hall, the lock-up ward of the state hospital where he was sent. He had been keenly alert to the surroundings when he arrived and immediately noticed the sweet, antiseptic smell flowing from the vent. For most of the first two days he spent in Rogers Hall Gene sat stock-still on the edge of his cot, trying to breathe as shallowly as he could, rummaging through the jumbled record of his memory to identify the chemical agent. At first he thought it might be some sort of tranquilizer designed to keep violent psychopaths docile, or perhaps the opposite, a stimulant to get him talking. At last he concluded it was a mild hallucinogen, for there were moments when he did not know where he was and thought he was back at Dover, staring at the nylon cord and the pistols on the table in front of him.

Gene saw the plot to make him appear insane, and he struggled against the effects of the gas. At first it took tremendous effort to break free of a hallucination, but realizing that it was an effect of the drug, he brought his will to bear, confident that he could outwit any conspiracy that he could so easily see through. Day by day the frequency and intensity of the hallucinations passed.

Three days later, when Irwin and Harris came, Gene told them of the gas—an "odor," he called it, thinking the lawyers would find the word "gas" delusional—and what it was doing to him. He told them that there was likewise a conspiracy to keep him in the dark about his case, about what was being said in the press. In a hushed, guarded voice he confided to them that the guard had refused to turn up the radio in the cell-block corridor when the news came on. He said he had been denied newspapers, and he knew that everything he said or did was being recorded by the hospital staff.

As he suspected they would, Irwin and Harris denied everything, confirming Gene's convictions. But when the gas did stop, following Irwin's and Harris's visit, and Gene was convinced that they had given up on that tactic, he became even more acutely aware of being denied the news. To test the conspiracy, he did not protest it.

Dr. Irving Kuo, the staff psychiatrist assigned to

evaluate Gene, could not get him to discuss the murders or anything else about his family. So one day he asked, "Is there anything you would like to talk to me about?" And Gene responded with a list of particulars on the news blackout.

"Have you asked for any papers?" Kuo said.

"No."

"Why not, if you wanted them?"

"I hadn't asked," Gene said with authority, "because . . . since the radio had been turned down and because I was never offered a newspaper, I presumed they would not have given them to me."

Armed with this conviction, Gene subdued his anger and spent hours filling page after page with a detailed and crabbed account of the mischief being worked against him.

". . . others are accusing me of being paranoid," he wrote, "[but] paranoia is when one imagines something is happening when in fact it is not. Now, since there is plenty of evidence [in this letter] that efforts were in fact being made to keep me uninformed, I submit that I was not paranoid." And he went on to catalog each hour of each day that he was denied the news, each promise of newspapers from one of the staff that was not kept—or not on time—and each time the radio was turned down. But he was careful not to behave in any way he believed could be construed as crazy. Dr. Kuo eventually found him competent to stand trial.

Gene returned to the Pope County Detention Center on February 29, 1988, confident that he had outwitted the medical machinations of Dr. Kuo and the staff at Benton, but still convinced that efforts to deny him the news continued. Gene never arrived at the truth but went to his death believing it was malice and not indifference that had kept the papers from him. In March he began to receive newspapers regularly, through free subscriptions from, first, the Russellville *Courier-Democrat,* and later the Arkansas *Democrat* of Little Rock.

By the time of his first trial, on May 9, 1988, Gene was in solid self-possession. His beard was full; he had lost weight; and his eyes, though sunken, shone with bright intensity. Aside from his nagging for back issues of the paper, he had been a model prisoner at the detention center, and he approached the trial date with only mild anxiety, repeatedly pleading with Irwin and Harris, "Don't betray me."

The venue for the trial was Ozark, the seat of Franklin County, a small town forty-five miles west of Russellville. Gene was being tried there for the murders of Kathy Kendrick and James Chaffin in Russellville —considered by the judge to constitute an "episode" separate from the killings at Dover— and Gene wanted a speedy trial, conviction, and execution. The hallucinations he had suffered at Rogers Hall had been difficult for him, and Gene did not want to have to stand trial for the murders of his family, relive all those moments, and see the gloating, vengeful eyes of his in-laws.

The town square in Ozark, where the courthouse sits, was clogged with police cruisers, vans and trucks mounted with satellite antennae, and the cars belonging to an overflow crowd of spectators. But the courtroom drama they all came to see did not take place. In his beard and rumpled street clothes, and with his head tucked down deferentially, Gene did not look the part of a mad-dog killer. Throughout the trial he was the most relaxed person in the room.

He appeared thoughtful as prosecutor John Bynum presented the evidence, perking up only occasionally at some detail of a witness's testimony, then letting his chin sink back into his cupped hand.

The defense was hog-tied. Gene blandly refused to

cooperate with them in any way and made it clear, through constant repetition, that he wished to be found guilty and put to death. After four days of testimony in which he did not take the stand, Gene got his wish. He was found guilty on counts of false imprisonment, attempted murder, and murder and was sentenced to death plus 147 years.

Gene smiled at the verdict and when the sentence was read, straightened his back, and asked Irwin and Harris to request that he be allowed to read a statement that he had been composing since his return from the state hospital. Judge Patterson agreed. Gene took the witness chair, perched a pair of reading glasses on his nose, and looked theatrically around the silent courtroom before he began to read from the paper in his hand. His voice was calm, steady.

"My statement is that if the jury renders the most proper and just and wise sentence of death in this case, I, Ronald Gene Simmons Senior, want it to be known that it is my wish and my desire that absolutely no action by anybody be taken to appeal or in any way change the sentence."

Judge Patterson started on the bench, concern creeping across his face.

"It is further respectfully requested," Gene continued, "that this sentence be carried out expeditiously. I want no action that will delay, deny, defer, or denounce this very correct and proper sentence.

"My attorneys have repeatedly counseled me to appeal. However, that is not what I want. I believe now and always have in the death penalty. To those who oppose the death penalty, I say, in my particular case, anything short of death would be cruel and unusual punishment.

"I am of sound mind and body and have been seen by psychoanalysts who can verify that I am capable of making a clear and rational decision. I have given clear and careful thought and consideration, so there is nothing that will cause me to change my mind.

"I only ask for what I deserve. Let the torture and suffering in me end. Please allow me the right to be at peace."

Throughout Gene's statement Judge Patterson's expression had deepened, and his eyes remained fixed on the ceiling of the courtroom long after Gene had finished. Although Patterson had never before sentenced a man to die, he had steeled himself for the possibility, reflecting on the profundity of the judgment and resigning himself to upholding both the law and the decision of the jury. But Gene's statement had plunged him into unfathomed legal depths. Arkansas has no mandatory appeal of death sentences, but a review is automatic unless the right is waived. No one before Gene had waived that right, and Patterson saw at once that he was being forced into constitutional issues he had not contemplated.

Patterson took several minutes to consider the situation, then explained his reservations and called for further testimony on Gene's competency before he would affirm the jury's verdict.

The day before the verdict was read Gene had created a brief legal skirmish by passing a note to Laura Schull, a reporter from the Russellville newspaper, during a break in the trial. His attorneys moved for a mistrial, but the note proved to be an innocuous communication complaining about access to newspapers and offering to meet with Schull in private. While visiting with Schull in his cell the following Sunday Gene told her, "Death shouldn't be feared. It's what comes before death that is to be feared. . . . I want to say to each and every member of the jury, never, ever, have any doubts as to whether you made the right decision."

That same day Gene agreed to meet with two of his

in-laws, Roger and Viola O'Shields. Still ignorant of the role Roger and Vi had played in trying to convince Becky to leave him, Gene continued to be toward them as he always had, civil but distant. He felt he could, through them, reinforce the court's assumption of his competency. They, for their part, hoped to learn something of the *why* that haunted all the family survivors. For Gene it was unnecessary, and for the O'Shieldses unrewarding.

Initially unable to face Gene, Viola asked her husband to visit with him first, on Sunday night, shortly after his interview with Schull. Gene acted genuinely pleased to see Roger, although neither man could find much to say. At last Gene became fidgety and began asking dissociated questions about where his family had been buried and whether a lump in Becky's breast was cancerous. Gene spoke as though she were still alive. Hearing the concern and sincerity in Gene's voice, Roger went cold along his spine, and he left the visitation room after less than ten minutes.

The next day, having reexamined Dr. Kuo and others who testified to Gene's competency, Patterson asked Gene, "Have you changed your mind over the weekend?"

Gene looked at the judge and smiled. "The sentence is just and proper punishment," he said, "and my decision is just as valid today as it was earlier. I will not change my decision."

Patterson set Gene's execution date for June 27, 1988, and Gene said, "Thank you."

Later that morning Viola returned with Roger to see Gene, hoping that telling him where Becky and the children were buried would elicit some answers to her own questions.

"Gene," she said, "will you, can you, tell us why?"

Gene coughed and looked away. "Well," he said, "the economic outlook was very bleak. We were three months behind on the mortgage payments, and all the cars were breaking down . . ."

"Gene," Viola said, "surely that's not the answer."

Still not meeting her eye, Gene smiled and nodded and said, as if in recitation, "When the time comes, I'll let you know. I'm not going to say anything that can be used by anybody. They might even subpoena you. I'll give answers at the proper time to everybody in the family, but I won't tell anyone everything. You'll have to get together to understand all the circumstances. There were reasons, but maybe you won't understand."

It was as complete a statement as Gene was to give.

Sensing Gene's adamance, Roger asked, "Gene, do you really want to die?"

Gene nodded.

"Why didn't you just kill yourself before the police got you, then?"

"Roger," Gene said, a note of scorn in his voice, "did you read the paper? Do you know what kind of gun I was using? What kind of ammunition?"

"Twenty-two, hollow-point," Roger replied.

Gene made a wry face and said pedantically, "They don't penetrate, Roger. They splatter."

Roger and Viola met with Gene several times during the next year while he was incarcerated at Arkansas's Tucker Maximum Security Unit, and received eight letters from him, but nothing he said or wrote shed any light on his motives.

Shortly after the trial Irwin and Harris told Gene that his sentence would probably be contested by some third party. On June 6, twenty-one days before his scheduled execution, Arkansas Churches for Life filed a petition before the Arkansas Supreme Court asking for a stay and a ruling that death sentences must be appealed. Gene responded with a fusillade of letters to the editor of the Arkansas *Democrat* blasting the court system, the Churches for Life, his lawyers, and the governor. Nevertheless, the state's high court did take the case under review.

On July 11, 1988, the court upheld the sentence, and Arkansas Governor Bill Clinton set a new execution date of August 9. But Irwin and Harris again cautioned Gene that other appeals were already planned. Gene paced his cell between periods of furious writing in which he railed against politicians, lawyers, liberals, Catholics, all of whom were in league against him. Other death-row inmates, fearful that Gene's execution would clear the way for their own, let it be known that they or their friends in the exercise yard would be glad to save the state an expense. For the rest of his days Gene would take all his meals and his daily tour of the yard alone, in the company of a guard.

Acting on another petition filed by Churches for Life, District Judge Thomas Eisele issued a second stay of Gene's execution on August 2, but on August 23 he ruled that the church group had no legal standing in the case. Eisele did, however, order Gene transferred to the Medical Center for Federal Prisoners in Springfield, Missouri, for further psychiatric evaluation, and he appointed a third attorney to review the case and advise Gene on the legal bases for appeals.

Gene refused to cooperate with the doctors in Springfield, just as he had with Dr. Kuo, and on December 29, a year and a day after his arrest, Judge Eisele declared Gene competent to waive appeal. But the ruling was a bitter victory for Gene. The postponements had allowed time for his second trial, that for the killings on Mockingbird Hill, to come to court. On February 6, 1989, Gene again found himself sitting before Judge Patterson, this time in Clarksville, another small town to the west of Russellville.

Gene could only marvel at the emotional distance he had placed between himself, his feelings, and the events of Christmas 1987. He watched the videotapes that the police had made when they exhumed the bodies from the mass grave on Mockingbird Hill and heard the testimony of the officers and betrayed nothing. His demeanor was that of a judge, intent and disinterested. Throughout the pretrial evidentiary hearing, in which Irwin and Harris tried to suppress the evidence that had been gathered before the search warrant was issued, and for the first five days of the trial, Gene searched every face as he entered and left the courtroom, smiling wickedly at his sister-in-law, Edith Nesby. He sat with his attorneys and followed the arguments impassively. And every minute he was taking the measure of the jury, calculating the odds of their recommending a life sentence. Despite his standing death sentence and the gruesome evidence presented on videotape, he could not shake the fear of being denied an execution. Newspaper editorials had lashed Irwin and Harris after the first trial, accusing them of abetting Gene in his death wish, and they were determined to put on the best defense they could muster in the face of his objections. Gene was fearful that their vigor might mitigate the jury's verdict, and he was determined to see that it did not.

Among the few people Gene spoke with during his first year in prison, aside from the O'Shieldses, was Anne Jansen, a television news anchor for a Little Rock station. He had seen Jansen on a black-and-white set in the death-row cell block, and her high cheekbones and wide mouth had reminded him of all the women he had loved—Becky, Sheila, and Kathy Kendrick. Gene wrote to Jansen, offering to speak with her in private and off the record. On Thursday of the trial, in one of their several meetings, he told her to remember the initials "MNM." When she asked him what they meant, Gene said she should be at the trial, and she would see.

The next day, while standing before the bench with his attorneys, in conference with the judge and Prosecuting Attorney John Bynum, Gene, whose good behavior had allowed him to be free of handcuffs while in court, suddenly lunged from between Irwin and Harris and struck Bynum on the jaw. Bailiffs had him in hand in seconds. Gene did not resist as they led him out and returned him in manacles. He smiled at Jansen, who was in the audience. He had accomplished his "MNM"—Mitigation Neutralizing Maneuver. He intended the assault on Bynum to erase any doubt placed in the jury's mind by his lawyers.

At 8:30 that Friday evening the jury returned from four hours of deliberation to pronounce Gene guilty of the fourteen murders on Mockingbird Hill, and at 11:08 P.M. they brought in a sentence of death. On Monday Gene returned to death row with a new execution date of March 16, 1989.

Gene continued his attack through the press on Churches for Life and its attorneys until he was moved from the Tucker facility to Arkansas's Cummins Unit, where his execution was to take place, and was placed in a small, windowless cell adjacent to the death chamber. Gene had chosen to die by lethal injection, only recently adopted as an option in Arkansas, and he had read everything he could about the effects of the "Texas mix" of sodium pentathol, Pavulon, and potassium chloride. Although he said that setting a precedent was a matter of indifference to him, Gene's death, had it taken place as scheduled, would have been the first execution in Arkansas in twenty-five years.

Seven hours before he was due to be strapped to the gurney for injection—while eating a last meal of well-done filet mignon, raw onions, sliced tomatoes,

American cheese, dinner rolls, one banana, and a 7-Up—Gene heard on the television in the hall outside his cell that the United States Supreme Court, acting on a request by another death-row inmate, Jonas Whitmore, had stayed his execution. When prison officials came to confirm the news minutes later, Gene's only concern was that he be allowed to finish his meal.

During the thirteen months that it took before the United States Supreme Court ruled that Whitmore had no standing to intervene, Gene lived in virtual isolation. He spoke to none of the other inmates, seldom saw his attorneys, and would admit no other visitors. On April 24, 1990, the court issued its decision, and on May 31 Governor Clinton signed the proclamation setting Gene's execution for June 25.

Nothing in Gene's demeanor or behavior changed. On June 18 John Edward Swindler, convicted of killing a policeman in Fort Smith, Arkansas, in 1976, was electrocuted at Cummins, preceding Gene by one week as Arkansas's first execution in more than a quarter century. But Gene showed no reaction. He was engrossed in his own approach to perfection, the pristine fullness of death. When asked what he wanted his last meal to be, he replied, "The same as last year." His only comment from the death cell at Cummins was a complaint about its lack of air conditioning and the fan that blew his long, silky beard into his food.

Gene entered the death cell on Friday, June 22, 1990, two and one half years to the day after the first murders on Mockingbird Hill. He ate sparingly throughout the weekend, napped, and watched television news broadcasts for mentions of his execution, still fearful that some last-minute appeal might postpone it once again. He had done all he could, made all the necessary changes to correct fate's error, and his sole anxiety was over the final act being in the hands of the state. He had fashioned the last link in the chain of events that would complete the circle around him, enclose him in perfection, but he had to rely on the law to forge it shut.

On Monday morning, June 25, Gene was quiet and composed. He watched the early TV news and lay on his bunk throughout the rest of the day until his last meal came at 3:07 P.M. He ate it slowly, in small bites. At five o'clock he watched the evening news coverage of his impending execution, then showered and changed into fresh prison whites. When asked about the disposition of his body he said, "No comment," then he lay down and slept until a guard awoke him shortly after eight.

At 8:48 P.M. Gene entered the execution chamber and got onto the gurney. He watched with apparent interest as the guards strapped him down, then looked at the ceiling when the medical assistants began probing for a vein with the IV needle.

"Let me clench my fist," he said, "so you can find one."

The curtains over the window separating Gene from the witnesses parted at nine o'clock. Among the fourteen people admitted by the warden were Doc Irwin and John Harris, Sheriff Bolin, and prosecutor John Bynum.

Gene's eyes fidgeted and blinked, but he continued to look at the ceiling.

A. L. Lockhart, Director of the Arkansas Department of Corrections, asked Gene whether he had any final words.

"Shouldn't the [governor's execution date] proclamation be read first?" he asked.

"No," Lockhart replied.

His mind aflutter, Gene said, "I want to say just a few words. Justice delayed, finally be done, is justifiable homicide."

Lockhart left the chamber and rejoined the witnesses.

At 9:02 the executioner began injecting the sodium pentathol through the IV tube in Gene's right arm. He felt a spot the size of a half dollar go cold in the crook of his elbow where he had once held Sheila's head. A rippling sensation swept over him from his feet, exploding in his head in a whorl of light. His neck began to go slack.

"Oh, oh," he called out.

All the strangling fears—of abandonment, of failure, of being unloved and alone—caught in Gene's throat. He began to cough. The gurney shook with his spasms for more than two minutes. Then Gene lay still and began to turn blue.

Lincoln County Coroner Keith Griffin pronounced Gene dead at 9:19.

On Wednesday, June 27, Ronald Gene Simmons was buried in a pauper's grave near the town of Grady, Arkansas, his body unclaimed by any of the five members of his family who attended. It was a hot day, and the ceremony was brief, ending with a prayer.

Amen.